HIGHER GROUND

LEAH LATIMER

Genesis Press Inc.

Sage

An imprint of Genesis Press Publishing

Genesis Press, Inc.
P.O. Box 101
Columbus, MS 39703

All characters in this book have no existence outside the imagination of the author and have no relation whatsoever to anyone bearing the same name or names. They are not even distantly inspired by any individual known or unknown to the author and all incidents are pure invention.

ISBN: 1-58571-157-8
Manufactured in the United States of America

First Edition

Visit us at www.genesis-press.com
or call at 1-888-Indigo-1

For
John R. Young, Sr. and Etta S. Young,
and
their children's children

"I'm pressing on the upward way. New heights I'm gaining every day.
Still praying as I'm onward bound. Lord, plant my feet on higher ground."

A Baptist Hymn

CONTENTS

Part Two
The Early Years, The Middle Years

Part Three
The High School Years

Part Four
Start Your Search Engines

Part Five
Detours Along the Way

FOREWORD
by Johnnetta B. Cole

Leah Y. Latimer tells us in the early pages of this volume that she is not an educator. That is true in the sense that her professional work is in the field of journalism. However, drawing on years of experience as an education reporter, her insights as a mother, and the concern she feels for all young people, she has given us a book that will systematically and effectively educate parents who are preparing African American children for college.

Why a book specifically addressed to Black parents and other adults interested in the education of African American youngsters? Why not direct Black parents to those publications that are written for the American public at large?

Quite simply, because helping our children to move to the higher ground of colleges and universities must take into account the fundamental fact that most Black American children do not begin on a level playing field with most White American children. They have been subjected to ". . . weak and watered-down courses, guidance counseling based on stereotypes, low expectations and standards, and schools without basic resources, where learning seems secondary." Such are the legacies and current realities of racism in our country.

What makes this book of enormous value is that Latimer takes into account the circumstances that surround being Black in America, but she refuses to let matters rest there. This book rests on the assumption that information is power! Once parents are armed with the right information, they can assist their children in overcoming those obstacles that have kept many Black youngsters out of college. Latimer calls for putting far more of the educational destiny of African American children into their own hands and those of their parents.

Without lapsing into the paternalistic tone that characterizes so many "how-to" books, this volume speaks respectfully to a range of parents. There is that extra push for those who need only a little help in order to bolster the possibilities of their sons and daughters entering and graduating from the college or university of their choice. And, there is so much here for those parents who hardly know how to begin to ask for what they need in order to make sure that their daughters and sons are accepted into higher education institutions and have the financial package to matriculate.

It is all here, everything you ever wanted to know and should know about the kinds of colleges there are, what colleges are looking for in an application, plus helpful suggestions on ways to pay for a college education.

The greatest value of *Higher Ground* is that Leah Y. Latimer tells parents what they must and can do to prepare African American kids for college. Three points are stressed. First, it is important for parents to be proactive. Rather than simply waiting for "something to happen" that will be of assistance to one's children, parents need to create opportunities that will enhance their daughters' and sons' possibilities for a successful college experience. Second, parents must start early in a child's life to pave the way for college. There is truth in the expression,

"College begins in kindergarten." Third, parents must assist their children not only with academic preparation but also in cultural and spiritual dimensions, for youngsters are being prepared not just for a college or university but for life.

This is an empowering book because it shows parents how they can concretely affect the educational future of their children.

Johnnetta B. Cole
President, Bennett College
President Emerita, Spelman College

INTRODUCTION

"Get all the education you can get. That's the one thing nobody can take away from you."

African American Folk Wisdom

Why Such A Book?

It was a fall not so long ago that public schools in a major city opened three weeks late. School children, nearly all 77,000 of them African American, enjoyed their Indian summer in the streets or kept themselves latch-keyed at home. Black teenagers there worked fast food jobs, if they could get one, watched daytime television, or fulfilled community service requirements.

Millions of children around the country, meanwhile, learned medieval history, algorithms, or brought home spelling lists and science fair instructions. College-bound seniors everywhere else prepared for admissions tests and worked on their application essays in English classes.

By the end of September, when children were allowed into their school buildings, they found the same out-of-date books and were still without basic supplies—not even enough toilet paper. A swim team stretched out on long tables to practice their strokes; their pool was condemned. That fall, some schools eventually were shut down again, sending parents and children scrambling. Some students were crammed into makeshift classrooms in churches and recreation centers. In some places, a teacher taught in the front of a room while another tried to instruct students in the back of it. One class, it was reported, was held in a closet in a church annex.

At one point, teenagers at the city's multicultural high school demonstrated outside that school. Some students at another high school refused to come to school at all.

As the parents in the city struggled with school closings, Black parents in a nearby suburb faced a twenty-five-year legacy of forced busing. Their children were shut out of special magnet programs, with their additional resources and highly qualified teachers, while seats remained empty in hopes that White families would be "attracted." Later in the year, they'd learn that the children from their well-to-do African American community scored next to the bottom on state standardized tests.

I saw firsthand the frustrations and the hopes of parents from both communities later that fall when more than four thousand of them pushed for positions at a private school fair at the city's Convention Center. At the annual Black Student Fund Fair, well-suited Black couples pressed against Black men and women in work boots and scruffy coats, all of them clutching brochures and applications from the representatives of a few dozen private schools.

I manned one of the tables as a parent volunteer with experience in dealing with private, independent schools. I talked to those who approached me with questions about reading, about building self-confidence, about commuting from the suburbs to the city, about extracurricular activities and about afterschool care. A couple whose only child was just an infant buzzed around the tables and grilled me about seventh-grade curriculum.

Compared to the previous years that I had volunteered at the fair, I fielded few questions colored by race. A man wanted to know about the number of Black teachers at a particular school. A woman in locs asked how the history and culture of Africa is taught. Others asked about the numbers of minority children. The overwhelming majority, however, wanted to know about math and science, how reading is taught, whether there are opportunities to learn music and appreciate art.

My audiences were intent—not because my spiel was so enlightening—but, I think, because I spoke with enthusiasm and delight about my own children's education, which had included public schools, and the progress they were making.

Many parents, in turn, spoke of their utter frustration and disappointment. There was a mother whose child was in a public math and science magnet school but couldn't read well and didn't seem to be getting what she expected in math. "If this is all the magnets are doing, what is everybody else doing?"

One woman told me she was desperate to find a new school for her daughter and had been on the waiting list of one private school for three years. Another said, sadly, "I don't see any future for the children at my son's school."

A father who walked away from my table with a grocery bag full of brochures and applications lamented, "I just want to see my child growing."

The waiting in line to talk to school directors. The straining to hear over the Convention Center noise. The anxious banter of people vying for the same break. The level of frustration at the fair that year was like a job fair in a town with high unemployment. The intensity of serious shoppers at a going-out-of-business sale.

"When is the next open house?"

"Will I get an application by signing up here?"

"Do you have financial aid?"

The truth, as I knew it, was that a small minority of their children would get into any of the schools represented there that day. Many parents would be discouraged by all of the necessary arrangements that had to be made, all the forms that had to be filled out. Some would be discouraged by fifty dollar application fees (not knowing fees can be waived). With tuition at private elementary and high schools rivaling universities—the most expensive $20,000 for day schools and $30,000 for boarding—there is never enough financial aid for all who need it. I thought back on a woman wrapped in designer clothing and layers of jewelry who wondered aloud how anyone could afford private schools. I realized, too, that some who could afford to pay all or part of the cost would not sacrifice their lifestyle to do it.

In the end, I knew it would be the parents who persevered whose children had the best chance of getting one of the coveted private school spots. Some adults had to get more information; arrange transportation to test sites, interviews, and school visits; fill out pages of forms and meet deadlines.

But the lesson here is not about abandoning public schools for private ones. (Even though government tuition vouchers that help low-income children attend private schools are gaining in support in some Black communities.) The lesson is that the children of parents who take the initiative, get information, and follow through are the ones who have the best chance of getting a good education—no matter what school they attend.

This, really, is why I wrote this book. To share information, insight, and advice that will inspire you to take the initiative, empower you to act, and help you follow through in doing what needs to be done to get what we all want for our children—an education that prepares them for college, an education that prepares them for the future.

In research for this book, dozens of high school counselors, college recruiters, professors, and financial aid officers from around the country were asked, "How prepared are African American students for college?" Removed from the glare of political correctness in which we love hearing about all of the positive things so many African American youngsters are doing, these college administrators and recruiters were candidly honest.

"African American students aren't setting the place on fire," said a man who counsels college-bound students in Chicago.

From another, "We have a lot of African American students in urban areas, or where there's poor school funding, who may leave high school with a diploma but are functionally illiterate." Even so, this admissions officer at a historically black college says his mandate is to "work with them."

Still another, "It's not uncommon in March to find a Black [college-bound] senior who has not taken the SAT [college admissions test]. In [an affluent White suburban area] they start preparing for the SAT in fifth grade."

Consider that a third of African American students in college must take remedial courses in basic skills. Also consider that forty percent of Black students who begin college actually graduate. That's a great improvement over the previous decade, when only a third of Black students who started college finished.

Well before college, African American children lag behind others on almost every indicator of academic achievement. Many of those statistics are included in this book. Stark and sometimes depressing, they are included here to show the great task before us.

Much of this lack of preparation for college is the result of the inadequacies of American education—weak and watered-down courses, guidance counseling based on stereotypes, low expectations and standards, and schools without basic resources, where learning seems secondary. Meanwhile, inflated grades and low standards give some bright young people an inaccurate picture of their strengths and weaknesses. Many do not know what they need to be competitive outside their own school districts.

The lack of serious preparation also is a function of what happens—or doesn't—in our communities and homes. Many parents simply do not realize how much getting a quality education for children depends on them. A lot of us just don't realize how much we actually can do (even those of us with few resources and not a lot of time), and wouldn't know where to start. And the more educated among us don't realize how much more there is that can be done for our children. Most of us just have no idea how much our children are missing out on.

Author Patrice Gaines recalls that her parents were happy just to have her finish high school and get a job. "They just didn't know what was out there, or how to get it if they did."

Our history and culture play a part in why it seems many parents are not doing much of what can be done for their children's education. I'm referring to those experiences, attitudes and beliefs that condition our thinking and sway our actions. You'll read later in the book how some cultural "truths" lead well-meaning Black parents to discourage their children from setting high goals and achieving. Such parents simply don't realize the power of education in overcoming the enormous obstacles previous generations of African Americans faced, nor how many actually overcame them and continue to overcome.

I have plunged into the affairs of a number of young people over the past decade. In working with some of them, I discovered that few had been charting a deliberate course to college (for a lot of the reasons previously mentioned). Their parents, many college graduates themselves, always hoped and assumed they would go. Yet there were so many of them, college-bound and in high school without having given serious attention to preparing for college.

Much of what keeps us from doing all we can do for our children is a lack of information that enables and empowers us to do more than we think we can. This lack of information also limits our vision of what our children can be. It keeps our aspirations for them low at a time when there are so many opportunities for them to soar.

Thousands of African American students are soaring. Our children are excelling in math, science, and the humanities, perfecting their talents and skills, and contributing enormously to their families, schools, and communities. Of those interviewed for this book, nearly all high-achieving African American students credit their parents or other adults for showing them the way to excellence when they were young children and for actively supporting their interests throughout their schooling.

Unfortunately, many parents don't realize how much our children can use our help, how important our active involvement is in determining their futures, and that the power of preparation for college is in the small details as well as the major decisions.

If you're not sure you know all there is or that you're doing all you could to start your child on the path to college, answer these questions:

- Have I researched all the possible school choices available for my children, beginning with elementary school? Or, hoping for the best, do I register at the neighborhood school without knowing what's going on there?
- Have I made sure my middle schooler is taking the courses she needs to be eligible for college-prep high school courses?
- Have I helped my young person compile a list of personal goals and ways to achieve them?
- Is my child taking advantage of academic and cultural enrichment programs inside and outside of school (many offered for free or low cost)?
- Will I allow my student to drop Spanish or science when he's "got all the credits he needs to graduate," not realizing he may need more years of study to be accepted at the college of his choice and compete for scholarships?
- Am I waiting until senior year of high school to help my child look for scholarships?
- Have I developed a financial plan for paying at least some of the costs of college?

Many parents who say they want their children to go to college, for many reasons, aren't taking the steps now to assure they'll get into the best school for them, if any. For most, it's a lack of awareness of all that is available, all that is possible, and all that must be done. Consider the following examples.

At the end of the first semester of her senior year, the daughter of two Howard University graduates still had not taken the SAT. She and her mother went to their first college open house the April before graduation not knowing that, at that point, the invitation was to high school sophomores and juniors. Having missed almost every deadline, she worked at Burger King that fall hoping to enroll somewhere the next year.

A high school journalism program participant was the first in her family college-bound. Her enthusiasm built as she checked off the list of schools she was interested in, then explained why she'd selected the one that was her first choice. "It has a bowling alley! It seems like a nice place to go to."

One young man applied only to a few small state colleges within a fifty-mile radius of his home. They were the only colleges he could easily name, and he and his parents considered anything else beyond the family's reach. Urged to expand his scope, he eventually applied to Morehouse and was ecstatic when he was accepted at Dr. Martin Luther King, Jr.'s alma mater.

A couple thought the small community college was all they could afford for their daughter. They never sought scholarships, affordable loans, or grants that might have helped her study at a more challenging, four-year college for equal or less than the full price they paid out of pocket.

A more poignant example of how lack of information can limit our ability to get the best for our children struck me hard in a situation I call "The Montessori School and the Trailer."

The Montessori program was in a gentrified neighborhood in a predominantly Black city. More than half of the children enrolled were White and middle class. The Montessori classroom was stocked with expensive educational materials—maps, puzzles, building blocks, a terrarium, geometric shapes for learning math, encyclopedias, a space for singing in a circle, and a corner for playing house. Highly trained teachers worked with preschoolers whose parents had made special efforts to get their children into this special public school.

Behind the school sat a trailer, young mothers in their teens and early twenties, and some middle-aged grandmothers, tugged preschoolers behind them. Inside the trailer was another publicly funded preschool program. But there was no integration here, all the little faces inside were Black.

I didn't go in, so I can't wrap this all up neatly in a black-and-white tale of privilege in the midst of disadvantage. Perhaps the workers in the day care trailer were just as dedicated, the trailer well-stocked. But who would not be struck by the symbolism: the children of the well-heeled all cozy and warm in a building, the babies of the lesser-to-do in a trailer out back.

Here is the point: The parents of the Montessori students made a deliberate choice, based on information about the availability of a "special" program. Then they went for it. They were able to act on their knowledge. Some pulled political strings, contacting their school board members. Others just got up early to get a good spot in the line to register for the program.

Parents have always sought something more for their children, like those at the Black Student Fund Fair, like the Montessori parents, and yes, like the babies in the trailer out back. Those who are successful at getting it, however, are the ones who get the information and take action.

I am not an educator, but I've been inside a lot of schools. As an education reporter for the *Washington Post,* I spent time in almost every type of school, sat in on hours and hours of classes, school board meetings and PTA gatherings. I've seen what works and what doesn't.

I've gone to college fairs, conferences, workshops and won fellowships for further academic study. I've interviewed school superintendents, college presidents, and top experts. Perhaps more importantly, I've just talked to hundreds of teachers, principals, guidance counselors, coaches, college recruiters, and successful students and parents.

Few parents who are not educators have had the kind of exposure to so many people, different kinds of schools, educational concepts, expert studies and philosophies that I have. I've approached it all with the critical eye of a journalist, but also as a mother and as a member of the community concerned about all young people. And I've studied schools and education without having a political agenda or predetermined educational philosophy to sell. In *Higher Ground,* I've put down what I've learned— basic information and practical advice—while presenting serious issues that need our consideration.

The book's approach is threefold: To inform you. To empower you. To enlighten you.

First, this book will inform you of much, though certainly not all, of what is available in helping to get children of color ready for college. Second, it will empower you, with information and practical advice, to take action on your children's behalf. To make the phone calls to teachers, counselors, and admissions officers. To follow up on the special program you read about on the library bulletin board. To insist on a teacher conference just because you want to get more details. To check your child's backpack and notebooks. To stay up with her when she doesn't have the self-discipline yet to finish her project. Most important, I hope you'll be moved to set a deliberate plan for reaching the goal of a college education for your child. You can do it if you're aware of the resources available to help you help your children

Third, as you read through *Higher Ground*, I hope you will be enlightened. Realize how much exists to help your children reach their goals—and there's even more than I've been able to lay out in this book. See the potential in and possibilities for your children. With information and insight, you won't have to settle for less than what your children can do or less than they deserve. There's a lot to learn, a lot to think about. But we've all got to start preparing our children now.

Who This Book is For

Higher Ground is for parents and other interested adults who:
- went to college a while ago and don't remember, or maybe never really knew, what it takes to be a top student.
- went to college a generation ago and need to know how things have changed.
- never went to college and need help guiding and advising their children.

Most important, this book is for real parents, not perfect ones. *Higher Ground* takes into account that some parents have to choose work over the school play, or a second job over helping with homework. *Higher Ground* acknowledges those of us who have good reason at the end of the day for being too tired to help out at the PTA bake sale.

Most mainstream books for the college-bound address families and students who are already on "the track" to higher education and doing well. *Higher Ground* deals in reality. Many of us don't know what "the track" is. Others face huge obstacles in getting and staying there. Among these pages, you'll find ways to accomplish as much as you realistically can, and find other opportunities and resources to compensate for what you cannot.

And please know that you don't need your own college degree to be an educationally savvy and involved parent. Sonya Carson, mother of pioneering neurosurgeon Dr. Benjamin Carson, raised her two boys in desperate poverty. But she limited TV and made sure they did homework and read books. Carson had no high school degree and could hardly read herself. Yet she motivated her sons and saw to it that they had the academic preparation to get into the University of Michigan and into Yale. To be college-bound, your children don't have to be perfect either. Dr. Carson, the innovator behind the technique for separating conjoined twins, had a rough start. He tried to stab a classmate, the story goes, when he was fourteen.

The specific goal *of Higher Ground* is preparing for education beyond high school. It's true, almost anyone can get into some colleges, even with dismal grades. There *are* a number of schools that are open to any and all who apply. With this in mind, I've heard some say you don't need all this stuff to prepare for college. But to truly be prepared for college means striving for excellence, whether your children are headed for prestigious universities or the local community college. Recall our often ignored legacy of excellence when some say it's easy to get into college: Frederick Douglass, W. E. B. DuBois, Zora Neale Hurston, Dr. Charles Drew, Paul Robeson, Mary McLeod Bethune, Dr. Mae Jemison, Colin Powell, Condoleezza Rice. Those who can, like the folks just mentioned, must be better than mediocre.

This book is about more than preparing just for college, though. It's about preparing for the future, preparing for life. It's about developing the mind, and also character and spirit. A student with the skills and achievements that will earn a spot in a strong college program also has the skills that can take him immediately into the workplace *if* that becomes the choice instead. In learning what it takes to prepare your children for college, you'll learn what they'll need to be productive, successful adults as well.

How to Use This Book

This book will tell you what you need to know to start getting your child ready for college, beginning with the earliest years of schooling. Your child may be just starting kindergarten, in his middle school years, or already in high school. Maybe you're chasing more than one child, running from elementary to senior high on Back-to-School Night. Wherever your children are, scan this book to answer your immediate questions and most pressing concerns. Then take the time to read the entire book.

Even if your child is very young, read beyond Part Two, "The Early Years, Middle Years," through to Part Five, "Detours Along the Way." It will help to know the road ahead, and to be aware of the challenges before you have to face them.

By reading the book all the way through, you'll be arming yourself with the knowledge of what is to come in your child's school life. You'll be able to develop long-term educational strategies. Prior knowledge is a common factor among almost all of the high-achieving students interviewed for this book. Through parents, guidance counselors, teachers, or their own research, the most successful students knew what they needed to do well before the time came to do it. In most cases, their parents made the effort to find out what a well-rounded, successful student needs at every grade level. But even the best prepared, highest achieving youngsters and young professionals interviewed for *Higher Ground* expressed some sentiment that "If only I'd known. . ." or "If my parents had only known. . ."

The world is changing so rapidly that some of the things we learned from our own college experience—the things *we* would have done differently now that we know better—are outmoded as far as our children are concerned.

On a related note, your African American student shouldn't expect the kind of advantage or special consideration in scholarships or college admissions you did a generation ago. Schools are no longer out to make up for past discrimination or to diversify their campuses to the extent that they were in the 1970s, 80s and 90s. "It's not about being Black, it's about test scores," an African American politician said of the impact of bans on affirmative action in higher education.

One of the most important things you can do as a parent is to understand how today's decisions will affect your children later on. In a real sense, there is a direct route from kindergarten to college. Reading to your child now and making sure she has a library card can develop the vocabulary and reading skills in an early grade that can lead to placement in a talented and gifted program. Which in turn can lead to advanced classes in middle school. High-achieving middle school students are able to choose from a number of highly academic high school tracks, from which top colleges recruit.

You need to see the big picture, to know the pitfalls, turns, and twists that lay ahead on the journey from young child to college graduate.

If your child is entering middle or high school, it's still a good idea to start at the beginning and read all of *Higher Ground*. Ideas and information directed at parents of older students are built on the advice and information about younger children. And you may be inspired with new ideas for your older child while reading about a stage you thought you both had already passed.

Whatever stage your child is at, don't agonize over past mistakes, bad decisions, or opportunities missed. Learn, repair if possible, but keep focused on the present and the future. Accept that there will be different levels of competence and achievement among the children you love. Don't plan on treating them all the same, because they aren't all the same. Count effort, hard work, and improvement among their successes, not just high grades.

Remember, also, that your child's education is a personal journey. It's not how fast she gets there, but what she brings with her, how she develops and grows. The person she becomes. Higher education is not the end, it's the means to a productive, successful, happy life.

I hope you will be proactive and aggressive when it comes to your children's education. Give it as much thought and attention as you do your jobs, your church, your volunteer and professional commitments, your social life, and your relationships. There's a lot you can do. But in the end, all we can do is our best. Then pray on it.

How Not to Use This Book

Each child, each family, is different. Keep this in mind always. Don't compare your third grader to your neighbor's, or press your teenager to do the same things the outstanding junior usher at your church is doing. What works for your cousin's husband's son may not work for yours. The path taken by your daughter's most accomplished classmates may be totally wrong for your young person.

In doing the research and reporting for *Higher Ground*, I was both inspired and overwhelmed by all the wonderful tips, advice, and outstanding opportunities available to minority students today. The information in this book is culled from more than two hundred interviews with educators, parents, students, professionals, guidance counselors, teachers and principals, college professors and presidents.

In addition I attended more than two dozen workshops, seminars, and conferences, and visited scores of schools of all types over two decades. I've read dozens of studies and reports. With all I've learned, however, I know that I still will fall short educating my children. There's no way I can do it all. None of us can, nor should we. Because no child can do it all.

So relax when you consider what all the experts, knowledgeable relatives, and books say. Read and absorb, but never force something on a young person just because you read it in a book.

Instead, determine what is right for your family and each child in it. In the end, you must be the expert on your own children.

An Interview with Howard University President H. Patrick Swygert

"One comes home from an exhausting day at work and then has children who need you to read to them or go over homework. But one must do that. There isn't an alternative."

What should Black parents' responses be to the dismantling of race-based scholarships and affirmative action in higher education?

There's a lot we can do. One is to support those institutions and organizations—the NAACP and its Legal Defense Fund—that are litigating these cases. Every parent can do that regardless of where your child may be in the education pipeline.

Just as every parent can send a dollar or two to the NAACP Legal Defense Fund and other such organizations, every parent can vote. The allocation of public resources is a matter of politics, ultimately. And so that dollar or two contribution and that vote are both intimately tied to educational policy. We should not overlook the relationship between the dollar, the ballot box, and what happens in terms of our children getting an opportunity for higher education.

The other thing that parents can do, or focus on now, is

understand the need for preparation for college—and I say preparation for college as opposed to preparation for a particular examination.

As difficult as it is—particularly for single parents—to find that time and energy, parents must find the time and energy to introduce children to books and literature. One comes home from an exhausting day at work and then has children who need you to read to them or go over homework. But one must do that. There isn't an alternative.

What else can parents do?

I think parents ought to start forming support networks, particularly single parents. We hear about support networks among women, and support networks among men. We need some support clubs and organizations of parents who say, "How can we come together outside of the PTA structure, outside of the school structure?"

What will college campuses be like in the future?

The technology is giving us an opportunity to offer soon, if not a virtual campus, then certainly close to it. And it is largely grounded in the notion that the learner has access to and is able to manipulate emerging technology.

That's different than in the past because although one needed to be able to manipulate some technology, the technology that was being manipulated—whether it was index cards or the library system or chemistry lab—was a technology that was fairly commonplace. The technology of today is the technology of the internet, of computer-based and computer-assisted learning.

The whole notion of wealth creation has taken a dramatic turn. We think of wealth today as not necessarily the capacity to manufacture things, but as the capacity to manipulate data. Well, a knowledge-based economy is more of a reality than not.

How important is technology in preparing children for college?

I'll give you two professions as an example of why youngsters have to understand, have to be comfortable with, and have to be able to manipulate technology:

It wasn't too long ago that many parents encouraged their youngsters to pursue one of two fields. One, of course, was medicine, and the other was the law. Both have changed dramatically and are changing rapidly. In both fields, technology is driving much of the change.

It's obvious in medicine. Today's health care worker relies as much on the computer as the previous generation may have relied on the microscope.

With all of this change taking place, it's going to take folk who can respond critically and are able to manage both obvious and not-so-obvious changes.

Let me go back to the printed page of the book, which sounds like I'm going backwards. But the fact of the matter is that some of the most difficult, the most sophisticated, the most challenging ideas, are still found in the classics. And those sophisticated reading skills are pretty much the same kinds of skills that are needed managing the so-called high-tech world.

It wasn't too long ago that most law firms were located close to the county courthouse or the city courthouse. If you were practicing law, you wanted to be close to the trial center. Today, you can practice law just about anywhere because the nature of the law that's being practiced has changed so dramatically. Again, technology. Technology is permitting lawyers and accountants and physicians, in a sense, to be somewhat removed from the old centers of action.

How can Black parents prepare their children for all of this technological change?

Just as we start by insisting that our children read, and read as much as possible, we have to be just as concerned that our children have access as early as possible to emerging technologies. Technology is moving so quickly today that there are very few opportunities to catch up. Your child, every child, needs a running start.

Imagine a child graduating from a high school without the ability to manipulate a computer. There is almost no field of endeavor where that child will not require some computer training or at least some familiarity with the computer. Whether it's a field where some form of higher education is required, manufacturing, construction, or automobile mechanics.

Well, if that's so, then imagine the challenge to those of us who have children, particularly in certain urban districts, who don't have those skills when they graduate. What are you consigning those children to? What kind of future will those children have?

You might say, "Well, they can make it up." Yes, they certainly can make up for that society-imposed deficiency. But to make up, somebody's got to be real serious and really committed to giving them an opportunity to make up. Wouldn't it be much better if they didn't have to make up for some deficiency in learning, and they had these resources and skills when they left high school?

Just as the book is important, the computer is important; it's not an add-on.

But everybody doesn't have $2,000 for a home computer. What should those parents do?

It should either be in the home or it should be someplace that a student can access, whether it be a Boys & Girls club, the church, public school, or private academy. It is reasonable to say that every child should have a computer in his or her life at some time during the course of his or her week. The idea of a child being subject to some systematic education with no significant computer engagement is hardly an education in today's world. It is that critical.

A parent can insist that "somewhere within my community my child will have a computer." We're doing less than a disservice, we're punishing, we're consigning our children to failure if we don't do this.

In not preparing for college, a number of students and parents rely on open enrollment schools that admit all who apply. What's your message to them about striving for excellence?

When I applied to Howard University undergraduate school in 1960, you did not see a large number of African Americans attending majority group institutions. And the generation before me saw even less. The world has changed considerably since then, and thank God it has. Youngsters coming out of school today have opportunities that my generation did not have. Youngsters have opportunities both in school and college choices, and in professional choices.

I don't want to sound like some soon-to-be old fogey talking about what it used to be like, but the fact is that there are some of us who believe that we can never relax, that we've not reached some point of nirvana that would permit us to believe that less than our best is good enough. We don't have the option of being mediocre. We don't have the option of not seeking excellence.

We are where we are today because of the sacrifice and the commitment to excellence of those who've gone before us. The Black middle class today traces its roots quite directly to those Black women and Black men, unseen, unheard of, and unacknowledged; who in 1,001 ways, job sites, and professions, blazed their own trails. And they did so because of their own excellence.

Some folks don't save for college because they think it'll limit their financial aid. Is that true?

It's hard to imagine that a parent or someone responsible for a child's welfare would make a conscious decision not to find, acquire, or save the resources necessary to at least partially offset the costs of college. As difficult as it is for many, many, many of our parents and those responsible for children, some contribution to a child's education, however modest, can be made by most of us.

PART ONE

What the Involved Parent Needs to Know About...

"Come prepared or not at all."
Advertisement beckoning Blacks north,
from Toni Morrison's *Paradise*

EARLY AWARENESS

Part II of this book discusses the early years of formal education, including what you can do to get preschoolers ready for kindergarten and what courses middle school students should take.

But why, you might wonder, would a parent of a child in preschool or junior high start getting information on college now? And why would a book about preparing for college go all the way back to fifth grade, or even preschool?

It's all about early awareness and advance planning: researching the road ahead before you reach it. Knowing what the choices are well before you have to make them. Realizing what opportunities lie ahead so you can position your child to take advantage of them. Understanding future requirements so you can start preparing your child at an early age to meet them.

It involves understanding how financial aid is awarded, and how and where you're likely to find scholarships—and what it takes to win them—so you can save and invest accordingly. It involves knowing that your child should take a foreign language and stick with it because most colleges require a few years of continuing language. It involves knowing what that excellent high school across the city requires students to master in elementary school and middle school.

Consider the study of mathematics, in which knowledge builds on knowledge, skills build upon previous learning. You need to know up front, for example, that your children will not do well on college admissions tests such as the SAT, and can't be admitted to most colleges without Algebra. As a result, Algebra I is called the "Gatekeeper to College." You need to be aware that your children's math instruction during the early and middle years will play a large part in determining when and whether they take Algebra I and other advanced mathematics required for college. Access to Algebra, believe it or not, is a 21st century civil rights issue: To deny or limit students' access to Algebra and other advanced courses is to limit their future opportunities. It's the 21st century equivalent of 19th century prohibitions against teaching African Americans to read.

Another example. If you'd like your child to win scholarships, it will help to know in advance, to have an early awareness of, the things that scholarship committees expect from the students they throw money at.

Are you aware that outstanding grades are not enough to win major scholarships? Most go to students who have good grades *and* have been active in their schools and communities, have developed a special talent or skill, have competed in sports or debate teams. Some scholarships seek out kids with average grades but who are leaders and active participants in school life. If you know this early on, you'll get your child accustomed to being active and involved, won't you?

Forward-thinking educators, including college presidents, are recognizing that tomorrow's high school students will have more paths to choose from if their parents are planning and preparing them today. As a result, private and state education organizations, and even residents of the White House have been trying to get the message out that parents should start thinking and planning for college early in their children's lives. Some of the most ambitious early awareness programs begin working with parents and children as early as third grade.

In recent years, the Campus Partners Mentoring Program at Xavier University in New Orleans matched college students with eleven and twelve year olds. College mentors helped the middle school students see how far they can take their education and showed what needs to get done to get there. In Riverside, California, the Passport to College project at Riverside Community College involved students, beginning with fifth graders, in campus activities. Meanwhile, their parents got information on financial aid.

Texas Christian University offered sixth graders and their parents seminars on college and career planning, financial aid, and admission. Most importantly, families learned what choices to make in middle and high school in order to be prepared for college.

Whether your child is in preschool or eleventh grade, Early Awareness for college involves Setting a Vision, Getting the Information, and Doing the Work necessary to give your child the best preparation possible.

Setting a Vision

If you haven't considered college for your child or if you've been thinking that a technical college or the small state school everybody else is going to is all your family can expect, set those thoughts aside immediately.

Look at your child who says she wants to be an astronaut,

your son who wants to be a surgeon, your other child who talks about going to Princeton one day. If their goals and potential seem far beyond what you can imagine, you need to reset your thinking. With knowledge and planning, much of what your little ones dream of can come true.

One of the saddest examples of lack of vision I've come across involved a mother of three young girls, the eldest eight years old. The mother was adamant that they not waste their time in college. Instead, she wanted each to get her cosmetologist license, something she knew would pay their bills.

"People go away to these big schools and then drop out. Nobody I know ever finishes," she explained. "Nobody I know ever got a job in something they majored in."

This kind of thinking, unfortunately, is part of our legacy. Renowned educator Carter G. Woodson noted it in the early 1900s in the classic work *The Mis-Education of the Negro*: "Negroes learned from their oppressors to say to their children that there were certain spheres into which they should not go because they would have no chance therein." If other young people can overcome great odds to become astronauts, neurosurgeons, and Ivy Leaguers, why can't your children reach their higher ground? They can if you open your mind to the very real possibilities, and let them enter whatever spheres they wish.

Start setting your own positive vision of their futures with these simple steps:

- Set realistically high expectations and standards for academic performance and personal behavior.
- Realize that even if you have no clue now what they may be, there are many options and opportunities out there

for our children.

- Realize that there are many people willing to help if you seek them out and programs that can be helpful. Realize that the history of African Americans is defined mostly by our ability to survive and achieve. Former Congressman Kweisi Mfume dropped out of high school in favor of gambling and drinking on the streets of Baltimore. The man who would become president of the NAACP turned his life around, getting a general equivalency diploma, then a bachelor's in urban planning from Morgan State University and a master's in international studies from Johns Hopkins University.

- Realize the potential, the possibilities, those perhaps unimaginable heights that can be reached by the children who now still wet the bed or can't remember their homework. Realize that with information and planning, you can help your child go far.

Getting Information

Once you've got the vision, you need the information and knowledge to work with as you and your child travel the road to college. *Higher Ground* is a good beginning.

Now, make it your habit to find out as much as you can about the opportunities and resources—people programs, special classes, etc.—available to your children now and in the coming years. Always cast your net wide, looking at school and community, private or public organizations, on the local, state, national, and international levels. These resources may help in academics, leadership, and character building, or in polishing your child's special talents and interests. They may simply help make life easier (afterschool programs, toy or clothing giveaways at Christmas, divorce counseling).

You must limit the distractions that keep you and your child from doing your combined best.

Get into the habit of accumulating information about your child and for your child. You need to:

- Find out early on what colleges are looking for and what they require. This will be discussed later in Higher Ground. In addition, start collecting college brochures and reading college guides for specific requirements. Older students can explore this with their parents.

- Consider what skills and talents make your child special. If it's not apparent to you, ask the day care worker, teacher, youth leader, or others who know your child's strengths. Then look for opportunities that will develop these gifts. Be prepared to abandon it all when your child's interests shift, as they almost surely will. Then move on to the next phase of developing interests.

- Explore the costs of different kinds of colleges. Attend a financial planning workshop or meet with a financial specialist.

- Become familiar with the college financial aid process. Attend financial aid workshops at high schools, churches, and college fairs. Middle school is not too early to find out how much college will cost and, based on your income, how much you will be expected to contribute.

- Evaluate where your child is going before it's time to go. Explore the local middle or high schools your child is slated to attend at least a year or two in advance. If you don't like what you see, start working toward improving things or look for alternatives.

Doing the Work

From the beginning, stress to your child the importance of doing one's best. Then help your child to do it. A parent or other interested adult must be intimately involved in a child's education and personal development. Few children excel without some older person showing them the way.

Monitor schoolwork, provide basic supplies, know the teachers, visit the school as often as possible but at least once per grading period.

Get involved in your child's school or classroom, even in a small way if you don't have the time to be a PTA officer: bring cookies for a class, help out at the book fair, chaperone a field trip, be a career day speaker.

Give your child as many different kinds of experiences as you can: trips, far and near, visits to museums, the theater, special exhibits. Expose them to people of color working in a variety of fields. Enroll your child in activities and programs he likes. Expose him to new things he might not try on his own.

Find mentors, teachers, or coaches who can help your child develop her special talents if you can't.

Prepare financially by making investments that will pay off in time for college. Or simply save what you can. For some of us, paying for college seems impossible, but setting aside even a few dollars, as soon as you can, will help with books (which can be a few thousand over four years), clothing or travel expenses—

things generally not covered by financial aid or scholarships. As you'll read later on in this book, the conventional wisdom that "the less money you have on hand, the more money you'll get" is just not true. If you have a decent income and haven't saved any of it for college, you may end up stuck with the kind of financial aid options you don't necessarily want (loans, which can lead to heavy debt over four years for you and your child).

This is just a sampling of things you can do to help your child reach college. By getting this book, you've already taken a step in getting the information you need to become a school savvy parent, able to help your child move successfully from kindergarten to college.

THE VALUE OF A COLLEGE EDUCATION

"…The excellence of knowledge is that wisdom gives life to those who have it."

Ecclesiastes 7:12

Good jobs and high incomes are what most people hope for their children's future. The relationship between income and education level is often talked about and will be discussed in the following pages. But jobs and money are just a part of any discussion on education. Learning how to live, that's the true value of a college education.

It allows us the chance to move to a higher level in those areas that truly define the quality of living. With a higher degree, your child can participate in a global economy, yes, but he may also find new ways to contribute to his community. He may be able to pull down six figures, but he can also appreciate a work of art as much as a video game, value a historical document as well as a pair of Timberlands, understand the maneuvering in a national election as much as those NCAA March Madness brackets.

With a college education, your children can move about the world in a way they might not otherwise. A college education is about having the intellectual means and sophistication to fully appreciate and understand our connection to our inner selves, each other, and our God. The traditional liberal arts education is about learning how to think, how to explore, how to understand and connect with the past and present in order to help construct a better future.

The value of a college education is also in being exposed to new ideas and different people, so that your daughter can know how to treat others and have high expectations about the behavior of those around her.

In more practical terms, a college education's value is about choices. Your daughter may choose to work the sixty-hour-a-week professional position, or be able to set a part-time schedule at pay that rivals another person's full-time check. She may take more time to raise children at home, go back to school, or pursue that business idea. She won't have to stay in a low wage job because she doesn't qualify far anything else.

Those whose services, skills, and talent are in great demand have more choices. The better educated, talented, and skilled your children become, the more choices they'll have in life.

With a college degree, your young person can pick and choose careers to a greater degree than those without one. This is not to say they will have it easy, but they will have more options than the non-degreed in a society in which a four-year college is as basic a resume place holder as the high school diploma before the 1960s.

The high school diploma lost its earning power with the move from an industrial work force dominated by good-paying blue collar jobs. Today's high-tech, information-based economy requires higher level skills and knowledge than most high schools are prepared to teach. The work force our children will have to compete in, for the most part, will reward workers who use their minds rather than their hands.

Those who don't believe education is necessary to achieve happy productive lives are right. And college may not be for everyone. But consider this: Do you know anyone who regrets having expertise? Do you know anyone who doesn't like the security of spirit and life that comes from knowledge? Who doesn't like the ease of navigating society that comes with skills and graces acquired through a good education? Have you ever heard anyone say, "I wish I knew less. I wish I had less education"?

As you talk to your young people about the value of a college education, keep in mind that it is a happy, well-rounded, productive life that is the real end. Higher education is just the means. And it should continue over a lifetime, if only informally.

When visions of big jobs and high incomes take over, ask if your dying wishes could ever include, "I wish I had spent more money, bought more *things.* " In the end, the quality of living is as important as good jobs and income. But there's no question that the two will make your children's futures more comfortable and secure.

Dollars and Sense

Money wise, here's what's at stake. High school is rarely enough by itself to equip one to earn a middle class income. This has been a running story, with some reports declaring that "as an economic credential, the high school diploma is dead."

This has not always been the case. Many of our parents clothed and fed us well, and paid for our weddings having never taken Algebra I. But they grew up in a different time, influenced by a different economy, when a man with a strong back and arms and a union card could earn a high wage. A woman willing to stand on her feet for forty hours a week in a unionized manufacturing plant could count on a good check at the end of the month, sometimes rivaling the pay of teachers and other professionals. But as William Julius Wilson tells us in *When Work Disappears,* those jobs have disappeared rapidly. And the wage gap between the degreed and the non-degreed has widened.

In general, those who go to college earn more than those who don't. Those with a two-year associate degree earn more than high school graduates, but not as much as people with four-year bachelor's degrees. Based on 2000 dollars, here's what the salary discrepancies look like:

College degree holder
Male	$42,292
Female	$32,238

High school diploma
Male	$26,399
Female	$15,573

Less than high school
Male	$19,225
Female	$11,583

Over a lifetime, the gap in earnings between those with a high school diploma and a four-year college degree exceed $1 million. The nation experiences highs and lows in unemployment. But in recent years, 9 percent of those without a high school diploma couldn't find jobs. About 5 percent of those with a high school diploma had a hard time finding work. But just 2 percent of those with a college degree were unemployed.

Even with college costs rising to levels that startle most of us, a college degree is still a wise investment, with a substantial pay-off in the long run. That may contradict some long held beliefs and even personal experience. Remember the woman previously mentioned who insisted her daughters become hairdressers? Experience had taught her that the doors of opportunity are not wide open for people of color. Why waste the effort and expense of education? This loving mother is stuck in the past, thinking back on the experiences of previous generations of Black folks and her own limited universe. She can't see all the real opportunities for Black youngsters who prepare to take advantage of them.

Something to think about: A college degree is not just a ticket out of a poor community. Teach your children that their educated minds and their professional skills can be used, and rewarded, within their own community. Success is not always someplace new. A better future may await them in the very places that prepared them for it.

The Possibilities

With a college degree, your child will have more choices.

Two-Year Associate's Degree

Computer technician
Commercial artist
Automotive mechanic
Heating/air-conditioning technician
Registered nurse
Hotel/restaurant manager
Medical laboratory technician
Dental hygienist

Four-Year Bachelor's Degree

Teacher
FBI agent
Investment Banker
Graphic Designer
Engineer
Accountant
Journalist
Public relations specialist
Insurance agent
Pharmacist
Editor
Dietician
Computer systems analyst

Graduate Degree/Professional Degree

Lawyer
Doctor
Psychologist
Veterinarian
Management consultant
Architect
Dentist
Biologist
Geologist
School superintendent
Scientist
College professor
Economist

African Americans have made their mark in so many fields that there are hardly any more "first Blacks." But many young people and their parents unwittingly miss educational opportunities because they don't know where, or if, they will lead anyplace. How can you earn a living with a degree in art history, a young man asked? He loved art and history, but was discouraged from pursuing this course of study because his family couldn't connect the dots from a degree in art history to a job. He could find employment as a museum curator, college professor, auctioneer, or as a six-figure salaried art buyer for a multinational corporation.

Don't discourage your child's dreams, even if they seem impractical. Everyone can't and shouldn't be a cosmetologist, computer programmer, or lawyer. Black people must explore and move into all areas of study and work. Let your child follow her interests and talents. If she has solid skills and a well-rounded education, she can probably make a good living in whatever field of study she chooses.

Different Kinds of Colleges

Throughout *Higher Ground*, the terms "college" and "university" are used interchangeably, as they are by most people. Colleges can differ in level and type of study, degrees granted, whether they are privately or publicly supported, limited by gender or founded on specific religious principles. Traditionally, universities are research institutions with professional and graduate schools in addition to undergraduate studies.

This book focuses on preparing youngsters for four-year programs that lead to professional careers and even more advanced academic study. You may not know what kind of college your student eventually will choose, but knowing the differences now can help in planning courses and careers. It may also help to realize that there are a variety of options, depending on your child's abilities and interests.

Colleges fall into two major categories, those with two-year programs and those with four-year programs.

Two-Year Programs

Most of these schools offer education and training programs that lead to associate of arts (A.A.)., associate of science (A.S.), or associate of applied science (A.A.S.) degrees. Admission to such schools are generally "open" rather than "competitive." That means they accept eligible applicants, who may need only a high school diploma or general equivalency degree. Within this group are:

- *Community Colleges.* These are public institutions that mostly enroll students from their nearby communities and offer academic courses, technical courses, and continuing education classes. Students pursuing studies as health care technicians, dental assistants, plant operators, and heating and air-conditioning specialists may choose a community or technical school. They also are a good alternative for the student not ready to move from high school to a four-year college. Most four-year institutions accept some course credits from community college students who wish to continue their studies and earn a four-year degree.
- *Technical Schools*, private or public, offer specialized education and occupational training in specific fields. In recent years, computer technician training (not the same as a major in computer science) has been a popular option.
- *Junior Colleges* typically are two-year private institutions. Some offer the same residential experience as four-year programs, attracting students from outside of their area.

Four-Year Programs

Colleges and universities confer bachelor of arts (B.A.) or bachelor of science (B.S.) degrees. These four-year programs lay the foundation for even more advanced study and professional careers. Universities embrace several individual colleges in one institution, such as the College of Fine Arts at Howard University. Universities also generally have a graduate school that offers advanced or professional degrees, such as a master of science (M.S.), master of arts (M.A.), doctor of philosophy (Ph.D.), or law and medical degrees. Admission to four year colleges and universities varies from the highly selective (students in the top 5 to 10 percent of their graduating classes, with SAT or ACT scores that put them among the top students in the country) to nonselective (high school graduates with minimum SAT or ACT scores).

Those are the basics. But colleges are so much a part of the social order that they have been categorized and nicknamed in ways meant to give you a quick reference of what to expect from them. The following are some further breakdowns of colleges your family might consider, based on values, interests, career goals, and preferred learning or social environments.

- *Denominational Colleges*: Some have obvious religious affiliations, such as Catholic University of America in Washington, D.C. Bennett College, one of the nation's two Black women's colleges, is affiliated with the United Methodist Church. Colleges tied to a particular faith vary in the degree to which the faith pervades campus life. At Georgetown University, students have rallied to have crucifixes placed in classrooms, while at fundamentalist schools such as Oral Roberts University, an evangelical lifestyle prevails. These schools do accept students of different religious affiliations. A popular commercial college planning guide notes that some colleges believe "atheist money is just as good as Baptist money."

- *Historically Black Colleges and Universities (HBCUs)*: Those colleges and universities founded prior to 1964 with the principal mission of educating Blacks. The White House Initiative on HBCUs includes 104 schools under this title. (Interesting note: Enrollment at West Virginia's Bluefield State College, founded in 1895 as a teachers college for Blacks, has been as high as 90 percent White.)

- *The Ivy League*: Eight hard-to-get-into, highly prestigious institutions—Brown, Columbia, Cornell, Dartmouth, Harvard, University of Pennsylvania, Princeton, and Yale. These universities accept students in the top 10 to 20 percent of their high school class, with average scores of 700 on individual SAT exams (verbal, math). Significant achievement in school and outside, extracurricular achievement, leadership, talent, and innovation are also considered in the Ivy League admissions process.

- *Single-Sex Institutions*: Students who might benefit from being away from the distractions of the opposite sex may benefit from private all-male or all-female colleges. In the Black community, Morehouse for men, and Spelman and Bennett colleges for women, stand alone. Morehouse and Spelman, however, are a stone's throw away from each other.

- *Service Academies*: Students earn four-year degrees in a variety of academic areas and are trained for service in the Army, Navy, Air Force, Coast Guard, and Merchant Marines. In most cases these highly selective schools provide free tuition, room and board, and a stipend in exchange for military service for a specified period after graduation. Service academies are open only to unmarried residents of the United States who are high school graduates, under age twenty-five, are at the top of their class, and have demonstrated high moral character. Other admission requirements vary among the academies.

Admission requires a nomination from your Congressman, the Vice President, or any one of a number of other military and government officials. These high-ranking officials don't have to personally know you, but you must apply for a nomination through their offices.

Public and Private Colleges

Most college students attend public institutions, where average annual tuition in recent years was as much as $15,000 lower than private institutions. The following list shows the types of colleges *initially attended* by Black students who eventually graduated and received bachelor's degrees.

Where do most students begin college?

	All Students	**African-Americans**
public four-year college	55%	57.3%
public two-year college	15.5	9.4
private four-year college	28.3	32.4
private two-year schools	1.2	0.9

Included in these figures are Historically Black Colleges and Universities (HBCUs). In recent years about 16 percent of all Black college students attended HBCUs, yet those schools granted nearly 30 percent of the bachelor's degrees awarded to all African American students.

WHAT COLLEGES LOOK FOR

"It's not the high school they went to, but what they did wherever they were."

Harvard Admissions official

While institutions say they want diverse campuses, a national survey of state college admissions counselors found the category for "race/ethnicity" placed near the bottom of the list of factors that can "tip" an admissions decision. Good grades. High SAT and ACT scores. They're the blunt and easy answers to what colleges look for in deciding who gets in and who doesn't. In general, schools look at the following factors. Priorities, or the weight given to specific categories, differ among schools.

- Grades in college prep courses
- Scores on the SAT or ACT
- Overall grade point average
- Class rank
- Difficulty in high school courses
- Special or unique talents or accomplishments (sometimes considered in light of obstacles)
- Leadership
- Active participation in extracurricular activities, in and out of school
- Student essay

- Recommendations
- Community service

The simplest way of determining what college admissions people value and what they expect from applicants is to look at their brochures. Some go into great detail describing the kinds of students they want on their campus. Some give specific guidelines—SAT minimums, grade point average, and class ranks:

A minimum composite score (verbal and math) of 800 is required. A comparable minimum ACT score of 20 is acceptable.— Hampton University

A Hampton recruiter at a college fair explained, "We'll look beyond the grades, but the SAT says a lot. You can't fake that."

Others let you figure it out yourself by offering a profile of their freshman class:

The Class includes 28 percent from college and post-high school preparatory programs which include 179 from navy preparatory schools; 73 from private preparatory schools and 77 who have completed at least six months of study at a college or university. Seventy-one midshipmen previously served as enlisted members of the Navy or Marine Corps.—U.S. Naval Academy

The Naval Academy brochure also listed the percent who, in high school, were student government presidents (11), National Honor Society members (60), varsity athletes (88), and placed at the top 20 percent/first fifth of their graduating class (78). Such information helps students see how they fit in-and are a good indicator of *whether* they would get in.

At those schools where competition to get in is keenest— where the average applicant has an A average and ranks in the top 5 percent of the graduating class—other factors must come into play. Usually these are the traits, talents, and experiences that set individuals apart (characteristics that can be established in your child's earlier years).

In a recent year, Cornell, a member of the Ivy League, received 20,000 applications for 3,000 spaces. With such a vast group of strong students to pick from, it still promises applicants a "thorough, individual review." In addition to grades, test scores, and class rank, it pays close attention to:

Intellectual Potential: In what ways have you demonstrated your passion for learning?

Character: Honesty, open-mindedness, initiative, empathy for others. Do the essays and recommendations in your application reflect these as strong personal attributes?

Involvement: Have you been a leader? Have you developed special talents or interest in music, drama, sports, politics?

College admissions professionals say they don't penalize a student for not taking challenging courses (Advanced Placement, Honors) if they aren't available at their school. They do, however, look for students whose high school transcripts show a willingness to work hard, take difficult courses and make the most of the challenging courses that are available.

A college fair representative for Harvard, echoing most college recruiters, says that a student's entire record is put into perspective. "It's not the high school they went to, but what they did wherever they were. Did they take advantage of challenging courses? If there weren't any, did they seek out other enrichment programs? Did they take chances and attempt new experiences? Did they rise to the challenge of leadership?"

Schools, you must remember, are building a community.

They want a well-rounded community. They don't want everyone to be a bookworm any more than they want all athletes. Still, it's okay if your child is highly focused on and excels in only one area, or has spent as much time on academics as playing the piano or taking care of younger siblings.

Don't try to force your children into the model college applicant. Let their little lights shine wherever they may. But make sure they get strong academics, establish good work and study habits, read for pleasure and out of habit, and are exposed to as many experiences, people, places, and things as possible.

In the end, for strong students, it may not matter that much what colleges are looking for. Such students, in beginning the search for college, should decide where to apply based on *what they are looking for.*

READING, WRITING AND EBONICS

Problem-solving. Technical literacy. Written and oral communication. Leadership and teamwork. These are some of the skills that will be necessary to negotiate a twenty-first century workplace that is multicultural, technology-based, and driven by information. Yet some things never change.

"The new basic skills? They're pretty much the old basics," according to Donald Stewart, then the president of The College Board. "Being able to read—and read analytically—and write, and compute."

Reading is the single most important academic skill in life. It is the route to information, knowledge, and ideas. Making sure your children read daily can lead to a lifelong habit that will stay with them even when their interest in karate wanes.

Most parents know that, and Black students made steady improvements during the past decade in reading and math. They were very far behind and our children still have a ways to go: Only 10 percent of Black fourth-graders and 7 percent of Black eighth graders are "proficient" in reading. Half do not read at the "basic" level. In math, about 12 percent of fourth and eighth graders are proficient, and about half are not on a "basic" level for their grade.

This is why so many people, from classroom teachers to high

school principals to recruiters from every kind of college (especially Historically Black schools), have the same answer when asked, what should parents do to prepare children for college? Their response: Focus on reading, for school and as a personal habit.

H. Patrick Swygert, president of Howard University, adds his insight on a number of issues at the front of this book. But he is adamant about parents' role in initiating and keeping a focus on this basic skill:

"As difficult as it is—particularly for single parents—to find that time and energy, parents must find the time and energy to introduce children to books and literature. One comes home from an exhausting day at work and then has children who need you to read to them or go over homework. But one must do that. There isn't an alternative.

"With all the technology that we have today and the emerging technologies that will be before us in the next five to ten years, being able to read and process what's before us and process it in such a way that we can analyze it critically, that we can dissect the various ideas whether it's on a monitor or whether it's on a printed page—that's the most important skill of any student of any age: the ability not to observe but to observe and to respond critically. One gets that by reading."

In more pragmatic terms, the SAT introduced in the fall of 2005 includes a new critical reading test (replacing the verbal skills test) that measures skills that begin to develop years before senior high school. Students who have been engaged in reading their entire life have expanded vocabularies, have developed critical thinking skills, and are at ease with different styles and forms of writing. This is the best preparation for those important college admissions tests—and it starts early.

The same goes for writing. In an age of information, writing skills take a strong place in the list of basic skills. Nurses must keep notes on their patients, and business people must be able to write a coherent and convincing plan for prospective clients. Psychologists and social workers and teachers and government supervisors are all called upon to write reports and evaluations. Engineers and accountants, too.

The new SAT also includes a writing test. Many school districts, acknowledging the increasing importance of writing, required classes in writing and basic skills tests in writing for graduation years before the new SAT writing requirement was announced.

The links between all of the language skills come together in writing. To write well, students must think clearly, and some of the best writers speak well. Good writers tend to read a lot, learning through deliberate study or just getting accustomed to the way effective language reveals itself on a page. The more you read, the more you see how strong verbs and succinct adjectives make strong sentences; how a stunning opening paragraph grabs the reader's attention or makes a point; how a funny anecdote or a tragic one compels a reader to continue.

Schools always have focused on the traditional academic skills that lead to strong writing: spelling, grammar, punctuation. But the teaching of writing has gone beyond the mechanics of grammar and spelling. Students now develop writing "webs" for character and plot development, study different genres in fiction and nonfiction, and can take courses in essay writing and preparing book reports.

Note of caution: With the emphasis on the "flow" of writing, many teachers are instructed not to aggressively correct grammar, punctuation, and spelling mistakes. Emphasis on such mechanics of writing is believed to "interrupt" the creative process. In the primary grades, when young children are not expected to have mastered spelling and grammar, this might be acceptable to you. By the older grades, however, one mother began to correct her child's "A" work. It was riddled with punctuation and spelling mistakes. An older son, she said, went through the same process. He never mastered spelling and grammar. She was not going to let that happen again.

Being Well-Spoken

When the school board in Oakland, California, declared "ebonics" a distinct language years ago, the uproar swelled from the almost universal belief that young people need to speak the language of the economy they expect to participate in. As comedian Chris Rock jokes, "In America there's two languages: the one you use when you want a job, and that other language."

Whether ebonics or so-called Black English is a legitimate language or not inspires political and cultural debate. But there is no question whether Black children should be required to learn to speak standard English. A Dallas, Texas, school board member's statement on the issue cut to the heart of the matter. "What we know for sure is that the speaking and reading skills of many Black children are still atrocious. It hurts them terribly."

This is what the Oakland school board was confronting when it wanted teachers to learn and acknowledge ebonics. Faced with a population that spoke the English of urban America, the school board sought to validate urban speech while teaching children to "code switch" or translate their home language into standard English. The educators didn't want teachers constantly correcting kids and telling them they weren't talking "right."

In one example, a teacher helped her students identify the differences between their speech ("I be going to the store") and standard English ("I was going to the store") by using both forms. This had been happening with little notice in California until the 1996 uproar. In fact, schools in New York, Michigan, Texas, and California are among those that have been addressing ebonics in similar ways. Even the Linguistics Society of America said using so-called Black English in classrooms was a useful bridge to standard English.

Depending on whom we're with and where we're at, many adults shift between dialects, from down-home talk to the King's English. It's like easing your feet in and out of a stiff pair of shoes. But just like there's a time and place for bare feet, at some point you need to put on our dress shoes. So, whether you love the soulful slang of so-called Black English, or whether it grates on your ears like stereotypical slurring, all American children must know how to speak standard English with comfort and confidence at school and work.

Experts are still divided on whether you should constantly correct your children's language—you don't want to discourage them from talking, after all. But there are many things you can do to help your child speak well. First, speak well yourself. Watch your own language. "Go barefoot" a little less often when your children are around.

Model good speech by summarizing what your child just said using proper English. He'll catch on.

If your own speech is seriously flawed, expose your children to others whose speech you admire.

Tell the older children you care about who know but avoid standard English that they can talk the talk with friends, but must present their formal selves in appropriate places, especially among adults. Says one high school language supervisor, "People form first impressions based on two things: your race and how you speak. Your speech is even more important than how you dress."

Keep all of this in mind when you think your young one talks too much. Do you find yourself frequently telling your children to be quiet? Talking is how children practice the speaking skills that will benefit them during oral reports at school, college interviews, public performances, and on-the-job meetings. Encourage children to talk and express ideas.

An outreach program of the Oakland school district working to improve student speech did so by helping both parents and children read more. See how everything keeps coming back to reading.

ALGEBRA, A 21ST CENTURY CIVIL RIGHT

"The ongoing struggle for citizenship and equality for minority people is now linked to an issue of math and science literacy."

Robert L. Moses, founder
The Algebra Project

"One of the central things we're saying is that the ongoing struggle for citizenship and equality for minority people is now linked to an issue of math and science literacy... It's important to make it clear that even the development of some sterling new curriculum—a real breakthrough—would not make us happy if it did not deeply and seriously address the issue of access to literacy for everyone..."

As a younger man, Robert P. Moses helped organized the 1964 Freedom Summer movement that helped blacks in Mississippi register to vote. It was not a small accomplishment, given the hate and violence waged against Blacks who dared try or encourage others to exercise their basic rights of citizenship. Within a year, the nation passed a Voting Rights Act that outlawed the customary practices and laws designed to keep African

Americans in the south from voting.

Now Moses has turned his passion for equality and justice to the education of disadvantaged children. His founding of The Algebra Project, in his own words, is based on the realization that, "The ongoing struggle for citizenship and equality for minority people is now linked to an issue of math and science literacy."

In most major colleges and universities, you'll see Algebra 1—whether your child wants to major in math and science or not. It's there because algebraic formulas and concepts set the foundation for more advanced thinking and analytical skills. Students who master rigorous math will be better prepared to tackle the entire college curricula, whatever their major. As you've read by now in the section on Early Awareness, Algebra I is considered "the Gatekeeper to College." For years, it has separated the college-bound from the rest of the high school student body. Students who are assigned to algebra are being given the approving nod from educators who think they are college material.

Keep this in mind in all of your young child's math instruction. By late middle school, she should at least be studying some pre-algebra. Tell teachers, if you need to, that your child is college bound (don't think they'll assume it because of your middle class bearing) and needs a foundation for advanced math.

Many students take it in sixth, seventh and eighth grade, but ninth grade is fine, too. In fact, math teachers increasingly say the push for early Algebra is more about parental ego and school system posturing than what's best for the average child (even those dubbed "gifted and talented" by their local school district).

If your child is slated to take algebra early in middle school, ask what he's missing by not taking the usual middle school math curriculum. Also ask, whether your child's middle school algebra class will be as rigorous and comprehensive as a high school class. One school system boasted about the numbers of middle schoolers taking Algebra only to be humiliated when testing of those students, at the end of the year, showed that they barely knew what equations were. And those kids presumably moved on to more advanced math.

Algebra and... Swimming?

My public pool offers summer swimming lessons in two-week sessions. At the end of each session, children are supposed to advance to the next level of swimming. Rarely, however, are they ready to move up. Everyone can see that at the end of the session, as most flail around the shallow end of the pool or barely make it across to the deep end. I asked an instructor why the sessions are scheduled for just two weeks (a total of eight, 40-minute lessons) when it's clear that most kids need more time, practice and instruction before moving on. The pool manager said the shorter schedule is less expensive and less likely to discourage parents who can't or won't invest the time and money that it takes to really learn how to swim. In short, it is a marketing ploy.

At the session's end, the parents who had the time and money to invest re-enrolled their children in the beginning swim class, giving them the time they needed to master those easy strokes before moving on. Others, without questioning the program, tended to find fault with their children and, either dropped swimming, or, hoping for the best, moved them to the next level. The latter group of children continued to fail and struggle in the pool that summer. A lot of those who have been moved up to the intermediate course dropped out. The first group of kids eventually became excellent swimmers, given what they needed (more instruction and practice) to master each level.

The same thing is happening in schools. Kids are rushed through or promoted without acquiring the skills to help them achieve at the next level. Many children who take Algebra I , even those who get A's, may learn enough to get by in their classroom but never fully master the subject. That, at least in part, explains the disconnect between high grades and low scores later on college admissions tests.

The reverse is true in other places. At some elite private high schools, it's not uncommon for ninth graders to retake Algebra I or Geometry even though they took it the year before in middle school. Few middle school students, the schools discovered, begin high school able to do well on a rigorous high school's Algebra or Geometry final exam. They can't show that they *mastered* the subject. By re-enrolling them in Algebra I or Geometry, the high schools and parents are giving students a chance to master the subject—to make sure they can swim well—before moving them on to the next level.

There are a number of reasons for making advanced math part of your child's educational plan, again, whether they are "into math" or not. "Mathematics Equals Opportunity," a report from the federal government, noted the jobs that once required little background in math now call for specific skills in algebra, geometry, measurement. probability, and statistics. An entry level automobile worker, for example, needs to be able to apply algebraic formulas and physics concepts to wire the electrical circuits of a car. And some major car makers require job applicants to pass mathematics and reading tests. A division of Chrysler and Mitsubishi, the study noted, tests all applicants for production and maintenance jobs on high school level mathematics.

Some of the fastest growing job areas are in computer technology and health services, the report continues, and these require substantial mathematics and science backgrounds.

The Bureau of Labor Statistics says the following jobs are among the many that require math and science:

- Chemical engineers
- Dentists and dental hygienists
- Occupational therapy assistants
- Physical therapists
- Roofers
- Tool and die makers

Robert Moses was among the first to identify advanced mathematics as a civil rights issue for the 21st century, as important as realizing the right to vote was in the 1960s. The main goal of The Algebra Project he founded is working with students in urban and rural areas to gain the higher thinking and problem solving skills that are necessary to participate fully in this nation's economic wealth. Those skills develop by taking Algebra. "Without these skills," according to Moses, "children will be tracked into an economic underclass."

Something to think about: The "Mathematics Equals Opportunity" report concluded that doing well in math depends more on taking higher level math courses than on what school you go to. Even if your child attends a school with a bad principal, constant disruptions, and crumbling buildings, if he completes courses in Algebra and other higher level mathematics, he'll have a good chance of excelling in math on college admissions tests and in college classrooms.

COMPUTERS VS. VIDEO GAMES

To the list of basic skills, higher education officials add computer literacy. You'd think that would be obvious by now. But personal computers are still a relatively recent phenomenon. As recently as 1999, when the first edition of *Higher Ground* was published, many people had not realized the importance of the personal computer in their children's school lives. If you still don't use computers at your job or home, you may not realize what your child will miss if he doesn't use this technology during and outside of school. But not knowing how to use computers and the internet today is just like not knowing how to make a phone call.

The basic skill of technological literacy means being able to use computers and the internet to retrieve and collect information. Using analytical and problem-solving skills, our children must be able to use and act on information. The full potential of computers for changing our lives and our jobs seems infinite.

Keep in mind the telephone if you don't already sense the urgency in getting your child online. What would your life, society, your business or job be like if you didn't have a telephone or didn't know how to use it? You'd be crippled without the connection, and at a disadvantage in your ability to communicate and acquire information. That's the role computers have assumed.

Beyond that, computers at home and in the community encourage a learning-to-learn approach beyond the classroom. The kinds of educational software used in schools for math, geography, reading, and writing can be purchased for home computers at a cost that is often less than the latest video game.

As a research tool, the internet is not just for college students and scientists. With a specific address or a keyword, a sixth grader can gather information for his French project from the website of the embassy of France. A science student can browse through the National Geographic files, the National Wildlife Federation, or public television specials for an upcoming report or project. And college-bound students can log onto the "home pages" of almost any college they're interested in, review lists of scholarships, and check out the federal government's instructions for applying for financial aid.

The fact that using computers is a basic skill is increasingly obvious as children progress through school. By high school, there are glaring disparities in the work of those who have easy access to a computer and those who don't. The differences are most obvious in reports and projects. The student with a computer can turn in a polished, professional-looking manuscript (spelling checked by the computer) with dazzling graphics and a Power Point presentation. A child without such word-processing ability turns in a handwritten paper or typed one, with hand-drawn charts. It takes the child on a computer much less time to craft a more sophisticated project.

Substance, not style, you say? Teachers, eager to encourage the neatest and most orderly work, struggle with whether to reward or give extra credit for polished work that comes off a computer.

But there's no denying the student who is on-line can gain the most current information in less time than it takes others to search the library stacks. Consider this student's project on global warming. Without leaving home, she got the most up-to-date data from the National Weather Service's website as it tracked El Nino's weather rampage. She found information on the internet about ongoing national and international efforts to control the weather phenomenon. She downloaded information they had sent her. As an afterthought, the student went to the public library, where she found a half-dozen books with information on global warming. The most current was seven years old.

Some schools open their computer labs to students before and after school, and during lunch hours. Your student should take advantage of this. But the fact is, not having a home computer is increasingly like not having a set of encyclopedias or a dictionary. Those with easy access are far ahead in the computer skills they'll need in college and on the job. Without the ability to log on regularly, students won't likely be exposed to as much information as those who can easily navigate the information superhighway.

If you can afford Sega, Nintendo, or Play Station, a stereo, wide-screen television, or family day at an amusement park, you can afford a home computer. (Some well-intentioned parents pay $60 to $150 for "computers" for their younger children. They're a nice start, but those are toys, not computers. If you don't know the difference, "computer toys" are what you get at toy stores. They even have printers. But if you can't buy software for them, they're just expensive toys. And some of them are no more useful, effective, or fun as a few good picture or workbooks.)

If you can't afford a home computer, you must make sure your child has regular access to one in school or in a public place. In school, find out how often your child will have time on the computer and what he will be doing. Computers in schools are used in a variety of helpful ways. Students may use them to do practice drills, to develop typing and word-processing skills that make the writing process easier and more fun. Some children can comprehend more quickly through a lesson on a computer than looking at a blackboard or listening to a teacher. In general, the computer is a teaching tool that should complement and enhance learning.

Press for specific answers about how computers are used at your children's schools. Some schools have computers, but they are too outdated to be of any value. Others have computers, even computer labs, but don't have the staff to help students spend meaningful time on them. Others have good equipment, but students must share with too many others.

If your child can't get regular quality time on a computer and the internet at school, seek out other places. Computers are in most public libraries, community and recreation centers, and youth centers like Boys & Girls Clubs and the YMCAs and YWCAs and other organizations have computers that students can use.

The value of computers is the ability to communicate and to use and manipulate information. All children need access to them.

Getting Along in a Multicultural World

When business people talk about diversity in the workplace and the need for multicultural skills, many African Americans assume they mean that White people need to understand and know how to get along with people of color. That's what I was thinking when Mary Ann French sent me an advance copy of her book, *40 Ways to Raise a Nonracist Child*. I asked her, "Why do Black parents need this?"

I answered my own question when I read the small paperback, with such sections as *Sensitizing Your Parent-School Organization, Think About How You Define Normal, Insist on Respect, Broaden Your Child's Social Circle, If Trouble's Brewing, Sound the Horn,* and *Challenge Self-Segregation*. These are issues all parents need to address. Knowing how to get along works both ways.

As the nation becomes more ethnically and racially diverse, African Americans, just like everyone else, will have to interact with people of different cultures, in neighborhoods, doctors' offices, shopping centers, schools and workplaces. In fact, Latinos are now the largest minority group in the country.

Yet many, many Black children are concentrated in predominantly Black urban schools, some never having known or had a friendship with a person of European, Asian, or Spanish ancestry. Even in integrated schools, students frequently clique up by race, eliminating entire groups of potential friends and acquaintances who could be a part of their personal and professional network later on.

If you want your children to take a place in the leadership positions of society and move about the country and the world, don't leave them racially isolated. While focusing on our own heritage and history, don't forget that we are not alone in this country, or this planet. Today's young people must understand themselves as well as those who will be their neighbors, employees, bosses and coworkers. They will need to know how to lead, as well as work as part of a team.

The principal of a predominantly Black suburban school, where one-quarter of the seventh and eighth graders are White, Latino, or Asian, laments that her Black students have a false sense of their place in the world. "Black kids clique up. Think they are in charge of the school and don't have to be bothered with anyone different. They don't realize that when they go into the world of work, it'll be a different story."

Indeed, by the time some unpack for college, they may find themselves "the only one" in class, in the dorm, in the choir. This kind of culture shock is repeated every year on predominantly White campuses where Black kids, who grew up without the burden of race bearing down on them in school, for the first time confront different kinds of people and cultures. Some adapt by running for the Black Student Union and sitting at the "Black" table in the cafeteria. They might be able to put it off for four more years, but the time will come when they have to interact in the real world.

For one Black accountant from Detroit, that time came soon

after graduation when he was invited to lunch during the final phase of a two-day corporate job interview. "I was a nervous wreck, unable to connect. I didn't know how to carry on a casual conversation with a White person. I know I sounded stupid and seemed socially inept."

All Black children need a strong, positive sense of their African American heritage (Biracial children need it, too). Introduce them to books on ancient Africa, the Middle Passage, the Harlem Renaissance and the Civil Rights Movement. Make sure they read the autobiographies of famous Africans and African Americans, and are exposed to culture and customs, such as jumping the broom, Negro spirituals, and Kwaanza.

But make sure they study other cultures and customs—and get to know people who are different from them. If your child lives and goes to school in a predominantly Black community, go beyond the boundaries of daily life for new and varied experiences with different kinds of people. Look for exchange programs with neighboring school districts, a scout troop in a downtown area that draws youngsters from all over. Enroll in an acting or dance troop at a university that attracts different kinds of children, or a citywide orchestra that is open to all.

Attend ethnic celebrations such as Chinese New Year and Cinco de Mayo parades. Read stories about Rosh Hashanna and Ramadan.

Black parents have to be vigilant, of course, about racism and cultural insensitivity. Connie Brown teaches third grade and is a loving teacher. Although most of her students are White, this African American teacher finds ways to assure that the culture and backgrounds of all kinds of people are explored and valued.

Mrs. Brown feels keenly about making sure all children feel comfortable with themselves in situations where they are in the minority. As a child whose family moved from Covington, Georgia to Cincinnati to a suburb of Washington, D.C., she learned about this first hand from teachers who were afraid to touch her dark skin, or wondered what was wrong with her (kinky) hair in front of her classmates. "I came home from school crying a lot. I felt inferior."

Almost every minority parent of a child in a predominantly White school has a story to tell of stereotyping, race-based low expectations, cultural insensitivity, or worse, a student is kept out of class for wearing an African headdress because "hats" aren't allowed. A social studies teacher gives awards for the best plantation designs. A third grade teacher is eager to label a Black child "language delayed" when he's really just shy (his parents know that he can talk up a storm around family and friends). A counselor tracks a student away from advanced classes, saying "You don't need to go to college." And to this day, schools hold separate proms for Blacks, Whites, and more recently, Latino students.

Combat such situations by listening and talking to your children and other parents as much as you can and visiting the school as often as you can. Don't coach or condition your children to look for racism everywhere. But watch and listen to how minority children are spoken to, treated, and perceived. Is it any different from the way other children with similar behavior or talents are treated?

Handle troubling situations with calm. Determine the facts; all stories have at least two sides. Give others a chance to explain their thinking and their actions and document rules, if they're used as a fallback. Sometimes frank conversation is all that is needed. If things don't work out after that, take your concerns up the chain of command.

Meet regularly with parents of all backgrounds to talk about things you have in common. This will strengthen the school community and serve as a model for your children about being part of a multicultural unit.

While being aware of negative attitudes our children will face in schools, teach them to respect and get along with those different from ourselves. Just as there's much that we can learn about ourselves, we can teach some of that to others. In turn, we gain insight and understanding about this rich tapestry of human experience that God created.

So why do Black parents need to raise non-racist children? In Mary Ann French's words, "Each generation brings with it another chance to restore balance and grace to our world."

WHAT OTHER PEOPLE'S KIDS ARE DOING

"We just don't know about this stuff until we luck up on it."
Tracey,
a single mother

Private tutors. Ph.D. mentors for school science fair projects. Professional editors for college essays.

Extra workbooks, on-line tutorials, educational software for the home computer. Distance learning classes in Algebra for sixth graders. PSAT and SAT prep classes for kids in grade school. Multiple tries at the SAT, starting in seventh grade. Some of the nation's top students take enough Advanced Placement courses to graduate high school with enough credits to start college as sophomores and juniors.

Some students ask to go to summer school to improve average grades or to get a head start on upcoming classes, or accelerate past their grade level. How about repeating an entire year of high school to improve grades and boost class rank. Senior year and your child's grades are just so-so? Enroll him in a "postgraduate" year or the 13th grade at a private high school.

Forbes magazine reported that there's so much private tutoring going on that for-profit learning centers for students in kindergarten through twelfth grade have grown into a $1 billion business.

That's not all. Each year, children spend summers on college campuses or travel abroad. Older youngsters and teens attend seminars with congressmen and explore the environment on the Chesapeake Bay. Teenage biologists tag turtles in Belize. Young thespians tour with professional acting troupes. The outdoorsy types test their fortitude in real wilderness adventures.

Art students work with professional artists, film buffs make movies with experienced directors. Others are starting their own businesses in young entrepreneur programs. Some young people leave inventor's camp holding their own patents.

What's going on here?

In an ever-increasingly competitive age, many parents, and students, too, are finding ways to get ahead, move ahead and stay ahead academically. For some, it's so much upper middle class posturing about the right schools and the right careers. These are the kind of people who are embarrassed if their child doesn't get into the Ivy League.

But more down-to-earth families are practicing educational savvy, too, by finding additional learning opportunities for their children in and outside of school. Both types of families are spurred on by the realization that students can accomplish much more than the normal school day and regular school year allow. This has led to a level of educational maneuvering and strategic planning (some call it a frenzy) that is more sophisticated than ever before, with opportunities for enriching activities far beyond what's offered at the local afterschool program.

Of course, your children can, and many will, do well without all this "stuff." But you need to understand that all of this is going on. Our students have to compete for spaces in college and for scholarship money with students who are getting every extra advantage.

Some of the most outstanding students excel because of the opportunities gleaned by parents who are serious and savvy about education. These opportunities, available to the students with the most savvy and involved parents, is a form of "affirmative" action that conservatives don't like to acknowledge. When it's time to apply for college and scholarships, they want to talk about "merit."

One of the most glaring examples of tilting the playing field involves the prestigious Intel Science Talent Search. For about $5,000 your students can travel to the former Soviet Union to work with Russian scientists on their school science fair project. If that's too far, there are colleges around the country that arrange for young students to work on their projects in a college research environment. Enroll in one of the five-week science fair summer research programs around the country.

With $100,000 individual scholarships at stake, did you think everyone else was working on their science project at the kitchen table? Come on. See how the academic playing field is tilted?

The societal implications of all this educational maneuvering and academic enrichment outside of school are enormous when you remember that children with limited opportunities will be compared with those who've had all the benefits and advantages of savvy, informed parenting. University of Colorado researcher Lorrie Sheppard summed up what's at stake when this academic opportunity gap widens beginning in the earliest grades. "A normal five-year-old from a lower [income] family comes to school without academic preparation, and is asked to compete with a six year old who has had several years of preschool experience and all the advantages that a middle class environment can afford."

Tilting the Academic Playing Field

Educational maneuvering begins for many families when they decide where to move or buy a home. Even before they have children, they investigate the public schools prior to making a move. What school does a potential neighborhood feed into? What's available at that school? These couples aren't just looking at master bedrooms. They're making real estate decisions on what schools their unborn children will attend.

- The tour guide at a private school let one mother in on this: The school's birthday cut-off date for kindergarten is age five by June 30. Most of the local public schools have a cut-off of either September 30 or December 31. The early cutoff date at the private academy means that most of the class starts kindergarten at age six or with their sixth birthday just weeks or months away. This is a form of kindergarten red-shirting. "Keep your son in a good preschool for another year," the tour guide advised the mother of a boy who was turning five in the summer. "When he starts school next year (at age six) he will be older, larger, more coordinated, and better able to pay attention, sit still, and read than the average kindergartner. You really want them to be older than the rest of the class, especially boys."

- In the early grades, parents also jockey to get their children into the so-called "magnet" schools that attract families with their special programs in science, foreign languages, mathematics. They leave behind others at what may be good neighborhood programs. Nonetheless, in one suburban school district, the media used the unfortunate label POOKS (Plain Old Ordinary Kids) for children not in a special magnet program.

- Summer school, a badge of dishonor when it meant you failed to do the work during the school years, is now a must for families who don't want to "waste" the summer.
- Among some communities, repeating a grade is not a stigma, it's a strategy. An African American girl in the eleventh grade told her mother, "I don't want to go into the twelfth grade with a C average. I think I can do better than I did." The mother agreed, and so did the girl's private school. They gave her an extra year on scholarship.
- In some well-to-do suburbs, kids routinely get into high school gifted and talented classes because their parents demand it. Some students do rise to the challenge of harder course work than their teachers thought they could handle. Later on, colleges are impressed by transcripts that show a student has struggled through a difficult course rather than taken the easy "gut" courses.
- Some parents and students, right or wrong, think being a big fish in a small pond is better than being one of many in an ocean of overachievers. This leads to high school-switching, the practice of enrolling in a high school that is less competitive than what a student is used to. In some

cases, it means moving from private to public school, or from a specialized public program to the neighborhood school. A higher class rank, top academic awards and leadership positions—those things that catch the eye of college admissions offices—may be easier to claim this way. Some students intentionally leave their private schools in order to win scholarships that target kids who have achieved on a national level in the public school environment.

- Then there is the thirteenth grade. Never mind that a student has a high school diploma. More than 100 private schools will take him in for a year of "postgraduate" study. The high school grad can spend this gift of time taking more advanced courses, boosting grades and improving standardized test scores. When he applies for college, it will be a more outstanding candidate that admissions officers will see.

- Entire communities get in on the act as well. A black women's sorority annually holds an SAT prep day. Hundreds of students cram into an auditorium for three hour of verbal and math coaching. A testing professional gives examples that are projected on a screen in the auditorium. It's a great show of community involvement but I've got to tell you, it's the extraordinary student who doesn't start nodding after the first half an hour.

- In one neighborhood, not affluent but upwardly mobile, parents pool their money and hire tutors for the dozen or so kids who are applying to a special high school programs. Admission is by test, and these parents hire the best possible test coaches: Math teachers from the school the kids are trying to test into. When you think about, who better to tutor a child than a teacher. During the summer, parents in an upscale suburb hired the teachers from their children's school for enrichment and tutoring. Imagine the head start these children have just by working with their own teachers before the school year starts.

For some schemes and strategies previously mentioned, you may find educators who disagree or are even appalled. In the case of kindergarten redshirting, for example, some studies show that children who have been held back a grade and are old for their grade level have problems later on.

Many of the things other parents are doing may seem impractical or not in a child's long-term best interest. The important point is to start thinking about your children's education and realize that much more is available than what you see. Realize that sometimes you can create opportunities and use the educational system the same way you work on advancing your career.

Most of the enrichment opportunities and educational choices listed at the beginning of this chapter cost money, lots of it. But lack of money can't be an excuse for not looking into them. Many programs offer scholarships to children who really need them. More and more opportunities are being made available to a wider circle of children, but an interested adult or parent has to be willing to get the information and do the work.

Tracey is one such parent. "Look at all this stuff folks don't want us to know about," she says, excitedly flipping through the summer school catalogue of a New England boarding school.

She is the single mother of one, has a modest income, and

can't afford any of the enrichment programs she sees—archaeology in Spain, marine biology and scuba diving in the Caribbean, Chinese language and culture in China. But she's undeterred. Filling out a stack of papers and meeting every deadline, she gets different scholarship funds to donate the money to cover the $3,750 summer-on-campus program. The next summer, her thirteen-year-old son spends eight weeks on the lushly landscaped campus of Northfield Mount Hermon in Massachusetts, far from his inner-city home.

"Incredible," she says, still amazed at all the school's other offerings. "We just don't know about this stuff until we luck up on it."

That's a misstatement, coming from Tracey. She doesn't luck up on stuff; she goes out and finds it. She is working the network of educational opportunities that has always been in place.

Tracey's example is important, not because of what she "got" for her child, but because she deliberately thinks about and takes action in the interest of her child's education. It began with her decision to use her grandmother's address to get him into a better public school than the one in her neighborhood. She had to plan that. It didn't cost her anything.

Among the things that have a significant impact on a child's future are the strategic planning and involvement of parents who keep themselves informed, learn how the system works, and take advantage of opportunity—in some cases create it. The lesson we can learn from Tracey, and others like her, is to seek information and use it to our children's advantage. All of us can try to do that. In Tracey's case, her moderate income forced her to look for "every dime" to pay for school and enrichment programs.

"Because I'm not making $60,000, I'm forced to ask questions. Opportunities are out there, but most people aren't as hungry as I am," she explains.

Talk to other parents, especially those whose children seem to be doing well. Find out what they're doing with their children, ask their advice. Talk to the parents of high-achieving, successful students. Don't be shy about asking, "How'd you find out about that?"

Don't assume that because you haven't heard about something that it doesn't exist. Each year, my state of Maryland holds classes and summer camps around the state called Maryland Summer Centers for Gifted and Talent Students. The fine arts programs require portfolios and auditions, some science programs require demonstrated achievement in advanced courses. But most are open to any and all who apply on time, while space is available. I often wondered why, with all of the black children enrolled in "Talented and Gifted" classes, so few attend the low-cost summer programs. When I speak to groups of Black parents around the state, I always ask about the Maryland Summer Centers. Without fail, I get blank stares from some parents who are obviously smart and involved in their children's education. But these parents just don't know about the program. When you think about it, if a program is sought-after and popular, there's no need to advertise.

So, how can you find out about things you aren't even aware of?

Besides reading everything on every bulletin board you come across and taking time to visit school guidance offices (or ask your children too), here's advice from Tracey. "Put yourself in the circle of parents whose children are doing things. Get to know the teachers who are involved in the most outside activities, competitions, projects. They know a lot."

One more thing. A *Higher Ground* reader told me the following family story: Her father went to the guidance counselor with brochures about a summer program for his daughter. The guidance counselor advised him against sending the girl, saying she worked very hard during the school year and needed time to relax and have fun during the summer. The father didn't take her advice. He filled out the applications and arrived with his daughter on the first day of the program. He was surprised to see the same counselor there, enrolling her child.

THE BLACK MIDDLE CLASS SECRET

The so-called achievement gap between children of color and Whites and Asians can't be blamed entirely on poverty and disadvantage and racism, as often is the case. They certainly don't explain this sobering fact: The children of our most prosperous and most educated Black families, as a group, don't read as well as poor whites.

It may be the best-kept secret among the black middle class, but the stats, facts and studies documenting The Secret have been around since the 1960's. "Middle class African American students just are not doing well by middle-class Asian American and White middle class standards," says L. Scott Miller, author of *An American Imperative: Minority Educational Advancement.* "People don't want to give ammunition to racists so they don't want to talk about it."

A few bold educators and social scientists—with no links to racist theories about genetics and intelligence—have started writing and speaking openly about underachievement and affluent Black students. They hoped to get African American parents riled up and moved to action when The College Board, the purveyor of the SAT, released the report, "Reaching the Top." In it, researchers including Miller detailed how middle and upper-middle class African-American students, as a group, lagged far behind their White and Asian-American counterparts. On the federal government's National Assessment of Educational Progress (NAEP), it noted, the average reading score for Black 12th graders *with a college educated parent* was two points lower than the scored by Whites *whose parents do not even have a high school diploma.*

There were scattered news reports about the middle-class achievement gap, but no national outcry, self-examination or call to action. Critics pointed out cultural bias and issues of fairness in testing. Some years later, members of the middle-class black community in Shaker Heights, Ohio, asked University of California Professor John Ogbu to find out why their well-to-do children, students in one of the nation's most highly regarded school systems, didn't seem to care much about academics and performed so much worse than their white counterparts.

Why is all of this happening?

For a lot of reasons, deep and complex, many of which historically have been beyond our knowledge or control. Many Black students whose families have means still attend schools with teaching and counseling based on racial stereotypes and low expectations, watered-down courses, inadequate resources, overcrowded classes, marginally-prepared teachers. In some schools, inflated grades give a false sense of accomplishment that holds students back from performing at higher levels.

And some African American students just have gotten it all wrong, avoiding high achievement as a way to stay true to the so-called Black experience. In the case of the affluent Black students from Shaker Heights, Professor Ogbu found that they, too, had developed an anti-academic achievement attitude. (See "Attitudes

About Acting White.")

Our own behaviors and attitudes come into play also, some of which unwittingly perpetuate underachievement. Are our homes filled with heavily-stocked bookshelves and magazine stands, for example, or video games and wide-screen TVs? Do we encourage the young to speak their mind and challenge us with questions and ideas, or do we too often tell them to "Be quiet?" Will we spend money for academic enrichment outside of school, or use limited disposable dollars for trips to Disney World? In short, do we value education in the way we live, or is it just something we say?

Some studies have looked for answers to middle-class Black underachievement by exploring parenting styles, parent's intellectual skills and their relationships with their children. In one, mothers get a full examination with questions about whether we are eager to praise or quick to criticize children, spend time reading to them and take them to enriching activities such as libraries and museums.

Household habits have been explored: Asian and White students, who may not suffer the effects of negative stereotyping and low expectations, generally spend more time on homework. Our kids spend more time in front of the TV. Meanwhile, Asian American students are forming "study gangs" in which good students help each other excel.

There's a lot more going on. For example, Stanford University professor Claude M. Steele has identified a form of test anxiety called "Stereotype Threat" that prevents African American students from doing well when they have to list their race on the test form. (The burden of race creates anxiety and stress that affects their performance. They do better when they don't have to list their race). And, of course, the tools that measure academic achievement are not perfect.

How much of the so-called achievement gap is due to testing bias? Depending on whether you believe The Secret or not, each of us must let go of fear and embarrassment and start talking about it, specifically asking our leaders these two things: Do the reports and stats really prove what they purport? If they do, what can we do about it?

I know The Secret confounds folks, like the mother I know who proudly displays on her refrigerator all her child's A-plus work. She was aghast to see her child then score near the bottom on standardized tests.

AFFIRMATIVE ACTION

"Colleges are going to be less forgiving of middle class Black under-achievers. They can't play the race card anymore."

Admissions official,
University of Texas at Austin

More than ever, students from all segments of American society are seeking college and professional degrees. Latinos, Asians, Blacks, the poor, and White women all are vying for scholarship money and space in institutions that, prior to the 1970s, White men pretty much had all to themselves.

But colleges and universities can't just expand and admit all who want in. As more students apply, more have to be turned down. One of the real reasons behind attacks against affirmative action admissions policies and scholarship programs is that the supply can't meet the new demands.

At places such as the University of California, Berkeley, the University of Michigan, and the University of Texas, many of the rejected are outstanding students. In one year, 29,000 students applied for 8,000 spaces at UC Berkeley. Nearly half of the applicants had 4.0 grade point averages. Still, the school had to send rejection letters to about 19,000 students. Many of them were the straight-A students.

Patrick Hayashi, UC Berkeley's associate vice chancellor at the time, connected those numbers to California's decision to ban affirmative action. "These are the forces that led to [the ban].

The 2003 Supreme Court ruling on affirmative action at the University of Michigan's prestigious law school upheld the way the school used racial considerations in it's admissions decision. However, it struck down Michigan's use of racial consideration at the undergraduate level, saying race can not be an overriding factor.

The elimination of and limits on racial and ethnic consideration in scholarships and college admissions is a reality Black parents and their children must face. It's true that the majority of college-bound students are not headed for the top schools where this is playing out. Selective schools like Berkeley and Michigan's law school attract a relatively elite group of students of all colors who come to college well-prepared and ready to compete. But it is unclear how widely applied court decisions upholding the ban on affirmative action will be at other public campuses around the country. The affirmative action backlash has forced educators to look at factors that limit academic achievement beyond race and ethnicity. In response to California's affirmative action ban, and the Michigan ruling, educators are looking at student applications to determine the impact of disadvantages linked to family income, parents' education, and the quality of their high schools.

Observers of education and the social order say the long-term implications are serious. Fewer Black students, especially middle class Black students who can't be considered "disadvantaged", may have access to the top echelons of higher education and academic research, places from which our country's political, business, and intellectual leaders often emerge. In the year after

California banned affirmative action in college admissions, the number of Black and Latino students admitted to the two premier campuses of the University of California plunged to more than half of what it had been in previous years, to a fifteen-year low. At Berkeley, 191 Black students were accepted, down from 562 the year before.

In the meantime, scholarships and programs that seek out deserving Black youngsters are also being challenged. The Benjamin Banneker Scholarship at the University of Maryland was dismantled after a Latino student filed a suit.

Donald Stewart, then president of the College Board and a former president of Spelman College, has been cautious about the future. "If parents are aspiring to the most selective institutions for their children, then they are going to have to contend with what is becoming a legal and political reality . . .

"[Colleges are] going to throw the African American student applications into the same pool as White and Asian students, and those students on average tend to score a lot higher on standardized tests and often have higher grades. The competition is going to be very, very keen."

Private scholarships are not being spared the affirmative action backlash either. At Northern Virginia Community College, a privately funded $500 scholarship for minority students (named after an African American English professor who died of leukemia) was targeted by a political science major. The young White man filed a complaint to the U.S. Department of Education. Although that scholarship money was raised for Black students from private donations, a public institution—the community college—could not award it based on race.

Another example, from the University of Texas at Austin, is the "Summer Success" program, which helped prepare minority students to enroll in the fall. Summer Success reportedly lost its university funding because of an affirmative action case against the state. The program continued, but only for those who could pay their own way.

The affirmative action backlash extends to the younger grades as well. In one suburban school district, an afterschool enrichment program for African American boys, who as a group were having the most difficulty academically and socially, had to welcome girls and students of all races. The focus could not remain on the young boys, who needed the help and attention so badly.

The response to the dismantling of affirmative action by college officials, however, is heartening. After California and Texas threw out affirmative action, university administrators began to seek ways to maintain their diversity, understanding its importance in educating individuals and in preparing them for the world.

In California, Texas and Michigan, public university officials now look not just at scores, grades, and class rankings, but at the conditions some students face in trying to get to college. Students are given an extra look if they are from poor backgrounds or high schools with limited opportunities yet overcome their circumstances. A new focus on student essays gives young people an opportunity to fully explain their academic records, special circumstances in their lives, or special achievements in the face of obstacles.

This is a bit of good news for those students who have fewer opportunities, for whom there has not been a kind of affirmative action that includes good preschools, private lessons, interesting and challenging courses, safe and well-kept school buildings, drug-free environments, travel, and coaching for the SAT.

African Americans should remember that this good news is colorblind; it applies to all students who have struggled or achieved despite odds, be they Latino, Native American, disabled, Asian, or White. The color in the minority talent pool is not just Black.

If the world were a pure meritocracy, head-on academic competition would be fine. But it's not, and no one knows this better than college admissions directors. They see the direct link between educational and financial advantage-the kinds of opportunities and maneuvering outlined in the previous chapter-and school performance.

For years, "merit," defined simplistically in some places as the highest test scores and grades, was the rallying cry for those who wanted to ignore the fact that student achievement has much to do with having financially secure, educated parents and all the opportunities they provide. By their definition, "merit" excluded many of those who struggled to do well without the advantages of an upper middle class family or community.

Even so, many African American students are competing at the highest levels of academia. One of them, Kwabena Blankson of Birmingham, Alabama, was an academic standout en route to Harvard when he was named to the USA Today academic all-star team. Blankson, with a 95.92 grade point average, played varsity tennis, was in the school orchestra and a string quartet while being student council president. He did groundbreaking research identifying antibacterial properties of the Ghanaian chewing stick and was named a National Merit Scholar.

Schools have always considered factors not-related to academics when deciding who gets in and who doesn't. Those who promote a focus on "merit" often ignore some of the traditional "preferences." As your child makes college plans, at a time when race-based programs are threatened, know that in addition to test scores, grades, extracurriculars, and character, the following politically correct "preferences" can give your young person an edge:

- *Legacies*. The child of an alumnus might have an advantage, particularly if the parent has contributed financially to the old alma mater. If you don't already, contributing to the annual giving campaigns at your old college is a good way you can give back and look ahead.

- *Academic majors*. Schools must fill their different departments with students. In recent years, business, social science/history, engineering, education and health-related fields have been the most popular majors. Listing any of them as a major would hardly make a student a standout at some schools. But if it's oceanic science your child is interested in . . .

- *Geography*. Students on southern campuses gain a wider perspective if students from the Midwest and Mid-Atlantic states are around. Similarly, West Coast students benefit if they can live and study on campus with young people from New England. Almost every college these days is talking about diversity, but most have always sought to expose their traditional students to young people from other parts of the nation. If you're in the Northeast, it may be to your advantage to look at other parts of the country (if your student is inclined to going that far).

- *Rural versus Urban.* Same thinking as above; whether you're big city or country, you'll be more attractive to schools that have few students like you.

- *Development.* This is another word for money, and it refers to situations where the school may gain a significant financial benefactor if the child of, say, a wealthy family, is admitted. The Association of American Colleges and Universities diversity website, quoting two researchers, noted that "access to higher education has never been based exclusively on academic merit; rather, colleges have historically favored those with the most money."

What does all this mean for African American parents and children? A generation ago, many African Americans rode the wave of affirmative action to good educations and corporate jobs. Black folks then were highly accomplished, but we also had the help of social policy that acknowledged prejudice and tried to make up for discrimination.

In today's talk of a color-blind society, people of color know racism still exists. Our children, it seems, may have to overcome it without affirmative action.

None of us can take education for granted. Our children cannot afford to do anything less than their very best. Middle-class Black parents especially can't afford to let their children lean toward mediocrity when so many others are excelling despite poverty, bad schools, and little family support.

In the quote that begins this section, a White admissions official of the University of Texas at Austin, speaking at a convention of educators, put the situation in blunt context for those who cannot claim poverty or social disadvantage, "Colleges are going to be less forgiving of middle-class Black underachievers. They can't play the race card anymore."

Another college administrator from Texas said, "You need to be more than qualified, you need to be competitive as more and more people qualify."

At a meeting of African American parents, a speaker noted, "It's not about being Black, it's about test scores."

Black youngsters can do as well as anyone on the tests if they read a lot, master the basic skills, take the necessary challenging courses, and work hard. In addition, parents must get the information and do the work to help children be qualified, and then some.

Later chapters of this book will detail the steps to raising a student who is not just prepared, but competitive.

Rae Lee Siporin, UCLA's director of undergraduate admissions now retired, said of the affirmative action backlash, "I think there's only one answer: preparation... The question is, do we have the will?"

PAYING FOR COLLEGE

"My parents didn't have a clue what to do. They thought if they didn't have the money in the bank that was it, no college. It was such a helpless and hopeless feeling."

Nathan McCall, Author

Don't let a young person you care about think that college is beyond their reach. With academic preparation, knowledge about financial aid and scholarships, and financial planning, most students who want to go to college can. Get this message to all the young people you care about, even if you're not yet sure exactly how it will be accomplished.

Lower income families need to know that financial aid is "need-based" and targeted at them. The neediest students may qualify for state grants as an alternative to loans that so many college students have had to take in recent years. Foster children and other wards of the state qualify for certain kinds of government-backed education aid.

Government and private money is set aside for children whose parents don't have college degrees, so-called "first generation" college students. Financial aid and scholarships are available to children of deceased or disabled veterans or police officers.

Writer Nathan McCall (*Makes Me Wanna Holler*) says a lack of early awareness about financial aide and scholarships almost cost him his future. His parents, based on the little that they knew, told him they couldn't afford college: "I didn't think about college again until my high school graduation ceremony. Then I saw all these kids marching, and they were getting all these scholarships. I said, "Damn.

"Pretty soon after that I got busted." (After serving three years in prison for sticking up a McDonald's, McCall got a scholarship and graduated from Norfolk State.)

Making a financial plan as early as possible will give your child more options when it's time to choose a college. Yes, money is available, but state and federal funding goes up and down. Students and their families inevitably pay more when funding is cut. Federal grants don't cover as much of the cost of education that they use to as tuition hikes around 14 percent annually in recent years. Special talents, high grades and test scores, and leadership activities and community service are the best way to qualify for scholarships and awards based on merit and competition. The trend among state and private schools is to offer more grants and aid to top students (many from well-off families) than to needy students (with lower grades and test scores).

Organizations of every kind, large and small, give money to deserving students, regardless of how much their parents make. Employers, clubs, associations, civic groups, major corporations, and local businesses award scholarships. (Resources and sources of information that can show you how to find money for college when your child is ready to go are outlined in "The Money Trail.")

College Costs

Understanding the range of costs among colleges and how

they can be met is important in setting your children on a realistic path to a college degree.

How much your student will need for college depends largely on whether it is a public or private institution she attends. The large majority of students enroll in public institutions, where costs are significantly lower than at private ones. Students who attend public colleges in their home states pay about half of what out-of-state students pay.

Tuition, room and board, books, fees, and expenses can put the cost for one year at $40,000 at a private college, $13,000 at a Historically Black University, or $4,000 (room and board not included) at your local community college. Here are national averages for one year of *tuition and fees*.

	Tuition and Fees	Tuition, Fees, Room and Board
Public two-year	$1,905	not available
Public, four-year	$4,696	$10, 636
Private, four-year	$19,710	$26,854

Books, travel, and personal and miscellaneous expenses can add another $3,000 per year.

Get an early idea of the costs of schools you think your child may be interested in.

Most families cover the cost of college through a combination of funds from these sources:

- family income and savings
- student job savings
- federal government grants
- state grants and awards
- low-interest school loans
- private scholarships and awards
- monetary gifts

Get as much information about financial aid and scholarships and how you can accumulate money for college, whether your child is still in the crib or rising to his senior year. Most families find a way, just as my own grandparents did in the 1930s when they traded the family sow and other farm goods for freshman year tuition at Virginia State College for Aunt Flo, the first of eight children to get a college degree.

Future Costs

Projected Average Tuition, Room, Board, and Fees for the Even Years 2006 to 2016						
	2006	**2008**	**2010**	**2012**	**2014**	**2016**
Public 4-year	$12,359.93	$14,363.27	$16,691.33	$19,396.73	$22,540.62	$26,194.10
Private 4-year	$31,206.60	$36,264.69	$42,142.62	$48,973.27	$56,911.05	$66,135.42

Note: The average tuition, room, board, and fees for the school year 2003-4 were used as the base for computing. The projections assume an average annual increase of 7.8% per year.

The reality is that most families have to contribute something to their children's higher education. In fact, it's expected. But too many modest and middle-income families realize too late just how much they'll be expected to contribute.

How Much Will You Have to Pay?

Don't let the high sticker prices shock you. Of students enrolled at four-year colleges and universities, nearly 70 percent attend schools that charge less than $8,000 a year; about 29 percent attend schools charging less than $4,000 in tuition and fees. After grants and other financial aid and award money is applied, most students pay even less.

In general, however, your student's college costs include tuition and fees plus added-on costs such as room and board, pocket money, lab fees, books, clothing, and travel back and forth from home and school. Many scholarships and awards based on achievement and talent do not consider family income. How much help you can expect from state and federal grants and loans depends on your family's finances.

All students should fill out a FAFSA, the Free Application for Federal Student Aid. Based on information you submit on the FAFSA, your family will get a Student Aid Report (SAR) that determines how your family will be expected to contribute toward your child's college. This is called your Expected Family Contribution (EFC).

After your EFC is determined, your student's need for financial aid will be addressed. "Need" is the difference between the costs at a specific school and how much the family is expected to contribute.

School A

Cost of Attendance (COA)	$6,000
-Expected Family contribution (EFC)	-$3,000
Need	$3,000

Once a college gets your child's report, her "need" is typically addressed by a combination of scholarships, government and college grants, low interest loans, and campus jobs.

But what if your student aspires to a more expensive campus? Consider the next example.

School B

Cost of Attendance (COA)	$20,000
-Expected Family Contribution (EFC)	-$3,000
Need	$17,000

Some wealthy private colleges guarantee to meet the financial "need" of any student that is accepted. If, after applying all other financial aide, your students comes up short $10,000, those schools will find the additional money (in actuality, they're just giving you a break on the rest). So don't limit your child's goals and choices too early because of advertised costs.

If the FAFSA determines that your family can pay the entire cost of college (for example, your EFC is determined to be $50,000 a year), your family may still qualify for low-interest loans.

In recent years, student loans have become a larger part of the financial aide package for students at all income levels. They leave students, and parents, too, with heavy debts to repay later.

Reasons to Save

There are few guarantees in financing college. The best plan is to try to save something. Some folks believe that saving for college is counterproductive, however. Because most financial aid is awarded based on need, the thinking goes, if you haven't saved, you'll "need" more money. Your child may learn the wrong lesson about self-help and self-determination from this type of mentality. That EFC (Expected Family Contribution) is based on income and assets beyond savings accounts. It'll be hard to make the case that you "need" financial aid because you haven't put money away when you're residing in a 3,000-square-foot home with an income of $80,000 a year. Here are some other thoughts about saving:

- Only the neediest among us get the government grant money set aside for those in need. The maximum for the Federal Pell grant, the federal government's primary college finance program for the poor, has been around $4,000 in recent years.
- Other federal financial aid programs for needy students depend on funding and are awarded on a first-come, first-served basis. There isn't always enough money to go around.
- Even with financial aid and scholarships, your student could come up short hundreds or thousands of dollars.
- Your student may have to limit his choices or change his plans if the family can't help out. That may mean he can't go to the prestigious university that accepted him. He'll survive, but some schools open more career doors than others. Different schools come with different opportuni-

ties, which have a lot of bearing on how much money a student can earn straight out of college and in the future. A study comparing the wages of college graduates showed that men who graduated from the nation's most selective schools earned 8 percent more than others. Women who graduated from highly selective schools earned 17 percent more than other college grads. If you prepare financially, your student may not have to settle for less.

- For those with a decent income but who haven't prepared financially or done the work that gets scholarships, financial aid may come in the form of debt. Educational loans, unlike grants and scholarships, have to be paid back by someone-you or your student.
- Your student may have personal and miscellaneous expenses that aren't fully covered by financial aid and scholarships. What about all those phone calls home?
- Having money on hand is always better than not having it.
- Except for the neediest students and, in some cases, the most outstanding, parents are expected to contribute to their child's higher education.

One college official drives home the point. "The message is to save and try to have as many family resources set aside as possible. If a student has not saved and needs financial aid, the bulk of that aid is going to be in the form of loans, not grants. And a student is going to build up indebtedness all through college and be encumbered by it just as she enters the job market or aspires to graduate school."

Getting more money by not saving, the official says, "Is a myth... There is financial aid and Pell grants, but that goes only to cover the cost of a very low cost institution. If a student is aspiring to a very elite institution, more aid is needed, and no aid program that I know is going to cover full need."

Start saving as soon as you can, as much as you can. Even if you think your child will qualify for low interest loans, grants, work study, and scholarships, your family will have less to pay out-and more options and peace of mind-if you plan ahead.

For those with the most limited resources, that money eventually may cover only the cost of books and travel to or from school, or perhaps just clothes, spending money, or calls home. However little it is, it will help to have some money on hand. It's never too early to start. And even a small amount of savings can make a difference later on.

At one financial aid workshop, a financial aid administrator agreed to take a look at a couple's finances and project the amount of financial aid their twelve-year-old daughter could expect in six years. It's worth asking.

Also, in the last few years many websites offer online, instant projections of how much financial aid a young child could expect based on information you input. All you have to do in an internet search for college costs calculators.

Ways to Save

Some of the most popular savings options are listed here.
- Certificates of Deposit (CDs). Short-term investments that guarantee a specific return at a specific time.
- Common stocks. Very high risk, moderate or lower risk "blue chip" issues, common stock offers potential income from both capital appreciation and dividends.

- Corporate and Municipal Bonds. Fixed income investments pay a predetermined rate of interest periodically and return principal at the maturity date.
- Mutual Funds. Invest your money with others in a diversified collection of stocks and bonds (portfolio) managed by financial professionals.
- Passbook Savings accounts. This traditional method allows you to deposit money at your own pace.
- Tax-Deferred Annuities. Deposit a lump sum with an insurance company and accumulate interest at a competitive fixed or variable rate.
- U.S. Savings Bonds. Can be purchased from banks, through payroll deduction, or directly from the U.S. Treasury. They're exempt from local and state taxes and from some federal taxes.
- Variable Life Insurance. Your premium is professionally managed to purchase stocks, bonds, money market portfolios, or other investments.
- Zero Coupon Bonds. Instead of paying periodic interest, these bonds offer a fixed cash payment at maturity.

Another method of saving for college is the Prepaid Tuition Plan, which allows you to lock-in prices for young children by making the payments years in advance. First offered in the late 1980s, prepaid tuition plans allow families to purchase tuition contracts to state colleges and universities. Depending on the options and payment plan chosen, the plans guarantee to cover a range of costs up to four full years of tuition. Some states have offered "portable" benefits that can be transferred to almost any college anywhere. Of course, a student still has to apply and be accepted.

Here's how one Michigan family used a prepaid plan. The father of three purchased a Michigan Educational Trust contract for each of his children, ages two to seven, for $8,165 apiece. The total bill was $25,000. The family paid it by taking out a loan the size of a car note. Ten years later, when the eldest child was ready for college, one year's tuition at the University of Michigan was up to $5,710. The eldest child alone could expect to pay at least $25,000 for four years there, but her price was locked in at $8.165.

Section 529 Plans

These plans are savings plans established under Section 529 of the Internal Revenue Code. These are plans that are operated by states or educational institutions to help families set aside funds for college. The earnings from 529 Plans are not federally taxed and your state may give you a tax deduction if you invest in its plan.

Section 529 plans typically are savings-based or prepaid. Educational institutions can offer the prepaid but not the savings plans. As you contribute to the plans you generally can direct the funds to investment vehicles of your choice. The assets are managed by a professional in the state treasurer's office or by an outside investment company hired as the program manager. Before investing in these savings vehicles do your research and/or seek the help of a professional.

Tuition savings plans can be purchased by others and given as gifts to grandchildren, godchildren, etc. If someone you know wants to do something for a favored young person, let them know about how they can put away money for college for the child.

Many financial planners question if the $25,000 in a Prepaid Tuition Plan might not grow in greater value over the years if it is invested in other, more aggressive savings methods. Talk this over with a financial planner.

And what if your student gets a scholarship? What if she doesn't get into the University of Michigan? What if he wants to go to school in another part of the country? What if the family needs the money before it's time to go to college, or for another purpose? What if your child decides not to go to college?

Most state plans address these twists of life through refund payout formulas. If your state offers a prepaid tuition plan, be sure of the terms. Contact your state's higher education agency, listed in the back of this book, for information on what's available in your state.

The following chart shows how much you could expect to have available for college by saving specific amounts each month in an account, such as a money market or mutual fund, that pays 5 or 8 percent interest. You'll see that regular savings can accumulate significantly over time, even at modest rates. The earlier you begin saving for your children, the less cash you'll have to set aside each month.

| | | In Order to Save $5,000 | | | In Order to Save $10,000 | |
| | | Monthly Savings Amount at 5% Interest Compounded Monthly | Monthly Savings Amount at 8% Interest Compounded Monthly | | Monthly Savings Amount at 5% Interest Compounded Monthly | Monthly Savings Amount at 8% Interest Compounded Monthly |
	Years to College			Years to College		
Newborn	18	($14.32)	($10.41)	18	($28.64)	($20.83)
Age 5	13	($22.82)	($18.32)	13	($45.64)	($36.64)
Age 10	8	($42.47)	($37.35)	8	($84.93)	($74.70)
Age 12	6	($59.69)	($54.33)	6	($119.38)	($108.67)
Age 15	3	($129.02)	($123.35)	3	($258.04)	($246.70)

| | | In Order to Save $15,000 | | | In Order to Save $20,000 | |
| | | Monthly Savings Amount at 5% Interest Compounded Monthly | Monthly Savings Amount at 8% Interest Compounded Monthly | | Monthly Savings Amount at 5% Interest Compounded Monthly | Monthly Savings Amount at 8% Interest Compounded Monthly |
	Years to College			Years to College		
Newborn	18	($42.96)	($31.24)	18	($57.27)	($41.66)
Age 5	13	($68.46)	($54.96)	13	($91.28)	($73.28)
Age 10	8	($127.40)	($112.05)	8	($169.87)	($149.40)
Age 12	6	($179.07)	($163.00)	6	($238.77)	($217.33)
Age 15	3	($387.06)	($370.05)	3	($516.08)	($493.39)

You may want to invest your money in aggressive, high-paying savings vehicles or choose safer investments with more modest returns. To reach your specific savings goals, talk to a bank representative or financial adviser who can help you set up an individual plan. Even if you don't have a high income, and especially if you do, putting money aside is more important than ever. Just as over reliance on affirmative action to get into a school is a poor strategy, so is not saving anything.

As you're saving, keep up with all the news about higher education financing locally and nationally. Many resources are new or developing, especially tax credits and deductions that help middle income families, or state merit awards to outstanding students. In Georgia, for example, the number of African American college students soared when lottery-supported Hope Scholarships were introduced. Any high school senior in Georgia with a B-average was eligible for the scholarship, which pays the costs of four years at a state college.

The federal Hope Scholarship Tax Credit can mean a tax cut of $3,000 far some moderate income families with two children in college.

Keep a good credit rating or clean up a bad one. Low interest educational loans may depend on this.

If you're ready to start searching for money for college now, see Part Four.

Finally, remember that crystal balls don't work and guarantees don't exist. No one knows what kind or how much state or federal funding for higher education will be around when your children pack up for campus. Political commitments shift, and so may society's willingness to help families pay for college. Who knows how high or how dry the scholarship well will be when your child is ready to go?

BEING INVOLVED
THE "CUTE YEARS" AND
BEYOND

*"Most people don't realize the role they play in the
education of their children."*

James P. Comer, M.D.,
Yale University Child Study Center

Parents and extended family traditionally have helped with
schooling as much as they could. One mother couldn't understand her daughter's work, but she dug earthworms in her yard
on rainy mornings so her daughter could use them for extra credit in biology. Another stayed up with her teenage son at the
kitchen table. She couldn't help with his advanced math but sat
there doing bills as a sign of supportant to keep him on task.

For all the ways we've learned to help our children at home,
parents previously remained virtually silent when it came to academics, leaving the running of school and the actual teaching to
the "experts." They accepted educators' words as law and truth.
They put the blame for not learning on the kids. It's not hard to
understand that parents without much education put their trust
in those who had a lot.

Beyond Bake Sales

To see how much parents' roles in education have changed, look to Dr. Marian White-Hood, a Principal of the Year. She wants to see parents at her middle school inside the school building no less than four times a year. She schedules opportunities for much more involvement than that.

Parents can take a walk through the halls, check out the cafeteria, sit in on a class, enjoy a class play, conference with their child's team of teachers, speak before classes about their fields of expertise. On weekends and evenings they can come in for workshops that show them what's going to be covered in the state functional tests, or explain the math problems the teacher will send home next week.

Those who can't come in regularly can check out the website for the most up-to-date news about school activities, or leave voice mail messages for staffers and teachers.

What's happening at the school in a predominantly Black middle class suburb is a well-coordinated parent involvement effort that makes it easier to stay in touch with teachers, know what's happening in the school and take an active role in the education at home.

Most of our children don't go to schools whose principals are distinguished as among the best in the nation. But the level of parent involvement at the school is a model for redefining the role of parents in public education. Making it easier to be part of your child's school life has become a national priority. And it became public policy with the National Education goals. "Every school will promote partnerships that will increase parental involvement and participation in promoting the social, emotional, and academic growth of children. "

The numbers bear out what's at stake if you aren't actively involved in your child's schooling. In families in which both parents are involved, 51 percent of the children are likely to earn straight A's. Among families in which neither parent participates at all, or at best attends one school activity in a year, the number of excelling students drops to 27 percent.

These numbers, from a survey of 17,000 kids in kindergarten through twelfth grade, helped fuel a movement to change the role of parents in school.

It's part of the equation: Parents must be involved at home and at school if our children are to get the kind of academic and social education that prepares them well for college and beyond.

That's why every year, local and national organizations promote these Back-to-School practices: Accompany your child to school on the first day. Meet teachers and exchange phone numbers. Tell them your expectations for your child.

The parents of African American children who go on to do well in the nation's best colleges have at least three things in common: They stay involved with their children's school, develop positive attitudes about learning, and monitor schoolwork at home.

One of the first things you can do to set your child on the path to college is connect home and school. Adopt a philosophy that learning is not limited to the classroom but is ongoing and can happen anywhere.

Develop a Positive Family Philosophy about School and Learning

Your children spend about 180 days a year in school. Those days average six hours. Do the math: more than half of your child's time is spent outside of school. To make the best use of that time, parents should make the home a place of learning and the world a classroom.

Start by furnishing your home with materials that say learning is a way of life: books, books, books, paper, puzzles, art supplies, maps, a globe, newspapers and magazines, educational games.

Recognize that teachable moments and learning opportunities can be unplanned, and happen anywhere, anytime. Do this by listening to your child and taking the time to answer questions. Stop to explain and discuss current events, the immoral behavior in the television shows they watch, for instance.

Make reading a regular part of home life. Expose your child to new things, people, and ideas. Take inexpensive trips to museums, community theater, concerts, folk festivals, parades, a farm, or a big city. Show respect for your child's school and teachers. Even if your child goes to a school that is struggling or faltering, show respect for the concept of school. If you've got bad things to say about what's going on, don't say them in front of your children.

Connect Home and School

Make sure your child has the basic school supplies at home. Set up a regular work space and work time. The kitchen table, with good light and no TV or radio in the background, is fine.

Take ten minutes on school nights to ask and check. Ask about the day's events, upcoming deadlines, and what your child needs to complete any assignments. Check notebooks and backpacks for the things kids "forget" to show their parents.

Help but don't do your child's homework. If you can't help, get on the phone to someone you know who can assist. If no one's available, send a note to the teacher explaining your child's difficulty or have your older child let the teacher know he needs help getting the work done.

Stay in Touch with School

Going to your child's school shows him that school is important and shows the school your child's education is important to you. Visit, at least once per grading period. That can mean simply going inside and chatting for five minutes with the teacher before or after school. If you have more time than that, sit in on classes, check out what's been going on in the cafeteria. Walk through the hallways and evaluate the condition of the building, the atmosphere of the place where your children will spend more than a thousand hours per year.

If you want to know how safe it is, don't wait for news stories. You can tell by sitting in the main office, the buzz center for what's going on around the school, for twenty minutes.

Most school districts have open-school policies, and in most areas, citizens, especially parents, have a right to visit at any time. Call ahead for an extended visit and always report to the office as soon as you arrive.

Call or send notes to your child's teachers about concerns or issues that might involve your child's schoolwork or behavior. Don't leave the teacher to guess what's going on, and don't wait until small problems become big. Also, pass on good news with notes or calls about something good about your child.

Be prepared when you have a conference with a teacher or staff member. Write your questions down in advance and ask how much time you will have to talk. Know what you want to get out of the conference: Advice? Information? Referrals to other resources? An agreed-upon plan of action? Before you leave, check your notes to see if your major issues have been addressed. If you need to, plan to meet again.

If there's a big problem, prepare to share the responsibility for solving it, no matter where you think the blame lies. Ask what the teacher/school will do to address it. Ask what the student can do. And ask what you can do. Make problem-solving a team effort— you'll get more cooperation this way in a situation that could otherwise lead to defensiveness and finger-pointing. That usually solves nothing.

Volunteer. With all the ways parents can now participate in schools, baking cookies is underrated. But schools still need to raise money. Your child will be boosted just by knowing you helped out. Look for other ways to be involved. Offer to be a guest speaker in a class if you have specific expertise or information.

Also look for ways to get your children's school involved with you. A newsletter, school handbook, voice mail or recorded phone messages, or an open house help connect parents to a school's daily life and regular goings-on. Suggest parents' workshops on specific parenting subjects, or even academic subjects your child is taking. Ask your school to schedule events so that working and single parents aren't stretched too thin during the week. Suggest a parent resource center where information from inside and outside the school is available for easy pickup. Schedule cultural events that include and welcome people of different backgrounds. In short, get your school's PTA and staff thinking about how to involve parents in positive ways, not just when problems arise.

Now that you fully realize how important it is that your family and school work together, get involved in your "village," too. Black social organizations popular in the fifties and sixties, such as Jack and Jill, formed clubs in which Black children could gather for cultural and social activities. Some of these clubs got a bad rap for being elitist; it cost money to join, by invitation. In many cities, only the children of the Black upper crust belonged. But the parents who developed Jack and Jill were right in building an intimate community in which African American children could focus on social skills, learning, and culture outside of school. This is what more Black communities must do. Community groups around the country are doing this with afterschool centers, weekend tutoring, mentors, and rites of passage programs, to name a few.

There is also much parents can do informally. Many African American women like to take time to gather and discuss their favorite books. We can use that same time and energy to organize children's book clubs/reading groups. Make it a social event with light refreshments, not an academic assignment. For help with this, check out *The Mother/Daughter Book* Club by an African American mom, Shireen Dodson.

Start your own culture clubs. Take turns bringing your children to museums, community theaters, and new exhibits. Keep everyone looking for free events or those group tickets that make learning more fun—and are less expensive than the latest Disney movie. Check the newspaper's calendar of events regularly for these opportunities.

Start a parent support network in your child's class or school. It doesn't have to be as formal as the PTA. Seek a casual network in which you can get on the phone and compare notes or share information. Discuss your own ideas for helping the children in your "village."

Good Fathers, Good Grades

The Million Man March, if it did nothing else, made Black men rethink their roles in the family. For the first time, some men learned and acknowledged how much their women and children need them.

Both boys *and* girls need their fathers, young babies *as much as* teenagers. That's nothing new, but now come documented studies that show that children need their father's involvement in school, too.

The Department of Education numbers mentioned at the top of this section, linking good grades to parental involvement in school, are not surprising. But the same study found that the straight A students had fathers who were more than just stern taskmasters about homework. Fathers who volunteered at school, attended meetings, chaperoned field trips, and met for one-on-one parent-teacher conferences were more likely to have exceptional students than those who didn't.

Howard University political science professor Alvin Thornton says the importance of school involvement by Black fathers cannot be overstated, especially for boys. "You do not see Black male children failing in any school where the father is actively involved in the educational activities of the school," Thornton says. "I'm talking about serving on committees, being PTA president. Not just fighting with the teacher about math grades, but modeling how to interact with the educational system."

Tragically, however, more than half the fathers in two-parent families and a whopping 82 percent of fathers who do not live with their children are not significantly involved in the schools their kids attend. Mothers have been carrying so much of the load for so long. But why should they, if your child can do even better when Dad is part of what's going on? If you know one of those absent fathers, or if you know one who's around but not really there for his kids, show him these numbers and Thornton's statement.

Staying Connected,
For the Parent Who's Not in the House

Not being nearby is not an excuse for not being involved. If you're not in the home with your child, you'll just have to work harder at it. Talking regularly with your school-age child should get you some of the information you may miss if you don't see all the handouts, announcements, or are not the first person teachers call with concerns or praise. If you're nearby, make the same effort to visit the school and meet teachers as the custodial parent.

Most public schools can't afford multiple mailings for individual students. So to help keep open communication about school matters, one parent can submit to the school office a set of self-addressed, stamped envelopes to mail a second set of reports and announcements to the non-custodial parent. If that's too much of a hassle, the custodial parent can photocopy them and pass them along.

If one of you cannot make it in person to a parent-teacher conference, find out if the school can set up a conference call. Or, bring your cell phone and keep the other parent on the line for a three-way conversation.

Beyond the "Cute Years"

This is the lament of middle school and high school educators: The years after age ten are the "forgotten years." Past worrying about day care, mothers and fathers start retreating from parenthood. You know it's true because all those who crowd preschool and primary grade events start slacking off in middle school and all but disappear in high school. There's no more urgency to "see him in his little costume," no scrambling to make sure there's film for the camera, no determination to take off in the middle of the day to hear his science project presentation. We coo less and less that "she's soooooo cute."

"You can't fill a closet on back-to-school night at a high school," one public school teacher said.

The tendency to let go evolves naturally, of course. Their physical statures—sometimes they're bigger than you—make it easier to treat older children and young teens as mini adults, capable of fixing their breakfasts and dinners, too. This professional mother's relief at her daughter's eleventh birthday is not uncommon. "I can do more night meetings now," she said, relieved that the girl now could "watch TV in her room until I get home."

Older children can do for themselves more, and we should let them. But these young adolescents need their parents as much as ever. This is a period when youngsters begin making "major decisions about values, standards, attitudes and personal beliefs," according to the National Middle School Association. Yet many youth spend less and less time with parents just as they are trying to define themselves and just as they are facing serious choices about drugs, sex, and school. Imagine the mother of the eleven-year-old with the TV in her room. What will she miss if she starts coming home later and later?

The National Longitudinal Study of Adolescent Health, a survey of 90,000 seventh through twelfth graders, showed that adolescents with strong emotional attachments to their parents and teachers are much less likely to use drugs and alcohol, attempt suicide, engage in violence, or become sexually active at an early age.

The study does not suggest that they need the same round-the-clock care and attention as a newborn, or that parents do a disservice to older children by being in the workplace. It just means that older children and youth need their parents as much as younger children, but in different ways-even if they tell you they want you around less and less. How many of us have waved to our junior high son in the school hallway. There's no more excited, "Hi, Mom." Instead, they recoil with embarrassment at the sight of you.

But this is the time when they need you to be there, too, if only at a distance.

A funny thing is happening at the middle school where Principal White-Hood insists parents come in four times a year. "Our kids are embarrassed if their parents *don't come*."

PART TWO

The Early Years, Middle Years

"Our young people can't get into the University of Texas not because of what happened in the twelfth grade but because of what happened in the second grade. "

Rev. Jamal Harrison Bryant

ESTABLISHING A MINDSET FOR HIGHER EDUCATION

Four of the McCray siblings have eight bachelor's and master's degrees among them. Telia, the oldest, holds a master's in Electrical Engineering and a Ph.D. in Transportation from the University of Michigan. Monique earned her medical degree from the University of Colorado Medical School, and is an ear, nose, and throat specialist. When I last talked to the family, Christophe L., an academic standout at North Carolina A&T, was working on a Ph.D. in Laser Physics from Hampton University. Rispba, the youngest girl, was on the way to getting a doctorate degree in molecular biology from the University of Pennsylvania. Meanwhile, Demetrius, the youngest, was making his way through undergraduate school.

How their parents, Christophe and Pensal McCray, raised five academic standouts has all the elements of parenting success: two committed, loving parents who instilled a love of learning and the importance of school, exposed their children to different people, places and experiences, kept strong ties to community and church, and set a deliberate plan for their children's education. Christophe J. McCray says the couple's strategy amounted to "intense, concentrated" love and support. "We trained them to want to be the best," says the proud papa. "Then we showed them how."

A piano teacher married to an optometrist, Pensal and Christophe were blessed to have the time and income to raise five children well. Pensal was a stay-at-home mom who worked full-time at preparing her children for college. Through the couple's experiences, there are lessons for everyone about how to raise children in excellence beginning with developing a mindset for education in young children.

It's one thing to want our child to go to college, but your children must want it, too, if they are to do all the work to get there and avoid the social pressures and messages to do otherwise. As they get older, children will more fully appreciate and understand how to set goals and work toward them. They'll learn the difference between quick and easy materialism—a focus on clothes, expensive shoes and designed bags—and the lasting value of education. From the beginning, however, parents of successful college students introduce higher education as one of the steps in life's journey: elementary school, middle school, high school, college.

Pensal McCray's approach was direct. "I told my girls when they were three or four that they would go where I went, Bennett College, in Greensboro, North Carolina. I told them they would be 'Bennett Belles.' I guess I sort of brainwashed them. I told my son he was going to North Carolina A&T.

"We talked about the importance of education and what it does-we told them it's really the only way out. It's a nightmare in Black America if you don't have it."

Most aren't as blunt or decisive as Pensal McCray, but children must get the message one way or another. Veronica Vella, an Industrial Engineering major at Georgia Tech, just assumed she'd go to college, a message she got by example and by word. "It was something I always knew was going to happen. My parents were always involved in my education."

Terri Brantley, a Political Science major at Columbia University, got the message almost as directly as the McCray kids. "My mom said, 'You will go.' Until the tenth grade, I didn't realize you didn't have to. I thought there was no break after the twelfth grade."

Some thoughtful educators feel the early elementary years are too early to talk specifically about higher education. They reject the idea of deliberately talking up college and the importance of doing well in school to young children. Early learning should be in natural response to innate curiosity, not motivated by the far-off prospect of a degree and a good job. To some, deliberate, calculating efforts to steer and prepare children for college at a young age may be inappropriate. A wonderful teacher I know at a school that draws mostly affluent families, feels this way. "We never related to our children nor do I with my students, the need to have good grades for some future goal," she says. "Students need to work their hardest for personal fulfillment now."

This is a wonderful philosophy. But in reality, it plays out most often for children from homes and schools that operate under the best conditions, places where they have the support and security that tells them they are of value in a society that also holds a bright light on their futures.

Children of such advantage accept as a given that they will do well in life-they don't have to be prompted or told. They expect it. Even the thoughtful teacher continues that her own children get the message indirectly that going to college is "who we are, who you are."

Unfortunately, most African American children don't get that message. In some communities, boys and girls believe they have a better chance of getting shot or going to prison than going to college. They live among the statistics. At last count, a third of young Black men in this country were on probation, parole, or incarcerated. Prison, not college, is a rite-of-passage in some communities. As slim as the odds are of a young Black man becoming a professional athlete—about ten thousand to one—our sons also have a better chance at the NFL or NBA than at getting a doctorate degree. Meanwhile, having a baby is the only achievement some young women count on.

Lillette Green-Campbell doesn't think African American parents can rely on children's natural curiosity to lead them to achievement later on. "I don't believe in my heart of hearts that Black children have that luxury," says Green-Campbell, the director of Bridges Academy, an all-Black independent school. Green-Campbell gives loud and clear messages to her students daily about how far they can go in life if they study and work hard and believe in themselves. It's imperative when popular culture and the media glamorize rappers and teenager NBA millionaires while ignoring Black professionals and scholars.

Begin to counter messages that Black children are not intellectually inclined by portraying college as one of the steps in a life of learning. Don't assume they'll get the message from school—some will, some won't. You must give it to them.

Explain what college is to little ones. In simplest terms, it's a place where older kids go to study what they want to be when they grow up. Point out colleges that are in your community. You may ride past some regularly. Do your children know what goes on there? Tell them.

Take advantage of children's programs on nearby college campuses, particularly any Historically Black College or University. Student drama groups produce plays that the public can attend free or at low cost. Some student groups have tutoring and other programs for children on campus. A university's School of Education may conduct their own early childhood or preschool programs. Enroll your child if it's convenient and affordable. Your child will see examples of young adults continuing their education.

Share your own experiences if you went to college. Recall your roommates, the classes you took, the parties you went to, the clubs you joined. College isn't just about classes and studying. Let them know about all the fun you had while you were learning. Introduce them to people who went to school with you. Let them know that these adults were once young (believe it or not) and they went to college to study.

Introduce them to college students. Young people in church are often college-bound, others are already enrolled. You children may not know that some young people are just working at McDonald's to pay for books.

At some point most African American children are confronted with negative peer pressure about doing well in school. You'll have to deal with these anti-achievement attitudes sooner or later. (See "Attitudes About 'Acting White'" and "Having the Talk.") Start battling that message now by making doing well in school the popular thing to do, and point out the role models who prove it, not just the studious, but people who excel in class and outside of it. Sean "Puff Daddy" Combs went to Howard University. Spike Lee went to Morehouse.

Michael Jordan, Grant Hill, and David Robinson made it to the NBA, for example, but they also attended the University of North Carolina, Duke, and the U.S. Naval Academy, respectively. They're good with the ball, but they also have something under the cap. Delante Hamilton, a Morehouse College graduate, remembers when he first saw college as an option for him. "When the show *A Different* World came out, I was in sixth grade," he says. "I just was surprised. The people I was used to seeing at that age weren't doing much, living with their parents. I had never seen that part of life."

Talking about college is a chance to start talking about possibilities, the beginning of career exposure. Use examples: If you want to be a nurse, you could study at Howard University's School of Nursing. If you want to run your own company someday, you could study management at the University of Pennsylvania's Wharton School of Business. If you want to be a police officer, you could study law enforcement at the community college.

Visits to the library can include looking at books such as Scholastic's *I Can Be* series. *I Can Be an Animal* Doctor or *I Can Be a Biologist.* There are several similar series of books on careers for students of all ages.

If you didn't go to college, point out professional people you know who did. Your child's teacher, principal, and school faculty went to college. Let your child know that's how they became educators. Your minister, the doctor and dentist, and others with whom children should regularly be in contact with also are college grads.

A twenty-seven-year-old mother of a second grader says she has always talked to her daughter about college. "When you go to college, you won't see me every day. You'll be living with your friends on campus." After so many of these conversations about going away, Laquisha, five, said, "When I go to college, I'm not going to go far, because I'd miss you." Laquisha was already familiar with terms like "campus" and "dormitory."

Her mother pointed out that friends and family who hadn't gone to college or had dropped out of school as pregnant teenagers, were less well off and working at dead-end jobs. "They can't do all the things we do; they can't travel, for one thing," she told Laquisha. Somewhat apologetically, she confides, "I feel bad. Maybe I shouldn't say those things about other people."

Maybe she shouldn't. While college is what you want for your child, other life pursuits should never be put down. Our ancestors were unschooled for the first two hundred years in America. We come from a people who toiled in the South's cotton fields and cleaned up after others. There's nothing wrong with honest physical labor or blue collar work that is done well and with integrity. That's what paved the way for our generation and those that will follow.

Mary McLeod Bethune, it is said, never lost sight of the value of less than glamorous work. When a train conductor snidely asked this woman of majestic comportment if she could make biscuits, she replied, "I am an adviser to presidents, the founder of an accredited four-year college, a nationally known leader of women, and founder of the National Council of Negro Women. And, yes, I also cook good biscuits."

Remind your young children that their elementary and middle school education is an important step in preparing for college. But you must do more than talk about the future. You must work with them in the present. The teacher who rejected early thinking about college is right when she notes, "Understanding and feeling the sense of accomplishment and achievement on a daily or weekly basis is probably the best preparation there is. A student who knows the satisfaction of learning will want to continue naturally."

EXPOSURE, EXPOSURE, EXPOSURE

Learning can happen in the backyard, in the neighborhood, downtown, on a trip to visit family, indeed almost anywhere. To keep her five children excited and curious about new things, Pensal McCray started exploring America. With their mother behind the wheel of the family station wagon, her children saw California, Toronto, Niagara Falls. While her husband worked, she and the kids kept the gas tank full, driving from Denver to Arkansas to Mississippi.

"We'd study the maps and decide where we were going to go," she explains. "We went to museums, to the World's Fair in Canada. We'd stop on the way back and pick peaches and things so we'd always have fresh fruit. We checked out the local places of interest. We took our time. It wasn't that expensive. My old college classmates put us up. I wanted my children to see the [United States] before they left the country."

That was fun, but McCray always knew her purpose. "Each place we'd go, we'd stop at a university or college. We'd buy little sweatshirts, look at the buildings. I'd say, 'One day, you're going to be going to college.'" My youngest was four.

"When they got older, they participated in the Denver Sister Cities program. They went to live in a home in another country. They have traveled the world. Kenya, Japan, France, India, South

America. Sometimes they went through youth ministry programs.

"Each time they went and came back, we saw a change. They were more mature."

The McCrays' house rules? No television on weekdays. Only two or three hours during the weekend. After- school hours were spent in the library four blocks away, where anybody who hadn't finished homework by the time Mom or Dad came to pick them up got left behind. The McCray children learned to love books, and also became fascinated with the science and medical collection on the library's third floor.

The McCrays kept their children on the go, swimming, dancing, music. They were members of the renowned Colorado Children's Chorale. "My daughter is thirty years old now," she says, "and you won't find a television in her town house."

A principal of an Afrocentric elementary school said that she believes minority children don't do well on standardized tests because they lack the exposure to sights, sounds, words, experiences, people, places, and things that others experience by doing things with their families.

"Those tests have as much to do with what they learn outside of school as inside. That's why the scores remain so low." The mother of a daughter, the principal said she had little money after her divorce. But, like McCray, she stays on the road, going to free or low-cost events that might give her daughter a new way of looking at things, to pick up ideas and information she might never get otherwise. "So many things are just a tank of gas or bus token away."

When author Patrice Gaines's daughter was twelve, she

brought her along on a trip to California. "It made such an impression, I tried to travel with her more. It didn't have to be some big visit. It was just so she could see people lived in a different way. Every learning experience doesn't have to cost a thousand dollars or be real fancy; it could be just walking in the fields where someone is planting peanuts."

Gaines, who was jailed for drug possession in her youth, scraped together money to expose her daughter to things she knew other families gave their kids. "I thought seeing things, doing things, was better than Mama telling her 'You can do this or that.' "

Things to Do

Wondering what you can do with your children besides renting the latest video, catching a new movie at the mall or going to the overpriced amusement park?

Museums: At public museums, don't try to see everything in one visit. Plan on spending time viewing a few specific exhibits, reading, looking and studying them in order to learn more. You can return again to look at things you didn't get to the last time.

Live theater: High school, college, and community plays are free or inexpensive, as are children's theater companies. Check local newspaper listings. Get together the young people you know and buy group tickets to professional theaters.

Live music: Children's classical music concerts, school orchestras, and community music festivals introduce children to musical instruments.

Nature: Zoos, working farms, botanical gardens, a beach, planetariums, aquariums, state parks, and science centers: They expand a child's love of animals and their wonder about the environment.

Historical tours: Don't be limited to, but certainly explore, African American roots. Visit the Martin Luther King, Jr. Center for Nonviolent Social Change if you're in Atlanta; the home of Frederick Douglass when you go to Washington, D.C.; the African Burial Ground Historical Marker in Manhattan; the Buffalo Soldier Monument in Leavenworth, Kansas; the Great Blacks in Wax Museum in Baltimore.

Other cultures: Celebrations, parades, ceremonies, traditions.

Travel: Day trips-find someplace to go in all four directions for major vacations by bus, boat, train, or airplane.

Civics: Check out the seats of power in your backyard. Visit town hall, walk the halls of your state capitol, tour the governor's mansion.

Worship centers: Visit different churches, mosques, or synagogues.

Ethnic restaurants: Not just the predictable restaurant chains.

Anytime: A trip to the grocery store, landscape nursery, well-stocked bookstores and libraries for author readings, a community park where ducks reside, a bike trail, fishing pond, another neighborhood.

Delante Hamilton, the Morehouse grad, discovered in his freshman year that outstanding students like him had a lot in common before converging in Atlanta. "It wasn't an accident that we all ended up together at the same place. Although we never knew each other, we followed the same path. Our mothers were taking us to the library, to museums, doing all the same things."

BASIC SUPPLIES

Every preschool and primary student needs the following learning tools in the home:

- shovels, buckets, sand or dirt, foam and water for play outdoors and inside
- outdoor play equipment such as balls, puzzles, blocks, board games
- crayons, markers, chalk, pencils and sharpener, compass, erasers, glue, tape, rulers, writing paper, drawing paper
- children's picture dictionary or first dictionary, children's encyclopedia
- globe, clock with moveable hands
- daily newspaper—some have Just-for-Kids sections
- a subscription to a children's magazine (in your kids' names)
- picture books, nature books, poetry books, true stories
- a library card
- access to a computer with educational software
- children's spiritual books, such as Bible stories, the Koran

In addition, for the middle years:

- a student organizer/assignment book to write down homework, a watch
- rulers (metric, English), compass, protractor, calculator (scientific, graphing)

- student dictionary, student thesaurus, encyclopedia, reference books or software (Collegiate and business reference books confound young learners. Buy the kid-friendly versions that they can understand and use more easily)
- pocket foreign language dictionary (French to English, Spanish to English, etc., depending on what language course they take)
- globe, atlas, world maps
- writing and drawing paper, pens and pencils scissors, colored pencils, markers, glue for projects
- spiritual books for youth, such as a student Bible, cultural heritage books, historical fiction, autobiographies, classic literature and novels, folktales, myths, poetry
- regular access (at least weekly) to a computer and the internet

Keep small, loose items in the same box or container together or else you'll give your child plenty of room for procrastination and disorganization: "Where's the ruler?" "My pencil's not sharp."

Getting your child to be responsible for her own supplies, keeping them organized, and knowing where to find them, helps her work in an organized fashion, free of excuses and disruptions. This will he vital in college, where staying organized and managing time are crucial to doing well in class.

Children also need a regular bedtime that allows them enough sleep (about nine to ten hours on school nights); a healthy diet (plenty of fruits and vegetables, grains such as rice, breads, pasta, lean meat, low-fat milk products); a quiet place for reading, doing homework, or daydreaming.

Something to think about: The mother of a preschooler bragged that her child already was computer literate. "She stays on it, and she'll play on it by herself for a good while. She knows how to use everything."

Many of the old basic supplies are on CD, but software and computers are not a replacement for books. Or for you. Children still need parents around to help them interact with computers and software and to interact with them. Older children certainly need supervision on the internet, where other teens and adult predators are eager to have contact with kids. While you stock your home with high-tech learning tools, make sure you don't turn them into high-tech babysitters. Besides, there's something about holding a book in your hands, old fashioned as that may seem to some.

BASIC SKILLS

In a bookstore, a young woman and her friend finished browsing the aisles of popular fiction and romance. One of them caught her baby girl by the hand and slapped it. "Put that down, you can't read," the young woman said, snatching a picture book from the toddler.

On another day, in a different bookstore, a brother searching the reference section warned the preschooler with him, "Don't move. Don't touch anything." The child obeyed, watching as other little kids around him fingered the thick embossed lettering on a picture book's cover or flipped through pages of nature books. A red-haired boy spread-eagle on the floor was absorbed by the silly pictures of *Cat in the Hat*.

Maybe you've seen this kind of scene before. It's a form of harsh parenting that keeps children "in their place" rather than letting them explore. Some well-intentioned adults do it in the name of good behavior. But such restriction can dull the spirit and the mind.

Like most children, African American preschoolers (three and four year olds) are capable and ambitious from the start. They have positive attitudes about school and perform as well as everyone else on so-called intelligence tests, according to a report by the Frederick D. Patterson Research Institute. For one, they recognize the letters of the alphabet and count to fifty as well as others. Ninety-eight percent look forward to going to kindergarten every day!

But they falter in a critical area: On average, Black preschoolers tend to test far below other children on vocabulary skills. When asked to put a name to pictures, Black children on average score about 25 points below White children. "This disparity may well be a precursor to the achievement gaps in reading and other academic subjects in subsequent years of school," the Patterson Institute reported.

Making connections between words and pictures is one of the foundations of reading. That's why it's important to talk to young children, to give them books to look at and read, and to read to and with them.

Increasingly parents are getting this message. Since the first edition of *Higher Ground* was published in 1999, home literacy seems to have taken off. The book reported back then that Black children got significantly less lap-book-parent time at home. The news is a lot better now. Among Black families, the percent of children read to frequently by a family member increased from 66 percent to 77 percent; more than half are frequently told stories and 77 percent are taught letters, words or numbers. These increases in home literacy activities, reported by the National Center for Education Statistics, are evident regardless of whether families had incomes at the poverty level or were solidly middle class.

There's still a color gap, however, with white children hearing more stories and being read to more often in the home. Make sure your child gets more, not less. Every college student interviewed for *Higher Ground* listed reading as one of the most important skills they need in college and the tool that best helps them explore the work, build knowledge, and acquire other skills. Those who didn't read a lot before college lament not having read more as youngsters. Those who did praised the parents and adults who faithfully took them to libraries and bookstores and made sure they regularly had things to read.

Your children must be accustomed to reading on their own, for information and for the love of it. This may be the most important idea you'll get from this or any book on educating children. Pediatrician Barry Zuckerman, speaking to a Children's Defense Fund conference on Preparing Children for the Twenty-first Century, called for a campaign to give books to babies at their six-month checkup. "We're not talking about teaching ABCs, but a love of books," he explained.

Babies and young children like being held close and talked to, and the love of reading can begin here. At home, make family reading a habit. Ten minutes a night for the youngest will do. Toddlers and preschoolers especially love hearing familiar stories, so you can get a lot of use out of a few favorite books; you'll be asked to read them over and over and over again.

If you have more than one child, try to spend some time reading alone with each one. It's also fun to read to the children at the same time, even if there's an age gap that makes a book too advanced or too elementary for one or the other.

And don't just read. Ask questions as the story unfolds. Beyond who, what, or where, ask your little one what he thinks about what the mean wolf did. Get her to solve problems presented in the story: What should the wolf do? Let them predict what will happen, or give alternatives to how the story might end.

For older children, establish a regular reading time. Set aside fifteen to thirty minutes, depending on age, every day. Those who think there's no time left in the day should consider what your children do after school and on weekends. The regular reading period can replace watching reruns on television or more time with a joystick.

At school, ask how reading is introduced and taught. In the 1980s and 1990s, entire states turned away from phonics, which teaches the sounds of letters and letter combinations. They abandoned reading textbooks, saying they are uninspiring and don't encourage a love of reading.

The whole language reading approach favors using literature to teach children how to interpret words from clues in a sentence or passage, and to recognize words by sight. Critics of whole language, however, say students don't fully master the skills and rules to decode the English language that come with phonics. In recent years a number of school districts have switched back to phonics instruction. If your child isn't progressing in reading, discuss the best teaching approach for him.

By third grade, a child can spend thirty minutes a night reading. A reading log with the name of the book, starting and finishing pages, helps children chart their own progress. Some get a kick out of seeing they were on page 18 on Monday and by Friday are on page 72. The reading can be great literature or popular novels and short stories, picture books, poetry, newspapers, magazines—even a comic book. For children who aren't strong readers, make sure they have simpler material so they can feel comfortable and successful when they read for pleasure. The goal is to get your children *used to reading regularly and on their own.* You're developing a lifelong habit, so while it may start out as a chore, you may find them reading spontaneously or looking forward to getting back to their book, even if they complain or need to be reminded.

I saw how this can work when, upon high school graduation, a young man I know spent hours in the library and a local book store café browsing the stacks and shelves. (To be honest, he spent a lot of time in record stores, too, a true hip-hopper.) He made a lot of purchases at the book store, and checked out a lot of stuff at the library. "I can finally read whatever I want," he said, relieved to be done with years of school reading list (including summer reading lists in high school). Don't miss the point. He spent his summer after high school graduation reading a lot-on his own. In the fall, he enrolled at Wake Forest University.

Keep dictionaries around that are for various levels-elementary, middle, high school, collegiate—so that words can be looked up quickly and at the child's level of understanding.

Don't think that older children don't want to be read to. Even if they can read well, many children enjoy listening to someone else tell a good tale. (Don't you?) Maybe it's just the time and attention from a loving adult, but it gets the child involved in reading something, with the benefit of hearing a skilled reader. Children generally have a higher level of comprehension when they listen than when they read. Letting them listen helps them learn and understand the material, and also gets them used to the sounds of an expanding vocabulary.

Don't be limited to books. Discussing news and magazine articles lays the foundation for an interest in community and world, whether it's sports or fashion or neighborhood news.

Children are likely to read more if they see their parents reading. Hopefully, you can make the time, especially if the TV is turned off. If the entire family is involved in quiet, low-key pursuits like homework, studying, reading the paper or the mail, or paying bills, so much the better.

This all may seem easier for parents who love to read themselves. For those who don't, keep that personal information to yourself. If you just don't like to read or don't seem to have time, start carving out fifteen minutes a day, even if you're just reading the mail, the newspaper, or going over your bills. Let your child see you reading.

If reading is not a part of your adult lifestyle because you have difficulty with it, check with a library about adult literacy programs and tutors.

Something to Think About: I'm always asking young people I meet, "What book are you reading now?" I don't hear as much about *Harry Potter*, but I do know a third grader who has discovered the old *Nancy Drew* series. And there are some teenagers who are reading classics (Shakespeare, Hemingway, Alice Walker). Sadly, though, too many of the kids I ask are not reading anything. So I prod, "Well, what book have you read recently?" Or, "What's your favorite book?" Many can't claim to have read an entire book on their own. It's hard to imagine that teachers (Math and History teachers, not just English teachers) do not regularly assign or require the reading of…books. So, ask your children, "What book are you reading now?" A responsible parent can't let the answer depend solely on what's happening at school?

What's Educational and Entertaining, and Free?

Introduce your child to the public library as early as possible. Sign her up for her own library card and take her for preschool story times or regular visits. Ask a librarian for a recommended reading list. They're usually available by age and grade level. In the summer many public libraries have children's book series and contests that offer free pizza and movie tickets to kids who read a lot.

Whatever the age, allow your children to choose some books for themselves. Books that interest them and are of their own choosing are the ones they'll most likely pick up without prodding. Choosing books on their own also encourages your children to explore more of what the library has to offer. If your older child has difficulty reading, let him choose some books that are simple and easier to read than what other children his age may be reading. This is an opportunity to read without pressure or struggle. A library adventure is so much cheaper than the movies or the mall. And in the library, they'll see not just kids, but teenagers and young adults reading and writing. They'll see that learning continues into adulthood.

As your child reaches adolescence, friends, going out, music, and other new social interests, plus more homework and school projects, will take up much of the time that even the most eager young readers used to spend with good books. By then, though, your child should have established a habit and pattern of regular reading out of natural curiosity and for his own interest. Encourage your adolescent to check the sports page of the newspaper to read about last night's game, or show her a magazine article you think she'd be interested in. His school English class should have regular reading assignments from novels, plays, biographies, myths, folk tales, and short stories. Social studies classes also have many opportunities for reading, beyond textbooks. Most schools today use an interdisciplinary method of instruction, connecting the life of Colonial America being discussed in Social Studies, for example, with reading assignments in English class.

Writing Things Down (for the new SAT)

Handwriting and penmanship. That was the focus of "writing" in public education just few generations ago. Today writing classes teach children how to organize thoughts, develop ideas and points of view, make a persuasive argument, explain things on paper and craft interesting passages. This should be the focus of writing in your child's school. They'll need it for life, and also for the new SAT, which beginning in the fall of 2005 will include three parts worth 800 points each: math, critical reading and writing (see "Bias and the Big Tests").

At school, ask if there's a formal program of writing instruction. There may not be, but students don't have to be limited to writing during language lessons or English class. Science, history, geography, reading, computer, and even mathematics offer opportunities to write about things. And so does class work, homework and exams. Explaining and interpreting things in writing is far more important to academic development and critical thinking than drawing than checking answer boxes.

If you don't see many opportunities for writing in your children's homework or the work they bring home from school, tell the teacher and principal about your concerns. The ability to express ideas, opinions, and thoughts, and to dispense information, is a critical tool in today's information-based society. "No matter what you major in, you're going to have to write essays and papers," says Cherise Bathersfield, a Northwestern University journalism major.

Before your child goes to school or even can read, she can practice writing when she scribbles lines on paper, draws pictures, and forms her first letters. Later, family spelling bees, crossword puzzles, and games of Scrabble or even waiter and waitress help with handling the written word.

Ask your children to write thank you notes, stories, lists-birthday and Christmas wish lists require no nagging from you-and let them see you writing fists and taking down notes. Children not yet writing can dictate their lists, notes, and even stories, and your older child can write them down. Read aloud the things you and your children write, so they can make the connection between written words and spoken ones.

Being Well-Spoken

For educators, the question has been how to teach some minority children to use standard English without denigrating the culture of their homes and communities. Parents don't have to have such delicate concerns. The pressing question is simply how to get them to use the appropriate language at the appropriate time.

You'll know if your child has a problem with speaking if he cannot at least "switch over" from the colorful but fractured talk used with friends, to grammatically correct English that should be used in class, when talking to adults, and speaking before a group or in an interview. If your children cannot move beyond the casual vernacular of Black slang, talk to their teachers about how school is helping them bridge the gap from cool talk to what in our society is the language of business and power. This is serious. Poor speaking skills are an impediment to writing and reading.

There are other things you can do. Take the time to answers to all those childish questions, instead of putting your child off. There are plenty of "teachable moments" to take advantage of, as when a child starts into the "Why?" of everything.

"The ball falls down because of gravity," one mother explains to her six-year-old. "It's a force you can't see that pulls things." Help your children develop a wide vocabulary by talking to them, reading to them, pointing out and explaining words to them.

One preschool teacher offers this simple advice in helping children with language: Use descriptive words and proper names of things when talking to children. Instead of pointing and saying "Bring me that," as some of us do, take care to speak in fuller sentences. "Bring me that pair of scissors," or "Pick up the box of pink tissues."

Beyond knowing how to apply the rules of standard English, young people should develop a comfort and ease in public Most of the outstanding young African American students interviewed for this book were well-spoken and articulate. Like a lot of pop singers, many got their first experiences before an audience in church. Later they moved on to classroom and school presentations, and oratorical contests.

Find opportunities for your child to speak in a group. This can be as informal as the family pageants held in a cramped living room. One sister reads a story, another recites a poem. The brother heckles. Your child may be able to participate in church services, reading a scripture or having a speaking part in a holiday pageant. Drama groups also help children with their formal, public speech.

Forget about having DVD player in the car. You can polish speaking and conversational skills during car trips, or at the dinner table. Family discussions can be a time to develop a logical argument, learn to listen, and articulate a position.

Early Math

While cuddling up with a book is a warm, bonding experience between parent and child, working together on math and science problems may not be as cozy. Yet, finding ways to encourage an interest and joy about math and science is just as important.

To begin, you need to know how much more mathematics is necessary than it was generations ago. Basic arithmetic—adding, subtracting, multiplying, and dividing—is just that, basic stuff. They must be mastered. And with calculators, even some math teachers say such computing is less important than understanding concepts and formulas. Your young child also must study the full scope of mathematics, defined as the study of numbers that involve shapes, patterns, estimation, measurement, and concepts that relate to them.

In the early years, help your child recognize that math and science are part of everyday living. Start counting everything-apples, candy, blocks, crayons, money. Sort things by shape, colors, sizes, and patterns. Talk about the numbers you use in telling time, reading a clock, measuring pancake mix.

In science, talk about the weather, how the toy works, the

changing seasons, electronic toys. Take advantage of children's natural interest in living things and give them opportunities to be around animals at zoos and farms, and insects and plants that can be found and grow in the neighborhood.

Make sure your child is getting a lot of opportunities for problem solving and for work that helps them see relationships and patterns, and that helps them think logically. These skills will be used in years to come in areas beyond math.

Look also for ways to help lay the foundation for higher level thinking about math. Second graders can make bar graphs to show how much candy they collect on Halloween, or can learn about fractions by slicing pizza.

The following are standards set by the National Council of Teachers of Mathematics for elementary and middle school math. The math teachers' group recommends that your child's math lessons involve activities beyond workbooks and flash cards. Children should have opportunities to:

- explore, investigate, estimate, question, predict, and test their ideas about math
- explore and develop understanding for math concepts using materials they can touch and feel
- look at math in terms of daily life and to see the connections among math topics
- use calculators and computers to solve math problems

Look through your child's math work. Ask to see or get a description of the math curriculum. Talk about the math council's standards if you don't see indications that your child is doing more than rote arithmetic.

As in reading, your negative attitudes or anxieties about math should be kept in check. They can be passed on unwittingly with comments like, "Ask me about anything but math," or "That's not the way I learned to do it."

Maybe you don't like math or weren't good at it back in your old school days. Don't make the assumption that your child will falter in math, too. Math teachers say parents pass on math anxiety or are too accepting of their children's math difficulties by explaining to them, "I wasn't good in math, either."

One grandmother admits she too readily accepted her grandson's lack of interest in going to a summer math program for gifted children. She "could understand" not wanting to do math. Later, she realized, "it had nothing to do with him not liking math or not being good at it. He was just lazy."

If your child's math assignments are truly beyond your understanding, ask the teacher and staff about arranging a math workshop for parents to explain what students are learning and how parents can help. The workshop can be conducted as part of a PTA night or weekend event at school. A lot of other parents are probably having the same frustrations.

Helping your child in the earliest grades to get a solid foundation in math will set them on a course to advanced math classes they'll need in middle school and high school.

THIRD GRADE TURN-OFF

*"Help every student to read independently and
well by fourth grade."*

Bill Clinton,
Call to Action for American Education

The beginning of the academic downturn for many minority children begins in third and fourth grade. This is the time when schoolwork in every academic area, more than before, relies on the ability to read. Also around this time, the dynamic of the classroom is changing, with fewer opportunities to move around and "play" than in the primary grades. Some kids have trouble with the changes, and it is exacerbated if they haven't acquired the basic reading and math skills needed to do the next level of work.

Family problems, being young for a class, health issues, under-funded and dysfunctional schools, limited English, hunger and poverty, lack of a secure home and neighborhood environment. These are some of the things that dim the lights of children who in earlier years were bright, curious, eager and able to learn. Writer Jonathan Kozol identified the impact of these kinds of social and school conditions on children's learning in 1967 in the book *Death at an Early Age*. In 1991 he published another book on poor and minority children's education, *Savage Inequalities.*

The same social and educational conditions Kozol wrote about back then persist today in community overrun by drugs, violence and poverty; and school districts where homework is out of the question because there aren't enough textbooks, teachers expect next to nothing from students, and classes can go an entire school year without a regular teacher. Even when conditions are adequate or even good, black children face particular challenges. There may be no Black role models and, especially in the case of boys, no Black male role models to connect with.

The number of things that can hamper learning are too many to list, but in the simplest scenarios, some children demonstrate frustration turning out and turning off. They begin to hate school, especially Black boys who may know they've been labeled troublemakers, slow learners, or jocks. (A study of a major urban school district showed that African American teachers labeled and stereotyped Black kids; not just White faculty.

By fourth grade the statistics show a downward spiral. As a group, Black fourth-graders fare poorly on almost every indicator of academic achievement and success; and they begin to get more than their share of suspensions and visits to the principal's office.

While many people of goodwill are still struggling to address equity in education, children whose parents keep track of what's happening at school have the best chance of making sure their children don't get turned off in third-grade. The alternative could be an early academic slide that has life-limiting consequences later on. The title of Kozol's book, *Death at an Early Age*, is not an overstatement of what's at stake.

Know what's going on at school. Every year you will probably have to start from scratch, getting to know your child's teachers and making sure they know you and your expectations for your child. If you drop them off at school, take a few minutes to speak to teachers about what went on the day before or last week. Call, email or send a note with your child when you have concerns.

Dr. James Comer, the Yale child psychiatrist renowned for his School Development Program in which parents and educators have worked together to turn around failing schools, says good parents react when problems arise, but that's not enough. "You need to make certain that [students] are developing confidence and competence from the minute they hit school. You prevent failure. You get in there early and make sure they're doing all right, and get them help if they're not."

For specific academic trouble, ask the teacher and counselors to help identify the problem. If tutoring is what's needed, it should be available you can find help for free. If the schools can't put you in touch with a church or community or school tutoring program, contact a local college. Tutoring younger children qualifies as a work-study job for some college students.

Ytasha didn't know until the middle of the school year that her son, a third-grader who talked about being a doctor, was assigned to a slow-learner track. His teacher at a predominantly White suburban public school said it was because of lower than average test scores from second grade. Ytasha did some investigating and came up with her own explanation about the test scores. "He was sick the week of that test," she remembered. To this day, she asks, "How could they put him in a slow track without telling me about it?"

For one thing, tracking, except for so-called Gifted and

Talented programs, is done quietly. The situation could have been averted if Ytasha had been in touch with the school and her child's teacher all along. "I just didn't realize what was going on," she said. Her son eventually was moved out of the class. He won a scholarship to a private New England academy for high school.

At the start of each school year, ask to see a curriculum, or get the teacher to tell you specifically what your child is expected to learn: some examples, double-digit multiplication, basic sentence capitalization and punctuation. Good schools will have these ready by Back-to-School Night.

Assess where your child is academically. Talk to the teacher about your child's progress a few weeks after school starts. Allowing for a wide range of development, look at the work of other children in his class that is posted on bulletin boards or on display in the classroom. Does your child's work seem within the range of classmates? Ask about standardized tests results? Ask about tracking.

Pay attention to early warning signs that your child is drifting away from his natural love of learning: he's bored, complains about teachers, doesn't want to go to school, avoids or fails to do classroom assignments and homework, is not involved in school activities. These may signal problems that are simple or severe.

Arrange for a teacher conference for each reporting period, whether it's offered or not. Is your child doing well? Moving along at an acceptable pace? Fine. But if he's starting to drift backward, or not moving forward, discuss what can be done help him.

Educators are accountable for how well their students do, so ask the teacher and a counselor what the school will do to prevent failure. And ask what you can do. Identify ways home and school can work together. Then stay in touch with the teacher, calling, emailing or sending notes about homework, a lesson your child doesn't understand, family problems that may be affecting schoolwork.

Outside, nonacademic interests can generate interest in school. Make sure your child has activities he enjoys and does well and has attachments to people who encourage and inspire his best efforts. Seek therapy or counseling for more serious problems.

Don't underestimate the impact of messages children receive directly or subtly. "[Black children] are picking up the messages from the world about what it means to be Black, about what it means to be a Black male. And you've got to counter the negative," Dr. Comer says. "Parents have to hang in there and counter the negative."

Dr. Comer refers to an incident he describes in his book *Waiting for a Miracle*. A White classmate mentioned that she knew his mother. It turned out that his mother, a domestic, had worked for the classmate's mother. "That bothered me," he remembers. But his mother saw no shame. "My mother said, 'You're just as smart, you're just as clean, you can do just as well—and you *had better*.' "

Thinking back on the incident, Dr. Comer saw what his mother was trying to do. "That was a direct counter of negative feelings toward the self, which are picked up. Black kids pick them up even when it's not intentional. [The White girl] meant no harm. But the condition of the society is such that [Black children] get negative feedback. Parents have to be positive and counter the negative."

Something to Think About: A difficult or slow start should not set in stone your child's future or potential. But if your child is well behind others, you both may be faced with a teacher's recommendation that she receive special education services. This should be considered carefully, as special education—a set of support services, not a place—is not a killer of college dreams. In the first twenty five years after the disability education laws went into effect, the number of young people with learning, emotional, or physical disabilities who went on to college tripled.

STAYING BACK, SKIPPING AHEAD

It was the last day of the school year. An inner city elementary teacher one morning found her school swarming with security guards. Police cars were parked out front.

The parents of Mrs. Brown's twenty-four preschoolers are mostly young, mostly unemployed, mostly unmarried women, and this day some of those who'd come to pick up their children's report cards had been slapped with really bad news: Their children had failed a grade, were "staying back."

The parents were outraged. "Staying back" was an embarrassment and near disgrace. There was cursing and threats. The police were called.

It is time for a new mindset. Staying back it never good news, but it shouldn't be considered a stigma or a failure that can't be overcome. In the best scenarios, it is an opportunity to mature, to catch up, to more fully grasp information and skills a child missed the first time around. Some people call it a gift of time. And in the past decade school systems around the nation have offered it, including Chicago's, by banning automatic or "social" promotions for children who haven't mastered their current level.

Some richer, suburban parents have made staying back palatable and even fashionable. In response to the move toward more rigorous academics in the primary grades, some school districts created transitional grades known as T-1 or T-2. The former are for kindergartners not ready for first grade, the latter for first-graders not ready to move to grade two. This calmed anxieties about "staying back" and gave some children a chance to make good; Some kids in the T-1 go on to first grade while others move up to second grade.

In upper grades, repeating a grade poses more problems. The National Association of School Psychologists warns that most children do not "catch up" when they are held back. Some do better at first, but fall behind again in later grades. In this case, being obviously older than one's classmates, and the "stigma" of staying back, embarrasses and further frustrates some youngsters. In the meantime they may get into trouble, continue to dislike school, and feel badly about themselves more than those who go on to the next grade. Many high school dropouts are kids who were held back.

If your child is a candidate for retention, get copies of test scores, recommendations, assessments. Ask to see examples of her work, compared to the classroom average. If the recommendation is made based on the results of a standardized test, get the name of the test and ask what the test is designed to measure. Specifically, is the test designed to determine whether a child should move on or repeat a grade? It may be designed to determine other things about ability, achievement, etc. Some tests are used inappropriately to hold a child back.

Make sure you inform the school about circumstances or stresses that may have affected the child's work. Tell the teacher if your child's behavior and interest in learning at home are different from the behaviors and attitude displayed in school.

If you have a choice, weigh the benefits against the negatives of having your child repeat a year. A classroom with children of different ages, summer school, and tutoring may be an alternative. In any case, we should all drop the stigma of failure from repeating a grade. A child is never to blame.

As for skipping a grade, this gives a parent a lot to brag about. But this too has its pluses and minuses. Socially, your child may be at a disadvantage being the youngest, less mature emotionally and physically. Social development is as important as academics.

Some of the best schools avoid skipping accomplished children ahead a year by offering more advanced work or enrichment classes during the school day without separating them entirely from their peers. Getting your child's school to teach him "where he is" rather than moving him up may be a better solution.

Some parents push their children along for reasons that have nothing to do with academics or ability. In order to avoid day care costs, many parents are eager to see their children move into preschool or kindergarten before they are of age. One principal discovered that one of her smallest, least capable kindergarten students was actually a three-year-old. Her mother was desperate and couldn't afford to pay for childcare. Free all-day kindergarten seemed like the only solution. Her desperation could have doomed her child to always being "least developed and slow" in her class.

SCHOOL CHOICE

Public education is doing great work with children across the country. You're blessed if your neighborhood school has dedicated teachers, adequate books and supplies, and administrators who maintain safe, drug-free learning environments. Many, many people are working hard to make public education work for all children.

Amid the many stories of public school success, there is failure and frustration. Reports in the 1990s declared that things were so bad in one urban school district that its students were called victims of "educational genocide."

These kinds of stories have incited calls to give more parents a choice in their kids' education. Here are some of the school options:

Tuition vouchers. Government funds used to help pay the costs for some students to attend private and parochial schools. In this, Republicans and low income Black parents have formed an unlikely alliance. The former, inclined against federal interference in family and local schools; the latter, desperate to save their children from failing schools. Critics say tuition vouchers take funding away from public schools and the kids left in them. Supporters say the use of vouchers will motivate public educators to do better.

Private voucher/scholarship programs. Wealthy individuals and philanthropic groups in recent years have pledged as much as $45 million to help families with low-incomes send their children to private schools. It's a preemptive strike to help disadvantaged children early in their schooling, rather than offering college scholarships later to students who are not fully prepared.

Charter schools. Run by parents and educators with public money, charter schools operate with little regular oversight from the local school district. Parents and staff determine the curricula and how money is spent.

Magnet schools offer public school students specialized study or environments in order to "attract" students who might not attend otherwise. Popular magnet programs focus on math, science and technology, foreign language immersion. Magnets schools can be more expensive to run that the traditional neighborhood schools. Some school districts are closing down programs in order to cut costs.

Black academies. At some schools the focus is wholly Afrocentric; others are Christian-based or follow an independent, private academy approach.

Independent, and boarding schools. Among private schools not affiliated with any religious denomination, about 5.5 percent of students are African American.

Home school. Once thought to be the white conservative Christian's escape from integrated public schools, home schooling is growing in popularity among some Black families. The numbers of Black children homeschooled by their parents (with help from home school academies) is reported to be from 80,000 to 120,000. State and local departments of education set requirements for home-schooling. Home school families must register with their state board of education and follow certain requirements. In some states, parents who home school their children need only a high school diploma; others require you to have a college degree. A homeschool can launch a child into a stable job in retail or into some of the area's most prestigious universities.

In *Morning by Morning: How We Homeschooled our African American Sons to the Ivy League,* Paula Penn-Nabrit writes candidly about her successes and her failures. Without cheerleading, she shows how homeschooling can be the answer for families with few options other than a poor public school system. And she also shows the social and personal costs, whether it's a lack of awareness of how "the world" works, to a carefree confidence that makes it hard to conform to the academic rules of formal education.

Evaluating Schools

It takes forethought and effort to find alternatives beyond your child's regular public school. Check out the school your child is slated to attend at least a year in advance. That fall is the time to start investigating options beyond the local school if you feel that's necessary. Private school open houses begin as early as October, and many start taking applications for limited spaces then. Also, visit schools during the regular school day, not just the evening open house.

If you're planning a move or new home purchase, investigate the schools that serve that area. If your child is in preschool, you'll still need to check out the middle and high schools she might eventually attend. Judge all schools by the standards that matter to you, whether public or private, Afrocentric or predominantly White.

Some specific questions to ask are detailed below. What you want to know upfront, though, is if the school develops the whole child (academically, intellectually, socially, physically, artistically) in ways that prepare them for success in college and life later on. In searching for middle schools, ask whether there's a a college preparatory curriculum. Specialized curricula such as Springboard, developed by The College Board (which administers the SAT college admissions test), builds into classroom specific lessons in critical thinking and analysis skills necessary for doing well on high-stakes tests and in college later on (every school should have an academic plan; by asking about plans to build critical thinking and analysis skills, you're looking for more than the basics).

Ask to see the curriculum or a summary of it, from the time a child enters through graduation. Expect it to look good on paper. (They usually do.) Look beyond that for how the school is run.

- What is the maximum class size and the teacher-to-student ratio? How many students go to the school and what is the racial makeup? Is the teaching and professional staff racially and ethnically diverse?
- For private and independent school directors, is the institution accredited, and by whom?
- Are children grouped by ability? How is this determined? What is the percentage of minority students in honors classes and special education and general tracks?

- Is Black history studied only in February or are the contributions of all peoples taught throughout the year as part of literature, social studies, math, science, and arts classes?
- Is the staff receptive to parent involvement and suggestions? Is there an active parent group? In what ways can parents be involved?
- How are children disciplined?
- Does the school value the arts, or is the curriculum totally dedicated to teaching "basic" skills?
- Are computers available, and how often will your child get to use one? Do students have access to the internet?

Sit in on a few classes. During your visit, are there routine interruptions during class time, or all the hallways and offices clear and quiet? While order is important, so is the intellectual life of a school. Speak with and observe the principal. Is she great with a megaphone but lacking when it comes to discussing books, current events, music with students, faculty and parents? Ask the principal to suggest some good books your child should be reading? A strong intellectual leader can tell you on the spot. A weak one will want to get back with you.

In public schools you should be able to get a report from the school board on how different schools perform on standardized test scores and their suspension and expulsion rates. Be careful how you interpret this information. If the test scores at your child's assigned school are below grade levels, ask about the factors that contribute to the school's poor performance. Are there many disadvantaged children, children whose first language is not English? Are the scores of special education students averaged in? How would those factors affect your child's learning?

As you visit schools, notice the demeanor of the children. Are they allowed to move around with appropriate freedom, asking questions and sharing their opinions and ideas? Do you see a lot of smiles? Consider the school environment. Is there order? Are teachers and staff in control without being authoritarian? Do they speak calmly or yell? Does the school seem secure and well-maintained? Look at the work that's displayed. Do you see "A" papers that are filled with errors? Do you see a lot of true and false and multiple choices papers (which promote rote learning) or opportunities to express thoughts in writing (which promotes critical reading, writing and thinking)?

Get a list of extracurricular activities and elective courses. If your child is interested in music, does the school have an orchestra or band?

For schools touting special programs, find out what percentage of students are actually enrolled in the science and math track, or the honors program. If those numbers are small, the tone for the entire school, set by the larger student body, may be different from what is being touted.

A year or two before your child is slated to go to high school, start visiting some. Keep in mind that you are looking at the school that will launch him into college. Start your research by attending open houses, back-to-school nights, or call and ask for a tour. It doesn't matter if you're checking out private or public schools. Are Advanced Placement and honors courses available? Is the school involved in any partnership programs with colleges in your area?

Get a copy of the previous years' graduation programs. Are

there many scholarship winners? What schools offer scholarships to the graduates? What do students do after graduation?

If you'll need financial aid for a private school, the private schools you're interested in should know of scholarship sources, including local funds for disadvantaged students or local and regional programs that help place minority youngsters. Or check the phone book for the organization representing private and independent schools in your area. They can give you more information. Finally, talk to parents of current and past students. They are your best sources of information on how a school really works, the pros and cons of attending.

Any one of the increasing array of school choices can provide a lifeline to a child who wants to learn but doesn't have a safe and orderly environment in the local school. But realize, too, that some of these alternatives threaten public education. Public vouchers, for instance, could siphon from public schools where the neediest children are left behind. And as more committed and aware parents opt out of public education, they take with them skills, connections, resources, and many of the children who could be high-achieving role models.

The African tradition binds families with many choices to those families with the least. What's best for our children includes what's best for our community. But in the end, you've got to do what is in the best interest of your own children.

In *Saving Our Sons: Raising Black Children in a Turbulent World*, Marita Golden says she was "haunted by the notion that I was copping out of the struggle and the race" by sending her boy to boarding school. Then a friend whose son was about to graduate from a boarding school spoke of the trade-offs of sending him away from his inner city neighborhood and his home. "The first trade-off is...he's alive."

THE COLLEGE PREP TRACK

A workshop for elementary school counselors included a discussion of what students will need in order to perform well on college admissions tests. "SAT prep cannot just begin in the eleventh and twelfth grades," the workshop leader said, passing out a list of vocabulary words. "SAT prep begins seriously in seventh grade. It's at least a five-year process."

Some kids—and parents, too—laugh off middle school or think it's okay to cruise through it because it "doesn't count." True, no college administrator will ever see what your child got in sixth grade math or eighth grade English. Doing poorly in middle school, however, may prevent them from taking or doing well in the kinds of courses college administrators will look for on that high school transcript.

Attention to middle school is so important if your child's goal is college. Making sure your child is assigned to and completes specific courses in the middle years will give him the preparation and record of achievement required to get into a strong academic program in high school. The high school courses your child takes, in turn, will determine if she meets admission requirements of various colleges and is in the running for academic scholarships. A weak middle school experience may result in wasted time trying to catch up in high school, with no time to take courses necessary to make your child competitive for scholarships. Worse, your child could be saddled with watered-down high school courses that are virtually worthless in the competitive, technology-driven job market, courses such as "consumer" or "general" math.

Sixth grade is the time to focus your child on the future. You may already have been talking about college, but now start talking with your child about how to get there. He must know that he can have a wonderfully bright and brilliant future. The options are there for those who know the way and are willing to work toward it.

Talk to your child about the difference between immediate and delayed gratification, wanting something of little lasting value now (manicures, trendy clothes) or working toward something that will bring them benefits later on (savings accounts, good grades). Program your children to expect the best, even if current circumstances are gloomy. If your family can barely pay the rent, don't let your child think he can't afford to go to college. Let him know that the government, colleges and private organizations set aside money to help out students like him. In short, the message is about continuing to read, studying well, doing one's very best, and taking challenging courses.

Your involvement and attention is critical. In a survey of the National Action Council for Minorities in Engineering (NACME), for example, 61 percent of minority middle schoolers said they planned to drop math and science as soon as they could. Although a huge majority in the NACME study had high hopes of going to college, the minority children were more likely than others to say they would drop math and science in a heartbeat. They didn't see the link between taking as much math and science as they can in high school and being prepared for (and accepted into) college.

The Gateway

The first section of this book talks about the importance of algebra, the higher level mathematics course that leads to more advanced study in high school and college.

In order to do well on college admissions tests and be admitted to most four-year colleges, your student must take algebra and geometry and, increasingly, higher level math. For decades, however, only certain students were given the opportunity to take it. The rest were stuck with Business Math, Consumer Math, and General Math—a repackaging and review of basic arithmetic.

That's changing dramatically. Today, school districts in Texas and Maryland, among other states, have made algebra a high school graduation requirement. Every student must take Algebra I, whether it's in eighth grade or tenth grade, whether it takes one year to complete or two, in order to get a high school diploma.

Teachers and other educators predicted doom when the idea of algebra for everyone started to spread. Some insisted that not all children are capable of advanced math. People feared a flood of failing and frustrated students in over their heads. Students, however, have proven them wrong. The number of ninth graders taking Algebra I in one predominantly Black school district jumped from 58 percent to 91 percent in six years. More and more elementary math curricula include the study of patterns, geometric shapes, and algebraic concepts. These help make an early transition from arithmetic to advanced mathematics.

Educators recommend that capable students take Algebra I in eighth grade in order to continue with other advanced math classes in senior high school. Other students may not be ready for algebra until later. Nationwide only 25 percent of students take algebra in eighth grade. Minority students are even less likely to take algebra in eighth grade.

Some schools have begun to introduce algebra in seventh grade. This may not necessarily be a good thing. Seventh grade algebra has become "good office water cooler conversation and bragging rights for parents," says one middle school math teacher at a predominantly Black middle-class suburban school. "It's usually not appropriate," the teacher continues, but parents want to move their children out in front. "One child got C's and D's in sixth grade math, and the parent was asking at the end of school if he could be placed in seventh grade algebra," the teacher recalled.

If your child is a candidate for seventh grade algebra, ask what your child will miss by skipping regular seventh grade math. Then ask about the rigor of seventh grade algebra. Some senior high mathematics teachers question whether seventh graders get a watered-down version of algebra that doesn't fully prepare them for advanced high school math.

Don't let your middle school child or her school make course assignments without your input. In the spring, information for the following year should be sent home. Find out from the school what courses are available the next year, which courses she will be assigned. When given a choice, get your child into the hardest courses she can reasonably handle. Consider also placing her with teachers that command respect, and subjects that excite her or spark her interests.

Be realistic, too. Pushing a child into a course that's too

advanced may lead to more failures than successes. This creates its own problems with self-esteem, dislike of school, and pessimism about the future.

College-bound middle school students should be on some variation of the following schedule:

Algebra I by eighth or ninth grade

Geometry or *Algebra II* in ninth or tenth grade and more advanced math every year until graduation

English, Science, and *Social Studies* (a combination of History and Geography) every year

Foreign Language (Plan on making a commitment to one language for several years. Colleges don't like to see one year of this, another year of that.)

Computer Literacy/Computer Science

The Arts (music, art, drama, writing)

Electives such as communications, psychology, or things your child just wants to try

While you're talking to your child about the future, parents still must aggressively monitor the education of young people who now tower over them and try to act grown-up. Remind your child of the connection between what they do now and their future options. Talk about careers, not just "What do you want to be?" but "What do you like to do? What interests you? What's your favorite subject?"

Explain how seemingly unconnected subjects relate to certain careers. How psychologists, high school counselors, and auto mechanics need to know advanced math. It's not just for accountants and scientists.

KIDS TO COLLEGE

*"The most important thing for parents is to go out
and look [for programs]. There's a lot, but the people
don't know about it."*

Carol F. Stoel,
Council for Basic Education

On Tuesday afternoons, twelve-year-olds at Goddard Middle School gather in the lunchroom to talk about the future. To some that's as distant as the hereafter. But each is asked to write down the vision they have for themselves. "What kind of life do I want when I grow up? What do I want to be? What kind of job do I want?" About half of the twelve boys and twelve girls can answer the questions with certainty. But they all put on paper some of their dreams: doctor, computer specialist, football star, police officer, neurosurgeon, fashion designer, lawyer, NBA player, electronics expert, rapper, video game designer, chemist, engineer. Dreams involve wishing.

On the other hand, goals require planning. What the students do during the next six weeks is try to turn their dreams into goals. With the help of two college administrators and volunteer graduate students, the young adolescents discover that to realize their dreams-now goals-they need to go to college. The also get an idea of what it takes to get there (courses, reading and writing skills). Most important, it becomes clear to most that there's a lot that they need to do in middle school to get ready for college. It's a difficult lesson for kids who rush home to watch reruns of *The Parkers*, but most seem to get it.

Not long ago you may have thought college and career exploration was premature for eleven and twelve year olds. But this "Kids to College" program was part of a wave of new projects established by educators, business people, and college officials to extend a bridge from college down to middle and even elementary school.

Partnerships between colleges and schools have long existed to provide volunteer opportunities for university students or field experience for college students majoring in education. But the "Kids to College" partnerships are focused on motivating younger students to attend college and getting them and their parents prepared for it early.

For colleges and private sponsors of these early college awareness programs, making young children aware of higher education is an effort to have a better prepared campus population and work force years down the line. It doesn't hurt, either, that the institutions are able to connect with students who may choose to attend their college one day. Private organizations associated with specific disciplines, science or the arts, for example, also sponsor programs to bring more students into their fields.

Some are limited to the students at a specific school, community, school district, or residents of the state. They can involve onetime visits to campus or year-long enrichment programs with summer on campus. Others invite students on campus based on teacher and principal recommendations or academic competition. Some are funded specifically for students whose parents are not college graduates or are at an economic disadvantage. They may offer campus visits and workshops on careers and financial aid, or a long-term commitment of tutors, mentors, counseling, and summer or weekend activities. Most require parents to participate by attending workshops in financial aid and academic planning.

"The effect on kids can be very powerful. Kids who stay in school will do better in school," says Carol F. Stoel, of the Council for Basic Education, who has tracked such programs.

Don't confuse the early awareness college partnerships with the many others on college programs. Universities and some for-profit groups operate camps and enrichment programs, by the college, a private sponsor, or the government and are likely to be free or charge a minimal fee.

Talk to your child's teachers and counselors about any special programs they hear about during the school year. Let them know you are interested, and ask them to recommend your child when that is appropriate. Many students are invited to programs that other parents and students never hear about, leaving many parents and kids to wonder, "How'd they know about that?"

You can also contact nearby colleges and universities. Start with the Office of Minority or Multicultural Affairs and ask about youth programs. You can track down some programs by contacting the local consortium or umbrella group of colleges in your area or state, and your state Department of Higher Education. Local chapters of groups such as the Urban League or NAACP usually know about programs specifically targeting children of color. If your child has specific interests, contact the academic departments of local colleges, professional groups and associations, such as the National Science Foundation, about youth programs they sponsor.

Ask about any and all programs for youngsters. You may receive information about for-profit enrichment programs and summer camps—sports, science, and computer camps are popular—that can cost from $300 to $4,000. These programs generally indicate whether financial aid is available.

Keep in mind that because of the reliance on outside funds, enrichment programs that are free or subsidized, come and go, change their focus, or limit their outreach.

"The most important thing for parents is to go out and look," Stoel says. "There's a lot, but the people don't know about it. Some programs go looking for kids and they can't find them." (See "What Other People's Kids Are Doing.")

ATTITUDES ABOUT "ACTING WHITE"

In the segregated schools that some of us grew up in, Black students were both valedictorians and the last in the class. We got all the honors and all the suspensions. We were class presidents and class clowns, belonged to the debate team or just hung out in the hallways. We were the varsity athletes and the student government leaders. We were whatever our talents and desire led us to be.

One of the casualties of integration—and this is not to wax nostalgic about "separate and unequal education"—is the loss in many schools of the Black tradition of academic excellence. Somehow, scholarly academic achievement is a Black-and-White (and Brown and Yellow, too) issue in the minds of some young people. Some Black students have bought into a notion that good grades, honors courses, speaking well, carrying books around, and being courteous is, well… "acting White."

Derogatory taunts against hardworking students have always been tossed around. Bookworm. Nerd. Brainiac. But some Black students are rewriting their history from trying to be the best to seeing how bad they can be.

Too many Black students, especially boys, avoid getting good grades, deny it if they do, are embarrassed if their names are posted on the honor roll or if they're called to the stage for the honor society. As early as third grade, they leave their books at school for fear of being called out for carrying them around. In some schools some of the rewards for academic success bring on more opportunities for taunting. Placement in predominantly White honors courses or academies can isolate high-achieving Black students from their friends and homies.

In her book, *Blacked Out: Dilemmas of Race, Identity and Success at Capital High,* anthropologist Signithia Fordham found that Black students have internalized the low expectations that some White Americans have of them. In rejecting White standards and values, and to maintain their own identity, many claim as a part of their culture the negative behavior they believe is expected of them. University of California professor John Ogbu found similarly distorted attitudes in research for a book on the underachievement of Black students from well-to-do families. (See "The Black Middle Class Secret").

In the meantime, Black students see entire states dismantling affirmative action programs and throwing out the rewards—scholarships and enrichment programs—for their perseverance and good work (See "Affirmative Action").

Some kids won't connect academic effort with the lasting rewards adults promise will come eventually. And now a new generation of Black children is finding it easier to embrace the negative, and reject as "White" those good habits and achievements that will be important in their futures.

Some smart kids have always learned how to fit in and do their work. Ralph is gregarious, quick-witted, fun-loving, and a big talker. Not particularly good-looking or well-dressed, he was pudgy but widely popular in his all-Black urban high school. Few but those who knew him well were prepared for what awaited him at the end of his senior year: Out of a graduating class of more than six hundred, Ralph was named valedictorian.

Ralph did what a lot of other young Black students say they do to cope. They act cool, clown around, but get their work done. One young man, a premed major at Morehouse, handled it this way: "I dealt with it by using different mannerisms with my friends. But with adults, when I had to show my intelligence, I would switch off my playful mode. As I got older, it was cool if you were smart and got your work done, and could talk the talk, too. It became an attractive quality to young ladies, an air of sophistication."

"Acting Black," by historical definition, is trying to get as much education as you can. After Emancipation, African Americans had "a greed for letters." So much so that schools, even Sunday schools, were crowded and had to turn away freed slaves. In her book about slave youth, *Stolen Childhood,* Wilma King notes that Blacks didn't like to be seen carrying books because they feared it would provoke White violence. How rueful and ironic that carrying books today can turn one Black child against another.

Teaching this history will go a long way in setting children straight about what, in fact, "acting Black" is all about. In your own house, continue to praise your children for good work, making sure they understand its connection to a life they want to have. That information is more valuable to them than the twenty dollars you promise for straight A's. It will give them some of the armor they'll need to face all sorts of negative peer pressure.

Enroll your child in an enrichment program in his favorite

subject. Praise and encourage their interests, particularly those that may not be typical in your neighborhood or family, whether it's writing poetry or collecting rocks.

Straighten out adults who put down children whose behaviors and interests aren't "Black" enough for them. "Oh, so you gonna talk White now?" a woman remarked, noting her nephew's good diction.

I can't stress enough the importance of giving your child opportunities to mix with other children of color who are serious about their schoolwork can't be stressed enough. One mother saw it almost everyday for eight years while she drove a carpool of boys to one of the best grade schools in her city. The carpool kids—all of them Black boys, in two different grades—routinely queried each other on who got what on what paper; who got the higher grade on a test; who was chosen to lead a project. The one-ups-man-ship got worse (I mean better) when they enrolled in an all-boys school known for a strong academic and sports programs. The athletic competition spilled over into the classroom. One boy got upset when another outscored him on a test by four points. One bragged that he was a finalist for the public speaking content. The machismo and posturing went on and on: "What honors courses are you taking next year? "Did you get approved for AP History?" "What did your brother get on his SAT's?"

Too bad the Morehouse pre-med major didn't have the same experience: "I wish I had known that there were so many young Black people working hard as I was, who had positive goals. I felt I was the only person who was staying up reading a book."

Of course, he was not alone, although the media and countless studies and statistics make it seem that way. Where school officials, teachers and parents work together to insist that young people perform at top levels, they do. And they do it proudly.

Having the Talk

Early adolescence is about the time many Black parents give The Talk, that frank, somber dose of reality that begins. "You have to be twice as good . . ." It has been a creed of generations ever since Black people started trying to do something other than "a day's work." Ellis Cose speaks to this in *The Rage of the Privileged Class,* his book on the frustrations of Black professionals who work hard and excel, only to find that they're still judged first by the color of their skin.

Your children must hear the truth about the world they live in. So speak truth to them about racism and its offspring-stereotyping, discrimination, and prejudice. Middle school is not too young for African American children to know that even with a college degree, Black people earn seventy-five cents for every dollar earned by similarly qualified Whites. They need to know that their ancestors were the "last hired and first fired" because of their color. It's only fair to tell them what they could be up against, too.

In candid, sober observations about the reality of racism, some Black parents find reminders of the Struggle and stern warnings effective. "We just tell them, `Black people don't have a chance in this country without education,' " says a father of five. Whenever you approach the Talk, however, include in it stories from our history of bloodshed for the right to read and go to school. It was against the law to teach Black children to read; Black schools got the worst of everything if they got anything at all. Black children walked miles to and fro in the snow—yes, they did—without shoes, trying to get to school. Our great-grandmothers had to dodge the rocks White children threw as they whizzed by in their school bus. Not just the public pools, but public libraries banned Black folks, too.

Children's Defense Fund president Marian Wright Edelman, in *The Measure of Our Success,* outlines twenty-five lessons for life. Number twenty three is, "Remember your roots, your history, and the forebears' shoulders on which you stand."

End the Talk—though you'll have to repeat it over the year— with uplifting, empowering messages. Racism may continue, but young people can determine their own direction, confront prejudice, and overcome unfair treatment with a well-trained mind. Focus on *Kujichagulia,* the Kwanzaa principle of self-determination in which Black people define themselves, rather than letting others define them. Muhammad Ali. Malcolm X. Colin Powell. Condoleezza Rice. Sean (P. Diddy) Combs. Oprah. There are plenty of examples, probably in your own community and family. Books of cultural pride and the autobiographies of successful African Americans will reinforce this message.

The Talk, by the way, traditionally also included this gem of moral direction. "Keep your dress down and your pants up." Adolescents and parents at this time should have ongoing, frank conversations about self-respect, peer pressure, sexuality, and drugs.

Motivation and Praise

Funny thing about kids. Sometimes what means most to them costs us nothing. Praise, your approval and words of encouragement, go a long way in rewarding and motivating your child. "My grandmother use to give out hugs and kisses for a good report card," notes one mother. " `Come here and get some of grandma's love,' she'd say. That's all we wanted."

Reward and acknowledge your children's improvements, efforts, and achievements with good words and more of your time. Promise to take her to the movie she wanted to see, take him for pizza or a football game at the local college.

Small "gifts" also mean a lot. Staying up an extra thirty minutes when it's appropriate, a chance to invite a friend over or to hang out at a skating rink.

If material tokens are important in your family, give books and magazine subscriptions as gifts, or gift certificates from bookstores and museum shops. They can involve a subject that your student is interested in. Ask friends and relatives to do the same.

Instead of giving cash for good grades (Even though I loved my Aunt Margaret for all those dollars for As), give a token that has attached to it a message about the value of the achievement. A college savings bond, a trip to the aquarium for a well-done science project, a book or special magazine issue on a favorite subject.

Don't fall into the cycle of always passing out "rewards," which when promised in advance are bribes. You don't want to de-emphasize the importance of good work by dwelling on material outcomes. In the end, excellence and achievement lead to their own, long term rewards.

BEYOND THE BASICS

Some of the most important lessons that young people need for college and life have nothing to do with scholarship. What good are awards and good grades if your children are inconsiderate, irresponsible and don't treat others with respect? How proud can you be if your children are ill-mannered, don't care about others and are not humbled by a power bigger than themselves?

In researching *Higher Ground*, I have met some wonderful and accomplished young people whose achievements are eclipsed only by their strong sense of self. They carry themselves in a way that makes you like and respect them. They display the good comportment and good nature of young people whose confidence is supported by proper social skills and knowing their place in their universe.

Are young people like this an exception? I hope not. But teachers from the most disadvantaged public schools to the toniest private ones say students, in general, carry themselves poorly, and lack common courtesy and the strong character traits that make good citizens. Yet developing good behavior and character is just as important as developing the mind and, as we'll talk about later, talents and interests.

One of the first and most important ways to address some of those things children need, beyond the basic academic skills, is to involve them in religious or spiritual training. In *The Measure of Our Success: A Letter to My Children and*, Marian Wright

Edelman tells parents to tell their children to, "Always remember that you are never alone." Having a faith in God can sustain young people through the most desperate or discouraging times.

Imagine going to college, leaving friends and family. If your child remembers he's not alone, he can call on God or Allah or Jehovah when he can't call you: in the dorm room, before a test, when friends fall out, if the grades aren't going well. Young people who know they can depend on Him are less likely to run to drugs for comfort, to people who don't care about them for friendship.

Jamal Harrison Bryant had been a "classic C student" in high school whose only ambition was to own a car by age twenty-six. Bryant had earned degrees from Morehouse College and Duke University. Bryant eventually did well in his studies because, he says, he tapped into the spiritual teachings of his childhood. "All the things I learned in Sunday school and church I didn't use until later. In college, my relationship with God was a stabilizing factor. That's important for everyone who's leaving home. "As long as parents keep instilling it, when young people find themselves between a rock and a hard place, they'll draw on it," he said.

Perseverance, responsibility, a drive for excellence, respect for self and others: These are some of the other things you must instill in the young people you'll have to let go off to college much sooner than you realize. In addition, they'll need good study habits, including time-management and organization skills.

Perseverance

Don't let your child keep giving up: quitting a team, dropping out of the scouts, opting out of music lessons. It may take a few trial and error experiences to find out what she's really interested in—letting her choose her own hobbies and activities will help—but after a while help your child stick with *something*. Sign a pledge or family contract to stay with it for an entire school year, or through graduation.

They may never develop a passion for that something, or excel in it, but your kids will learn to make and keep a commitment, to follow through. Don't let your children get used to quitting when things get difficult, unfashionable, or "boring."

Responsibility

Tiger Woods's father, Earl, often tells this story. Once, when the golf champion was four or five, Tiger got in the car ready to head for the course. "Dad, did you get my clubs?" he asked.

"Whose clubs are they?" Earl Woods responded.

"Mine," Tiger said.

Earl Woods sent his son back to bring along his own clubs.

At that young age, he also sent him the message that a child must do for himself whenever he can, or be prepared for the consequences. On first hearing that story, Earl Woods sounded a little rough on the preschool prodigy with the wide eyes and star smile. But Woods was correct in insisting that his then little boy learn to haul his own load. The earlier we give our children responsibility, the easier it is for them to learn how to handle it.

The Drive for Excellence

Accept that there will be different levels of competence and achievement among the children you know. All children, however, should get the message that if they do their best they'll achieve personal excellence.

Excellence has many definitions. In the same family one child's excellent work may be different from another's. Count effort, hard work, and improvement among your child's successes, not just high grades. Everyone can't be the best, but they should *do* their best.

Set standards realistically high, but don't make excuses or set them so low that your child feels good about accomplishments that are just average. A junior high math teacher said he didn't know how to respond when a student came to school wearing $129 Jordans that he got for getting a D in math. As the child told it, his mother said, `At least you didn't get an 'F.'" The teacher wondered, "How can I motivate that child now?"

Whatever Happened to Citizenship?

Hats on in buildings. Combs riding the back of the head. Walking in front of people without saying, "Excuse me." Butting into adult conversation. Cursing without caring who hears. Underwear showing. Dropping the door on whoever comes behind. Banging the phone down. Guys hanging on girls like lamp posts, and girls thinking that's okay. Ask a question or to do something, and you get "Yeah?" and "What?" These are far too common, while "please" and "thank you" are hard to come by.

We know better, but somehow in our haste a lot of us don't get around to teaching the rules of good manners and conduct, or enforcing them, until we are embarrassed by our kids in public. Granted, the transgressions mentioned above are mild-although our grandmothers wouldn't think so-when you consider guns in school and attacks on teachers. But pay attention to the part of your child's report card that evaluates attitudes and behaviors. Get specific examples if your child's behavior and attitudes are characterized as only satisfactory, or worse.

When talking about grades and tests, ask your child's teacher about everyday behavior. Let teachers know the kind of behavior you expect from your child and what will not be tolerated. Some teachers don't bring "small things" up because they don't know what your standards are. Unfortunately, some assume that your child's tacky behavior is just a reflection of you.

It's impossible to talk about basic courtesy without also mentioning the important character traits necessary to be a truly successful, productive young person. Big jobs, money, and accolades are unimpressive without honesty, courage, compassion, and respect for self and others.

Pay attention to the messages and values you may be unwittingly instilling in your children, through words and deeds. Do you treat people with respect and courtesy, or do you bad-mouth the teacher and the school within earshot of the children? Do you talk more about expensive cars and designer clothes than ways to help others? Do you buy your children more toys and CDs than books and software? If the cashier gives you more money back than you having coming, do you pocket it and brag later about how you got over?

Here's what a principal of a predominantly Black middle school says. "Some of our children are spoiled: cell phones, beepers, TVs in their rooms. There's a lot of the 'me' attitude. I see a lot of conflict about my pencil, someone stepped on my shoe. I deal with that 'me, me, me' stuff all the time from affluent African American children."

Good Work Habits

Ask any college student, and you'll hear that lack of good work and study habits, poor time management skills, and poor organization are among the main reasons for college hardship or failure.

Tige Nishimoto, who's pursuing a degree in information systems at Northern Virginia Community College, offers this hindsight. "I wish someone would have sat me down and taught me the fundamentals of good study habits... Good study habits, typing skills, analytical thinking skills, the ability to organize and prioritize are some of the most important skills you'll need in college."

Joel Brown, a business major at Morgan State University, repeats a common theme. "The most important skills I discovered I need in college are study skills, time management skills, writing skills. In high school, I didn't have to study that much."

Good work habits and an attitude of excellence are best set at an early age and by example: seeing you working hard and doing your best, getting to places on time, keeping your home and personal business in order, not wasting time, keeping your promises, setting your priorities and following through. These will help build responsibility, punctuality, an ethic of hard work, and an organized life and mind.

Assist your child in organizing his young life—dressing, packing lunch, keeping track of his things. Helping your child put toys back in a box and, later on, cleaning up after himself and washing dishes, are the first lessons in responsibility, work, and independence. Keeping supplies together, knowing where his shoes are, putting his laundry away, having his backpack packed and books together in the same place before going to bed—in doing all this, you're teaching him how to plan ahead, budget time, and take care of himself when he leaves home.

You or an older child can do it for them quicker and better, of course, but then when would your child ever learn? In the long run, things will go more smoothly with your teenager if you let her fumble around at times trying to do things on her own when she's little.

Praise them for their efforts, and don't make chores and responsibility a form of punishment. Expect kids to leave a book they need for homework at school, forget what the assignment was, run out of the house with the project that's due today under their bed. These are learning experiences, too. You may not be able to bail them out of trouble all the time. They'll need to suffer the consequences of some of their mistakes so they'll remember not to do it the next time.

By third or fourth grade, your student will need to track his school assignments with an assignment sheet, book, or calendar. In the beginning, it can be a sheet of paper at the front of the notebook to write down that night's homework or a reminder about Friday's spelling quiz.

An assignment book becomes a must in middle school when different teachers, different classes, short-term and long-term projects confuse and confound even the most organized. Your children should also have a calendar to chart their own activities. A clock or watch helps keep track of their time on school nights.

Time management derails many kids with good minds. College students interviewed for this book say that allotting enough time every day to tackle a continuing flow of work and readings, and setting interim goals and deadlines, is another college-killer.

For more information on helping your child develop good study skills and work habits, especially if you're the disorganized type, organize a workshop for parents of younger children and one for older students at school, church, community centers, or the public library. Ask a teacher or counselor to conduct it. As in all things, if you want to learn more about it, read and ask questions.

Learning to Set Goals

Young children and adolescents do not easily make the connection between today and the future. Continuing conversation about the great things that may await them is helpful. This chat with an eleven-year-old youngster with two professional parents indicates how some kids connect the present and the future.

"Why do you want to go to college?"

"To get an education."

"Why do you want an education?"

"To get a good job."

"Why do you want a good job?"

"So I can buy a house and food."

"Why do you want those things?"

"So I'll be happy and can take care of myself."

Beyond basic understanding, this child understands that he can make decisions and control his actions, and that his actions have consequences. He can choose to go to college or not; and that choice and action—or inaction—largely will determine his adult options.

The African American child who understands this is empowered. Empowerment contributes to self-confidence and good self-esteem—the ideas and opinions one has about oneself. This will matter even in the daily choices he has to make and in facing peer pressure: whether to try to get a B or not study, whether to start a fight or walk away, whether to stay enrolled in chemistry or drop it. Imagine the child who has no sense of self-determination.

There's an often told story about a teenage mother who never had dreams, much less goals. She felt she had no control over her todays or her tomorrows. "Life just happens," the girl thought. By nineteen she had three children.

Talk about short-term goals in the early years: get a star on the math test, finish reading Sharon Draper's *Tears of a Tiger* by next week, clean a room this weekend so you can visit a friend. Set medium-range goals for older children, too: getting an "A" in behavior for the grading period, trying out for cheerleader next spring, saving enough money for a new CD.

Your adolescent should start developing at least a mental plan and mindset about his educational goals. Different from dreaming—which is nothing more than wishful thinking—goals require planning and work.

By middle school, help your child set some goals by talking together about likes and dislikes, favorite subjects and hobbies or things she wishes she could do or just wants to know more about. Discuss the kinds of classes and education those careers require. Get more information about these things from the school or public library, or by talking to people involved in these areas. Middle school students can visit businesses and attend career fairs. Encourage your children to explore clubs and activities that are related to their interests, or to volunteer in a place where they can get an up-close look at a possible career. They can see what the job is like. Mention the subjects and classes that will help get her to college and let her know that doing well in middle school will help make the transition to high school smooth.

Explore their specific long-range goals, too. "I want to go to the University of Illinois and become a veterinarian." The details likely will change several times, of course, but having a future outlook will keep them going when it would be easier to slack off in school. Goal-setting has four parts:

State the goal (college).

Set a time period or deadline for reaching it (end of twelfth grade).

List the steps to reaching the goals (take challenging courses, study well, develop your talents and interests, participate in extracurricular activities).

Be flexible and have an alternate plan. Set a new deadline and additional steps, if necessary, to reach the goal.

Continue to say good things about your child's efforts. Every child does something that's praiseworthy, even the smallest accomplishments. Those who don't have any sense of achievement, who are weighted down by failure, may not set their goals high or may refuse to try. Why would a kid who's failing two classes want to talk about college?

When kids fall short of their goals, explain that we learn from mistakes. Let them know that obstacles and struggle are not life-limiting. Insist that they keep trying and set some goals that they can easily achieve. Having the tools of learning, exposure to life's possibilities, practice in setting goals, and working toward them is what you must seek for the children you care about.

Most of us know smart people who haven't done well in college or life. Young people who lack a strong work ethic and family values and morals to guide them, no matter how intelligent, will have a hard time facing pressures and temptations that can crush careers and even destroy lives.

Joy Bowman, an industrial engineering graduate of the University of West Virginia, notes that "lack of focus on who you are, your purpose in school, and your ultimate life goals makes you a very easy candidate for falling prey to some of the evils of society that seem to be ever present on college campuses." Ms. Bowman comes from a family with a strong religious tradition. Their motto, "We've Come this Far By Faith," speaks to the need to rely on something greater than our own abilities.

DOES YOUR 13-YEAR-OLD HAVE A RESUME?

In developing your children's interests and talents, your goal is not to pile up achievements and bragging rights. You're teaching them to live their lives to the fullest, to get involved with life rather than watch it go by. "To get off the sidelines and into the game."

By the end of middle school, some students have accumulated enough experiences and activities to build two-page resumes. They can list volunteer service, participation in organized sports, academic and other kinds of competitions, attendance at special programs, awards and honors from school.

You want your child to be well-rounded, with interests and meaningful activities beyond academics. In later years these outside activities and skills will stand out on a college application (Don't list middle school activities on college applications, as some students are tempted to do. By high school, your student should be used to being involved in activities and developing his skills at a higher level. The middle years lay the foundation for accomplishments in high school student.) Colleges are looking for fully developed people who can contribute to their campuses beyond the classroom. A student who's been diligently developing his talents over the years is also in position to compete for scholarships and awards based on those specific interests.

Start by identifying talents and natural interests. Every child is "gifted and talented" whether or not the "giftedness" shows up on a test or school honor roll. Some of your children's talents will be too obvious to ignore. He's dunking at twelve, has a voice like Luther, or can spell words you never heard of. But some of our children's talents may not be so apparent.

The "talented and gifted," and "gifted and talented" programs that some public school districts operate are a reconfiguration of the old tracking system (remember "honors" versus "basic" classes?) In some large urban schools, students in a single grade, say seventh, were divided into as many as twelve classes by descending levels of "ability." You knew you were smart if you were in 7-12 at Taft Junior High, and you never even got to talk to anyone below 7-10. Where official tracking was thrown out, "gifted and talented" classes emerged.

Most in-school gifted programs use recommendations and standardized test scores to determine who's eligible. Increasingly, however, "giftedness" is determined by parents. In one neighborhood high school, from 30 to 50 percent of the students are enrolled in gifted classes, most at their parents' insistence. Which is why the whole concept of "gifted and talented" programs in public education offends many people. It can set up a separate and unequal system—"gifted" classes get additional resources and in-depth study, as well as some of the best teachers—that largely benefits families who already have the means to boost their children's school performance. The labels applied to children in the programs are an abomination. If some in the school are "gifted and talented," what are the rest? Non-gifted and untalented?

Whether you agree with ability grouping or not, children *are* different. Many gifts may seem to have nothing to do with school and academics, but are no less valuable if acknowledged and developed. A child who loves to make up poems and tell tall tales. The car pool kid who sings along with every song on the radio. The young person who's always asking "Why?" The one in the family who always figures out the restaurant tab before it comes. The doodler who creates elaborate labyrinths on the backs of napkins. The social butterfly and chatterbox who easily attracts friends and engages strangers. The kid who puts together hundred-piece puzzles and invents new creations for Legos.

A number of researchers have promoted the theory of multiple intelligences, seven areas of innate ability and talent:

- *verbal-linguistic intelligence* (the poet, storyteller)
- *logical-mathematical* (the family tabulator)
- *visual-spatial* (the "Legomaniac")
- *musical* (backseat crooner)
- *bodily-kinesthetic* (athletes, dancers, folks who are good at making things with their hands)
- *interpersonal intelligence* (everybody's friend)
- *intrapersonal intelligence* (the independent child who keeps to himself and likes to work alone)

Whichever category your children fit in, encourage their interest, actions and activities. Provide opportunities for private or group lessons. Sign them up for community teams or Little League, school clubs and church groups that are involved in interesting things. Scouts develop leadership skills and expose children to all sorts of new activities outside of their communities.

Find a friend or mentor who shares your child's interest or is a pro at the thing he wants to study. Whether it's playing an instrument or African dancing, stamp collecting or football, give your child the chance to show what he can do outside of the classroom.

Some children deny an interest in anything except the current popular trends. The video game junkie or budding rap artist may resist invitations to take swimming or join the chess club. You'll have to take the lead and expose them to activities they might not experience on their own. Without spending a lot of money up front, find free activities and one-day or short-term classes he can sample. Recreation departments and your local park service offer seasonal classes for nominal fees. Public museums conduct one-day workshops for free or the cost of supplies.

Keep reading your newspaper calendar section for concerts, plays and live theater, children's lectures and workshops. Share your own hobbies. If you don't have any, try to take time for yourself. Children will understand the benefits of a full life if they see you taking advantage of opportunities, trying to improve yourself and trying new things. Over the years, these interests may shift and change. And a child may lose interest in extracurricular activities and hobbies you think are a natural for her. By middle school, encourage them to find something and stick with it. Developing talents and interests now will get your child accustomed to taking on new challenges and persevering through what they take on. Eventually they'll grow and mature with the satisfaction of mastering a skill.

A Record of Achievement

The following resume is that of an African American thirteen year old in the eighth grade at a predominantly Black public school. He attended a private African American elementary school. He is the oldest of three children.

His mother believes, as many parents of successful students do, that you've got to get your child interested and active, seek out opportunity, and keep looking ahead. When asked to put together a resume to demonstrate how much a young person can accomplish, it was early spring and she was busy calling around and getting directories of summer programs. Her son likes to enter science fairs, so she was specifically looking for a science program where he could gather information for next year's project.

Jamal's resume demonstrates how much a young person can accomplish, in this case, at relatively low cost to his parents. Many of the enrichment programs he attended were subsidized in whole or part by universities, major corporations, or private education or professional groups.

In some cases, one opportunity opened doors to another. By participating in some major competitions and activities, your child's name may be picked up by colleges interested in students with specific talents. New Mexico Tech gets the names of middle school students from state science fairs and the Odyssey of the Mind competitions. Over the years, it had invited these students to the campus and keeps their names on a list of young scholars.

Middle School Resume

EDUCATION

8th grade courses: German, Geometry, Algebra II, Physical Science, English, Humanities, Physical Education, Geography

School Activities: Exploring the Planets Club, Southeastern Consortium of Minorities in Engineering (SECME)

Awards: City-Wide Science Fair (2nd Place-Engineering) "Testing Airplanes in a Wind Tunnel," City Wide SECME Mousetrap Car Competition Team Award (3rd Place), Junior Beta Honor Society, Honor Roll

Grades K-6 Courses: Spanish, Heritage, Social Studies, Algebra, English, Computer Literacy, Science, Physical Education

Activities: Marching Band

Awards: City-Wide Science Fair 2nd Place-Engineering) "Model Rockets and the Space Shuttle," Honor Roll, Science Award, Social Studies Award, Math Award, Scholarship Award, Outstanding Student Award

ENRICHMENT Programs

First Light (Carnegie Institute), a Saturday Science Program

Smithsonian Institute Air and Space Museum, Summer Camp

NASA Space Camp, One Week Summer Program

NASA Goddard Space Flight Center, Rocketeering Course

Concordia Languages Village, Two-week Summer German Studies

Center for Math, Science and Technology, summer course for middle school students

SPORTS

Soccer League

COMMUNITY ACTIVITIES

United Methodist Church-Acolyte, Usher, Youth Choir Member, Youth Fellowship, Youth Speaker

IF THEY'RE GONNA PLAY SPORTS ...

It's just too easy to think that all Black boys are natural athletes. One mother battled this when a school board member asked if her son, new to the district, played sports.

"Yes," she said, indicating his skill in basketball, baseball, tennis, and swimming. "Good," the board member said. "We need some jocks."

"He's no jock," she replied. "He also paints, plays the piano, and likes science. And he's an honor student." The school board member seemed stunned.

It's easy to be flattered by that kind of excitement and praise over a child's athletic ability. At Saturday morning tee-ball and tennis, and afternoon peewee football games, you'll hear a lot of moms and dads talking about the scholarships they're hoping for. As in, "She's gonna need a scholarship. That's why she's here. Haven't you heard about all the tennis scholarships they can't give away? They're looking for Black kids who can play tennis."

In their zeal, it's easy for parents and coaches to lose sight of what's important. That's what's happening when basketball leagues schedule games for ten-year-olds at nine p.m. on school nights.

With the Title IX legislation that requires equitable school funding for male and female sports programs, and new developments such as professional women's basketball, the parents of young girls have joined the sports dreams crowd. As the years pass and reality sets in, however, fewer parents still expect college recruiters to call. Ironically, with the pressure off and reality setting in, sports become a lot more fun for many families.

Those who coach young people caution that young children should get involved in sports for the physical activity and lessons in teamwork, friendship, and competition. If an athletic scholarship is a realistic goal (it will be apparent by the middle of high school), parents of student-athletes should know from the very beginning that they can't expect their student-athletes to just get by on academics.

In the past decade, eligibility requirements for participation in the National Collegiate Athletic Association require even the most athletically sought-after to take a "core curriculum" of academic classes and meet minimum grade point average and college admission test scores. Student athletes, like other students, must get on the college prep track in middle school.

IF THEY'RE GONNA WATCH TV ...

Think of what's on television, and radio, too, and you can't help but boil with concern over the media diet of the next generation. Any responsible adult with a child at his or her side winces and cringes when the lewd talk, risky behavior without consequence, gratuitous violence, and sexual overtones appear suddenly on screen or voiceovers. This sends most of us on a remote control scramble or knobswitching fervor.

The average child watches three hours per day of television. Black children, on average, watch more than everybody else: Our kids sit in front of that stuff for more than five hours each weekday.

If they're going to watch television at all, young people should be limited to one to two hours a day of quality programs, the recommendation of the American Academy of Pediatrics. So approach television with thought, planning, and discrimination. Rather than plopping down to see what's on and staying in front of the tube for the broadcasting parade of shows, teach kids to watch selectively. Your children should get into the habit of asking, "Can I watch *Raven?*" rather than just, "Can I watch TV?" Check the TV listings and read the reviews in the newspaper for special or new programs you may be interested in. Look for shows that inspire an interest in getting up and doing something else-adventures, shows that introduce children to literary stories, science, and nature.

Discuss the things you like and don't like on TV. Point it out if you disagree with the actions of a character, if the setting is unrealistic or unnatural, if the actions and events offend you. Turn off a show if you really don't like what you see, don't mindlessly surf for poor alternatives. Find something else to do when the programs you're interested in are over. If you believe, as many do, that television can be educational, this is the way to watch it.

Even long hours in front of public television's acclaimed educational programming, such as *Sesame Street* followed by *Barney*, take your child away from "active" play and experiences that develop physical and social skills. More worrisome, the flashing and fast moving images on the television screen have been linked to attention deficit disorder in children who watched more than two hours of television a day as toddlers.

Young children don't distinguish between programming and commercials, and even some older youngsters think you really can jump higher depending on the cost of a pair of athletic shoes. Identifying the motives of commercial pitchmen, talking about what you see and hear, is a viewing skill you should pass on.

Something to think about: If you can afford to give your child her own television, set up in her bedroom, ask yourself if she can *afford* to have it. That is, what are the benefits of giving a child or adolescent the potential for so much private television viewing? If you can come up with more benefits to you (electronic babysitter), as opposed to benefits to the child, resist the temptation to put a TV in a child's bedroom.

HIGHER GROUND

IT'S YOUR HOMEWORK, TOO

A parent's major task in keeping home and school connected involves homework. Its purpose is to give your children a chance to practice and review what's been taught, explore subjects beyond what can be done in class, get a head start on upcoming lessons, learn to study and do research on their own. All of these are necessary skills and habits they'll need for higher education.

Homework, however, can take as much out of parents as it does out of the kids. Let's face it, being involved with homework, indeed all of our children's affairs, requires work from us. But you've already worked all day, and by the time you get home you still have clothes to wash, dinner to fix, and lunches to pack. Plus, you told your friend you'd call or go out tonight.

If you want your child to be the best she can be, homework is an additional, unavoidable chore for parents, just like making sure there's dinner on the table. Yet who hasn't had the same sentiments expressed by this mother at a back-to-school night.

Parent: "They won't have homework every night, will they?'"

Teacher: "Probably not on Fridays or holidays."

Parent: "Oooh, thank God."

At an expensive private school, almost all the parents in one sixth grade class complained outright about too much homework.

Mother: "He needs help with all this homework you're giving. I shouldn't have to teach him. I have my own work to do, I have dinner to cook."

Father: "You don't cook diner."

Mother: "Go to hell."

Meanwhile, parents in one well-to-do African American community complained when a new superintendent required homework on weekends for elementary and middle school. The community, whose students were second to last in state rankings, had a long history of complaints about the inadequacy of their schools. Yet when the new leaders tried to introduce "rigor" into the schools, enough parents balked that it led the local news.

We all have lots to do. That can always be a good excuse if you choose to not treat homework as an essential part of your child's education and future. Suggested guidelines for the amount of time your child spends doing homework depends on the child's age and grade level:

- primary through third grade, up to twenty minutes a night
- fourth through sixth grade, from twenty to forty minutes
- grades seven through nine, up to two hours

Pay attention to these guidelines, which come from experts at the Department of Education. In our zeal to have our children do well and get ahead in school, some of us impose inappropriate homework requirements, especially on younger children. One young mother was frustrated that her first grader hated homework, saying the little girl fussed and cried and balked every night. No wonder—the mother was requiring the six year old to study and do sheet work for an hour. What she got was a frustrated child—six-year-olds don't have the attention span to sit at a table for an hour doing "home work"—and a candidate for early academic burnout.

At the start of the school year, ask your child's teacher about homework policies and expectations. In middle school this information may be included in a school handbook or other written materials sent home during the first days.

Teachers say you can best help your children with homework by making sure they have the basic tools and supplies readily available. For younger students, you may have to help them determine the things they'll need in advance, especially if it requires a book or other resource you'll have to borrow or get from the library.

They'll also need a quiet, well-lit place to study that is free of distractions, such as talking, television, and radio noise. If your house is small and generally noisy, you could establish a quiet time when everyone is doing homework, reading, paying bills, etc.

Make sure your child has enough time for homework (not doing too many other things), and that you or another older person are available to help or to check on it at some point during the evening. Try setting a regular time for homework.

As children move up in elementary school and begin middle school, they'll likely get long-term assignments or projects that are not due for weeks or months. Monitor these closely, and don't just ask your child if they're working on the project. If the teacher is not doing so in school, you must help your child learn to manage such work. Check the project's progress weekly. Look at it—don't just ask about it. Offer guidance the way you would if you were talking to someone at work about how to meet a specific deadline. If your child knows he must be able to show his progress every week, he will not be able to put things off until the last minute. And he will learn the valuable skill of meeting deadlines.

It's clear when a parent (or both) has done the work for a child. You walk in your child's class and roll your eyes at the Powerpoint presentation that a first-grader supposedly put together. Then you help your child set up his castle made up of blocks. Which child has learned more? Which child has pride in his accomplishment? Perhaps both? But the fact is, all that parental input usually isn't necessary. Teachers are grading on the standards of children's work. They're not grading parents. So, explain directions, give examples, help purchase supplies, or do projects together. But please, don't take over your child's project (So you'll get an "A").

On the other hand, if the homework is beyond your knowledge and your child is struggling, send a note to the teacher the next day explaining the difficulties. If your child is unable to complete an assignment for whatever reason, send a note to her teacher with the explanation. She may be given a chance to make it up, and shouldn't be penalized if you inform the teacher of special circumstances.

If problems with homework are regular and continuing, your child may have bigger problems in school. Start talking to the teacher immediately, before things get worse. Some schools and community groups have after-school homework sessions or hotlines staffed by teachers. If homework seems too easy, tell the teacher this, too.

Some programs, by design, do not require homework, such as

Montessori programs, which were designed in the early part of the century with the expectation that children would spend their time after school fully engaged with their families. Even on the occasions when children have no assigned homework, they can "make up some homework" or "find something to study," as many parents say. And every child should have a reading period each evening, right?

Many children try to finish their homework before their parents get home from work. Encouraging this will give them something to do while you're away. But don't set television or anything else up as a reward for doing homework, as in, "You can watch TV when you finish your homework." You may find your child rushing through work better done with patience and thought because he wants to watch whatever is on the WB network. Instead, set a specific time period for study and review, getting things in order for the next school day. When homework is done, look and see if the homework *is* actually done, and done thoughtfully, without signs of haste (sloppiness, silly mistakes).

By the way, don't limit television as a form of punishment. You'll assign it more value than it's usually worth. If it's an educational show, you probably don't want to limit it as a punishment for a different reason: Education always is to be encouraged, never held back, as it was during slavery.

STAYING INVOLVED

At Home

Stock your home with the basic learning supplies.

Set aside a regular time for homework, reading, and other quiet activities.

Keep reading to your children even after they can read alone, and let them read to you.

Compile a home library. Get used books from yard sales, secondhand stores, if you need to, or swap books with friends and neighbors.

Plan learning adventures to the library, museum, a country farm, the zoo, live theater. Expose your children to the things in their community, and travel beyond it.

Send children to school rested and on time. Make sure they get enough physical activity and a healthy diet that includes plenty of fruits, vegetables, and grains.

Don't over-schedule with activities or overburden children with chores. Allow time just for lazing about.

Show interest in what your children want to tell you about their daily adventures. If leaf collections or the biology dissection are part of the day's excitement, show some honest enthusiasm.

Make a folder to collect flyers, brochures, pamphlets, and the names of people, books, and programs that could enrich your child's education.

Check notebook and backpacks to find the things kids "forget" to show you. You're not snooping, just looking for teachers' comments, crumpled-up bad grades, and even good things that get lost in the mix. Some of the things you find will open up a door to conversation with your child. Some things you may just want to keep in the back of your mind. Of course, you can ask your child to show you or go through their things when you have a quiet moment.

At School

Meet your child's teachers at the start of school. Let them know your expectations that your child will go to college one day.

Talk with your child's teachers at least once during each grading period, but as frequently as possible, even to exchange informal information about his likes and dislikes, new and old habits.

When you ask questions of teachers and staff, be specific, as in: "What did he get on the last few tests?" or, "Is he having difficulty with fractions? He seems bored. Do you see that, too?" Or, "She's been complaining about going to school lately. Do you have any idea why?" In other words, don't ask general questions that will give you a general response you can't act on, such as, "How is he doing?" One mother was told her healthy, athletic son was doing "fine" in physical education. When report cards came home, he got a C in phys ed, with a minus for effort and attitude. This is not what she expected from a report of "fine."

Pass on good information about your child: "She just learned to ride a two-wheeler," "He's being confirmed this Sunday," "He says he wants to be a biologist"—not just problems or bad news.

Come to parent-teacher conferences with questions and comments written down in advance.

Talk informally to your children before conferences to find out their problems, concerns, things they might be wondering or worrying about.

Organize a parent support group for the class, not just the regular PTA group. A smaller support group is a way to help each other, share notes and information, help individual teachers.

Volunteer at least once during the school year. Show your child that school is important enough for you to put in an effort there.

Attend school events that are important to your child.

Keep going to school even when your kids start to tell you not to (around middle school). Find new ways to be involved, going on field trips and being classroom mom may not give your child the sense of independence he needs at this time. But don't follow their lead totally. If you haven't already, join governing boards, PTA committees, booster groups. Even if the kids say it embarrasses them, keep going to school.

Something to think about: One of the jobs of today's teachers and principals is to encourage parent participation at school. They're attending workshops on ways to make school more inviting to parents from a diversity of cultures to make parents feel more comfortable coming to school and being involved with the events and people there. Some of them are being evaluated on how good a job they do in getting you involved

In the Community

Organize culture clubs or reading clubs for the children you care about.

Reach out to other children by taking a neighborhood child, a relative, or your child's classmate along with you on excursions they'd enjoy but might not otherwise experience.

Develop your network of like-minded parents who are "in the know." Pass along interesting information that other parents would appreciate having.

Arrange book and toy swaps. Pass on things your child has outgrown and pick up more usable items for free.

PART THREE

The High School Years

"Almost all the jobs that pay enough to support a family now require higher levels of literacy, language fluency, and technical training."

Project GRAD
(Graduation Really Achieves Dreams)

PARENTS IN THE PROCESS

The high school years can be the most exhilarating—and also the scariest and most frustrating. The decisions our children make at this point, more than ever before, will determine the course of their lives. And so you must be a part of their decision-making.

If you started planning for college years ago—putting away money, getting your child into a daily reading habit, participating in school activities, making academics a priority at home—you probably already see the benefits. By now, your teenager considers college a natural step after high school.

With that mindset and some specific goals already in place, it will be easier to guide and push your youngsters to do the things necessary to graduate from high school with the credentials and skills for college success.

Just starting to plan? If, like so many other parents, you are just discovering college is a real option for your children, or you're late in realizing you need a specific plan of action to get them there, don't panic. There's a lot that has to be done but there's also time to do it.

At the start of freshman year, or as soon as you finish *Higher Ground*, get your students thinking about this sober truth: *What they do for during the high school years, in school and out, will deter-*

mine whether he gets into the college of his choice and earns scholar-ships to help pay for it.

High school freshmen start with a clean slate. The missteps of middle school won't find their way onto a high school transcript. There is much that can be done in the next four years. All high school students should enter knowing the importance of those years and that their own actions will determine their future. With the support of parents and other adults, they can direct their own course. Late bloomers and underachievers should be told this. The most self-disciplined and motivated should be reminded.

Robin Hall got a reminder, a jolt, really, in her senior year. In high school she says she was "hanging out" a little more than she should have, and her grades, while good, told the tale to those who knew she could do better. "The beginning of my senior year, my counselor, a White guy, said I'd never get into a good school if I didn't get a 4.0 for senior year. He didn't see it happening. I showed him. I got a 4.1."

Hall went on to major in accounting at Hampton University.

Review with your teenager—the start of each school year is a good time—the reasons for doing well in school, the reasons for going or not going to college.

Common reasons for going to college:

    to prepare for specific career or profession

    to make more money than you might otherwise (See "The

Value of a College Education")
to get away from home
to delay going to work full-time
to learn new ways of thinking, meet new people, share new
experiences
because everybody else is going
pressure from parents

Common reasons for not going to college:
job interests don't require college
can't afford it (See "Paying for College")
not worth the investment (See "The Value of a College
Education")
not academically prepared (Read about Morgan State
University's Horace Moo-Young in "What Else Are
Colleges Looking For?")
family responsibilities (See "Teen Parents")
family not in favor of it (Show them "The Value of a College
Education"
never thought about it, not enough information to make a
decision (keep reading this book)
friends aren't going (share this book with them)

If your youngster is approaching junior or senior year, you
both will have to hustle.

One of the first things to discuss with the young person who's just considering college is the variety of colleges and universities and the range of ability and interests they accommodate. (See "Different Kinds of Colleges.") College is still an option for students who aren't high achievers.

You should also involve your youngster in the family's finances. Start talking about how much a college education costs. The figures may seem overwhelming. But even if you don't have a fat bank account, your young people should know early that money doesn't have to be an obstacle, as you'll find out later in this section. Even if you're living in the projects. Even if Dad won't pay child support.

Scholarships await those who've worked hard to get good grades, served their community, or developed their talents. The neediest poor and low income students can get financial aid from a number of state and government programs. New grants and programs have been developed to help middle-income families. Low interest educational loans are an honorable debt for those students and families with few other options. Pledge to help your student find the resources to supplement what the family can afford.

If you haven't already, start putting away money for higher education, whether it's in an old mayonnaise jar, savings bonds, or certificates of deposit. Taking the effort to set aside even a small amount shows your young person that college is a real and tangible goal, not a distant dream.

If academic readiness is a problem, try to stop the cycle of mediocrity or failure now. Students promoted to senior high with below average grades nonetheless may not have the basic skills in reading and mathematics to do high-school-level work. Don't let the problems worsen before you intervene.

The summer before freshman year, arrange for a tutor or remedial help. Ask counselors and teachers about summer school (especially if your child is not recommended). Ask anyone you know about people and organizations that can assist with the cost of additional instruction. Some local communities have private school-scholarship funds that also will help pay the cost of summer enrichment and remedial classes. College students are paid through federal work-study jobs to tutor youngsters. Contact a local college for help. Ask about college-prep programs for high school students.

Parent's roles are changing by the time children grow into teenagers. Your high school student will have more friends and peers to give advice. Your daughters and sons probably are more interested in what other young people are doing than in what you thin.

In a natural bid for independence, they'll make more decisions and choices about school and activities on their own. And they don't want to let you in on all their "business." This period of adolescence typically is marked by rebellion, too. So changes are kids often will want to do the opposite of what you suggest.

Give them some slack. As you begin to let for of your young person, you empower them to thinking and do for themselves. Self-reliance and independent decision-making skills will be critical during the college years. Whether they stay at home or go away to live on campus, they'll very soon be making major decisions without any help from you. Letting them make and learn from small mistakes now is part of getting them ready for the freedoms and responsibilities of college.

Your role becomes less authoritarian and more supportive, like a coach. You explain the rules of the game and make sure your students plays by them. You provide the equipment, support and training necessary to perform well. You offer guidance, call some of the plays, and try to stay aware of what's happening on the field and off.

But don't leave them completely on their own. Despite the way they act sometimes, even if they're bigger than you, can drive and cook for themselves, teenagers still need a close relationships with the family. And perhaps more than ever, when decisions about school really are life-defining, you must continues to advocate for your children and be an activist when it comes to their education.

You shouldn't be overly involved in history projects anymore. And your chaperoning every party and field trip could stifle your teen. But show up at school at regular intervals, nonetheless. You still need to show interest and be involved in school and activities even if he can take the subway alone to the track meet or negotiate with the teacher himself about that "C" in biology.

You'll still need to do some of the same things you've always done. Schedule parent-teacher conferences and come prepared with specific questions. Call a teacher that your child has had trouble with, just to check in. Attend school events that are important to your youngster. Your high school student will have more teachers, and that means more effort on your part in maintaining a home/school connection. Make sure you get an email address for each teacher. And log on to the school's website routinely.

Continue to make sure your child has the tools of learning in the home, although you can leave the school shopping to him.

Monitor homework, even if it's just checking in to see that he's working on something on school nights. College preparatory high schools where courses are difficult and standards are high assign two to three hours of homework each school night, plus homework on the weekends.

If your child is still developing organizational skills and his level of personal responsibility is not yet high, you still may need to ask to see his assignment book, and query him on what needs doing. Notebook and backpack checks are a good way to start each grading period organized-and to find those things crumpled at the bottom.

Some parents also like to help their child clean out the school locker. You'll be lucky if your biggest surprise is a long lost sweater (does it belong to you?) and a library book that is two years overdue. But you'll also see firsthand how your young person manages his "business." Like the work space at a job, is it orderly? Can he find what he needs when he needs it?

Basic Supplies

    student organizer, agenda, or assignment book
    small tape recorder as a backup for in-class note-taking
    color-coded notebooks/binders
    black and dark blue pens, highlighter markers, rulers
    encyclopedia, atlas, globe, almanac
    subscriptions to daily newspapers, news magazines, and periodicals of interest to the student dictionaries (more than one, so that various approaches to words can be compared), a thesaurus
    foreign language/English dictionary for foreign language

courses

spiritual books, such as the Bible, Koran, biographies

a public library card

regular (at least weekly) access to a computer and the internet

scientific, graphing calculators for advanced math courses

BACK TO BASICS

The previous section of this book began with helping children establish a mindset for higher education. Continue to expose your teenager to people, events, and places that light up their imaginations and lift their aspirations. By high school, your children know many successful people, at school, in the community, at church, at the doctor's office or hospital or community center. Make sure they are told that the same kinds of successes they see others enjoying, whether it's in their neighborhood or on TV, are within their reach.

The following section on career exposure will help get your young person to understand the possibilities that await her if she gets a college degree. You can also involve her in career-focused youth leadership programs through local churches and community programs. African American sororities and fraternities offer opportunities for personal and academic development that encourage college. Contact a chapter in your area and ask about cotillions for girls and beautillions for boys that stress these aspects. In recent years, African American families and organizations are conducting Rites of Passage to direct teens through the tumultuous years from childhood to adulthood. Such programs, often with an African theme or Afrocentric concepts, focus on character and cultural pride.

Regular reading outside of school assignments is key to building the critical reading and language skills that will determine placement in advanced classes, and to more self-assurance in completing the writing and research assignments that are necessary in higher level academics.

If your child has not yet taken algebra, contact a counselor and together set a timetable for taking it. As noted earlier, taking algebra is not an option, it's a necessity for students who are going to college.

While there's a flourishing market for courses that prepare students for college admissions tests such as the SAT and ACT, the best preparation for the verbal sections is a lifetime of reading beyond school. The best preparation for the mathematics section is advanced math, beginning with algebra. If your students have not made reading and math a priority, they must do so now.

Your young person now would probably rather send instant messages to friends than sit on the sofa and read with you. But you can discuss the nightly news at dinner or debate the latest political scandal over a cold drink. For your part, encourage reading outside of school by acquiring materials teenagers are interested in. Several magazines on urban culture, sports, fashion, and popular culture. Get your teenagers their own subscriptions to the magazines they like to browse through at the grocery store, and also sign them up for a subscription to a news magazine, such as *Newsweek or Time* or *Jet*.

Also look for books that address the African American teenage experience and books about famous African Americans, particularly those who have overcome great difficulty. Some examples are *Makes Me Wanna Holler,* Nathan McCall; *No Free Ride,* Kweise Mfume; *The Autobiography of Malcolm X,* written with Alex Haley, and Maya Angelou's series of autobiographical works, beginning with *I Know Why the Caged Bird Sings*. Ask the school librarian for recommended high school and college-bound reading lists. In school, your college-bound student should be reading classic literature, too, from Shakespeare to Charles Dickens to Toni Morrison.

Encourage your young ladies to join one of the book groups that are so popular among African American women. Or help start a book group specifically for teenagers that meets at homes, school, library, church, or recreation center.

Involve kids in managing money, and then budgeting their own spending money while saving or investing for college. Help them accumulate enough to deposit in a savings account. More sophisticated savings options, such as certificates of deposits, stocks, and bonds, are not out of their reach, either. Learning how to manage money is a skill they'll need beyond high school.

Your student should also be developing time-management and study skills, including note-taking and using the library and internet for research. College students interviewed for this book routinely named these as among the most necessary skills. High school students should also master:

Note-taking—Taking down information gained aurally or from written material to aid in the review of facts and information. Learning to write key words, identify conclusions and important facts. Rereading material for key points in headings, summary sections, and in each paragraph and chapter.

Report writing—Identifying main points, making an outline, writing a first draft. Revising or editing and preparing a final draft.

Research—Using various resources in a library, such as index-es and bibliographies, computer databases, computerized directories.

Organization—Setting a schedule for completing multiple assignments, plotting the steps necessary for long-term projects, and tracking their own progress by setting inter-im deadlines.

Time Management—Making choices and allocating enough time to get all assignments done well and when they're due, in addition to doing things that young people want to do.

Studying regularly—The practice of reviewing old tests, re-reading hand-outs and previously assigned chapters, re-doing math quiz problems that are likely to show up on the final exam. Going over lessons in order to better understand what's been taught. It takes a mature student to do this nightly, regardless of whether there's a test com-ing up. The students who study regularly without being told to) are the top students in a school.

If your students are disorganized, consider a special summer or weekend course in study skills and organization. Community colleges offer classes on "How to Study" or "Becoming a Master Student." College freshmen enroll in these as remedial courses. You can find workbooks on this subject in bookstores and libraries.

Finally, the best way to prepare for college is simply by always doing one's best in high school, beginning in freshman year. Your child starts high school in ninth grade with a clean academic slate. This is the beginning of building a record that will determine the direction of her young adult years. Talk about this often, especially when the young people you love want to blow off homework, or don't think it's that important to pull a "C" up to a "B."

A WINDOW ON THE FUTURE

Marian Wright Edelman, founder of the Children's Defense Fund, asked a Black teenager caught looting and setting fires during the 1968 race riot in Washington, D.C., what kind of future he expected to have if he stole and burned down his own community. "Lady, I ain't got no future," he answered.

Don't expect young people to work hard and postpone immediate gratification if they can't realistically look to something better and more lasting than their current situation. They need to be able to envision a positive future. In this regard, the value of meeting and getting advice directly from people of color from varied professions can't be overstated. These role models demonstrate to young people that they, too, can have a successful future.

They still may not have a clue about what they want to do with their lives. Plenty of students begin college without knowing what they want to major in. But career fairs, occupational handbooks, informational interviews, and contacts with African American professional organizations will help them see the possibilities.

Most high schools will arrange or announce career fairs or bring in guests to share their careers with students. Your young person should be there. And so should you. If your high school hasn't been arranging visits from college representatives, suggest forming a school committee that can put one together annually. Or arrange your own trip to a college fair. The same can be done through churches and community groups.

Role models are equally important in giving young people information and advice on how to achieve their goals. To get the most out of career information sessions, discuss with your child his values, strengths and weaknesses, and still developing interests. This is one of the first basic steps in formal career and college planning. Ask questions about what is important to your child: Making a lot of money? Having time to spend with family or on personal interests? How does she want to live? Does she want to travel? Is spending sixty hours a week at work okay?

A common exercise is to have young people imagine their adult life. Does it revolve around family? Having nice things? Doing good for others and making a difference? Perfecting a skill or talent with hours of dedicated effort? Gaining celebrity or fame? Working alone or surrounded by people?

A common question of anyone trying to determine a career or a career change is, "Can I earn a living doing what I like do?" Your child's love of art, even if he can't draw, may lead to a prestigious museum as an art historian, or to the corporate world as an art buyer-someone who, literally, is paid to shop for artworks for deep-pocket companies or individuals. If he does draw well, is always doodling, maybe he could earn a living illustrating scientific texts, animating Disney films, or producing his own syndicated comic strip like "Boondocks" by young Aaron McGruder.

Don't be negative or discouraging of the seemingly impractical or farfetched. Despite our grandparents' beliefs, African

American professionals are not limited to teaching, preaching, or a good government job. If your child expresses an interest in something for which you see no practical occupation, do some research. Review the U.S. Department of Labor's *Occupational Outlook Handbook,* available in public libraries. Check out career books in the school guidance office and library. Ask the French teacher about careers for a student who wants to major in a foreign language.

If your child has definite career interests, freshman year is the time to start looking through college guides and identifying schools with strong programs in the subject and their admission requirements.

Also, help your child set up "informational interviews" at companies or organizations and with individuals. Have your student send a letter requesting a brief interview in which she can ask questions about education and training requirements, colleges they recommend, the employment outlook, and what's involved day-to-day on the job.

This is good interviewing experience in a non-pressure situation. Students interested in professions such as law, medicine, accounting, journalism, nursing, business, engineering—almost any field, really—should check out African American professional associations. Making contacts with people in these organizations during the high school years will put your young person in touch with some of the best professional networkers. These are the people who have contacts that can lead to other opportunities—most professional organizations award scholarships. Students who are already involved in the organizations, high school and college mentoring programs, and internships are in good position for the scholarships such groups award.

Career choice is an ongoing conversation with your young person over the next few years. Beginning it early helps young people make more sense out of the formal information they should receive in school or outside career workshops. It is also good motivation when students make decisions about how they will spend their high school years.

YOUR BUSY GUIDANCE COUNSELOR

You've heard the complaints if you haven't made them yourself. The guidance counselor is always on another line when we call, or off to a meeting when a student comes in for help. They never tell us all that they know. They can't answer our every question. They won't necessarily arrange college visits or pitch our perfect child.

We're constantly under-whelmed by them, wondering what they're doing that they can't make sure we know everything there is to know about courses, requirements, colleges, scholarships, summer enrichment programs, essay contests, poster contests, and every other thing that could possibly benefit our student.

This all-too-common negative perception of the high school counselor results from two things. One, the guidance counselor in a large public high school is responsible for 407 students. Social problems, personal counseling, and dealing with disciplinary actions-not just college application deadlines-take up a counselor's time, though they're not social workers. Two, much of what parents and students expect high school counselors to do is beyond their job description.

Audrey Hill, a past president of the National Association for College Admissions Counseling, says the mandate of the public high school counselor is to help students complete their graduation requirements on time and to leave with a plan for higher education, work, or further training. In her words, "Our role is to be advocates for the student and to make sure the student gets through the educational process—and leaves with their ego intact. We do that. And we try to encourage parents to be involved."

Notice she didn't say the guidance counselor's job is getting students into college. The guidance counselor at a predominantly Black urban high school is quick to correct the misperception that she should "get kids scholarships and into college."

"A lot of people have never really been in contact with their child's counselor. And I'm willing to bet you they haven't read anything that's come out of that guidance office. Whenever they say, 'My counselor didn't do anything for me or my kid,' then I have to talk to them about who's responsible."

Says another counselor, "There's an attitude among some parents that things are supposed to fall into your lap. Literally, I've heard, 'No one told my child that there was this scholarship.' Well, there's a room where you go where the information is. It's there all the time. But there's this handholding they want."

Also, sad to say, you can't assume that your guidance counselor is aware of everything that can help your child. A study by NACAC found that some guidance counselors in white suburban districts lacked knowledge of Historically Black Colleges and Universities (HBCUs). "They didn't give me specific information because a lot of schools I was interested in were Black colleges they never even heard of," an African American student reported.

Kim Manley, an admissions officer at North Carolina A&T, says she graduated from a predominantly White high school in

North Carolina never having heard of Howard University or most of the other HBCUs. And she realized later that she didn't get the information about scholarships for minority students that she might have received. "I didn't get the information I needed from a majority White high school," she said.

High school guidance offices are not created equal. Those with more resources start holding College Nights for parents and students in the fall of junior year, and meet individually with students, and again with a student and her parents at least once during junior year and again in twelfth grade. For seniors and their parents, the guidance office may hold monthly evening workshops or quarterly College Nights that guide parents and students through filling out applications, financial aid issues and Q&A sessions with representatives from colleges. Or, the guidance office may hold one mass meeting in the auditorium.

Audrey Hill's advice is that parents and counselors work together. With all that's at stake (potentially tens of thousands of dollars in financial aid and scholarship money for four years of college for one student), Hill says parents shouldn't be shy about taking the lead. "Call the counselor. Ask questions. Parents and students have got to learn to be more aggressive, more assertive. That's the real world, otherwise your child will continue throughout life to lose out."

All families should expect to get, and counselors in most school districts are required to give, some basic information at the start of freshman year that answers the following questions:

What are the graduation requirements-the courses and numbers of semesters/years of study?

Does the school award different kinds of diplomas, such as

Honors, Merit, College Prep, General? What are the different requirements for these?

What are the prerequisite courses, classes my child should take in ninth and tenth grade in order to move into more advanced courses?

What arrangements can be made to take advanced courses not available at the assigned school?

What elective courses are available (and recommended) to college-bound students?

How much time should my student spend on homework each night?

What is the grading standard/scale? Does the school assign a class rank? How is this determined?

Do students need a minimum grade-point average to participate in extracurricular activities, including sports?

What accommodations and support does the school district have for students who have employment and/or family responsibilities?

Sometimes this information is sent home or arrives through the mail. Some schools arrange meetings the spring and summer before high school. During these "bridge" programs incoming students and their parents meet individually or in groups with a counselor. Soon after school has started your child should meet with an adviser about his plans for high school and beyond.

If your child is in a special academic program or college-prep high school, preparing for college is a given. If your child is in a general education track, she should make clear her desire for higher education, even if her plans are not definite. Career interests, however unfocused, should be a part of this freshman year discussion.

If parents are not included in general discussions held at school, introduce yourself to the counselor. Through a note, email, phone call, or visit, arrange a meeting similar to the regular parent-teacher conference. This is the time to make sure the counselor knows your student's goal is college and that you expect the school to assign her a college-prep schedule and consider her for academic and other enrichment programs outside of school.

The counselor can be your child's most important ally in the next few years (although your students may be reassigned over the course of four years), especially in the college admissions process. Get to know the counselor and be known. Early on, your student should get into the habit of stopping by the guidance office to see what's new, read the bulletin boards, pick up brochures. Many opportunities go wasted because students don't know about them (the guidance counselor won't tell every student about every opportunity). Inform the counselor about new interests and plans. Let the counselor know about outside activities and accomplishments, as well as problems and achievements within school.

This also is the time to collect as much information as you can about all the four of the high school years, not just the first one, as well as college. You and your child need to understand the long road ahead, not just the initial steps.

Bring Everything Home, Read Everything
Every notice, every handout, every flier posted on a bulletin

board has the potential to change lives. Essay contests, art contests, scholarships, free tutoring, internships, study abroad programs, enrichment programs, student stipends, mentor matching, free training, workshops, seminars, college and career fairs. Schools receive and make this information available all the time. The school guidance office should be stocked with stuff to take home.

Get your college-bound kids in the habit of accepting everything that's handed out. Ask them to pick up pamphlets and brochures even if they don't seem interesting on first glance. You can throw them out later.

Parent and student should start reading it all, along with all the mail. Did you see the sewer and water bill announcement for a $1,000 scholarship for the best "Water in Our Lives" poster? Your union newsletter probably gives deadlines for applying for scholarships. And a scholarship for local kids may be part of the deal between zoning officials and the developer of a new shopping center. This kind of information crosses our paths all the time. But most people don't take the time to read it. Then we wonder how so-and-so found out about it. Consider the following:

"What's this about?" a visitor at a community center asked the recreation worker, pointing to a notice about scholarships to George Washington University.

"Oh, yeah. They can't give those scholarships away," the rec worker said.

Long story short: The visitor, her younger sister starting twelfth grade, took down the phone numbers and made some calls. The next fall, her sister, and her sister's friend, enter George

Washington on full, four-year scholarships set aside for low-income students whose parents do not hold college degrees. No one at their small Catholic high school had heard about the local scholarship program.

You can get into the habit of information-collecting a lot earlier, of course, but by high school parents and students should start keeping their eyes open and collecting phone numbers and information that can open up opportunities and resources. The library and bulletin boards in churches, libraries, and community centers are also sources of valuable information. Jot down phone numbers and email addresses if you can't get an extra copy. If your child can't take advantage of some of the information for another year or two, keep it along with all the materials of potential interest in a folder at home marked "Opportunities for (child's name here)."

Now that you know that guidance counselors don't know everything, realize that even the most dedicated may not get around to telling you all they do know. Kim Even as an honors student, she says, "They only tell you about the scholarships they want you to know about."

In short, the most assertive students—or those with the most assertive parents—get the most positive attention. Don't wait for information to come to you. In most major public senior high schools, you and your child will have to go after it.

Louanne Johnson, the ex-Marine Corps officer whose experience as an inner city high school teacher inspired the film *Dangerous Minds,* puts the responsibility for getting ready for college on those whose futures are at stake. "Who suffers if a guidance counselor falls short?" she asks in her candidly funny book,

School is *Not a Four Letter* Word. "Put responsibility on the student."

WHAT ELSE ARE COLLEGES LOOKING FOR?

This is the list of factors that the flagship campus of a state university in the Northeast considers when admitting students:

Grades in academic subjects Standardized test scores (SAT or the ACT)

Quality of high school course work

Grades in intended major subject area

Progression of achievement (did the student show improvement over the years)

Class rank

Essay/personal statement

Recommendations

Extracurricular activities

Extenuating circumstances

Underrepresented by home state/ region

Underrepresented racial/cultural group

First generation college (neither parent has college degree)

Special talents/skills

Community involvement/Community service

Demonstrated leadership

Academic endeavors outside the classroom

Breadth of experiences

Learning disabilities

Children/siblings of alumni
Children of faculty/staff
Work experience
Language spoken at home

The order of priorities depends on the school, but most selective colleges consider some combination of the top ten on the list, in varying order. In general, state colleges and universities have less flexibility than private ones, and most apply a more formal set of objective criteria. States with the largest public college systems often apply a specific admissions formula, assigning eligibility to various state schools based on one or a combination of the following: grade point average, class rank, college admissions test scores. Because of the volume of applications some large state colleges receive, admissions professionals focus on their top criteria, and may or may not consider other factors except those that distinguish one student from all others. Often, state university admissions officers are bound by law to apply specific criteria.

Meanwhile, high schools around the country increasingly are declining to assign class rank, that is, ranking graduating seniors based on grade-point averages. Officials cite grade inflation as one reason, with more students than ever before accumulating straight A averages. One school reported having more than a dozen students with perfect averages, naming them all co-valedictorians. Years ago, only one or two students in a school stood out with those kinds of grades. It was easy to identify the valedictorian and salutatorian.

Schools are also rethinking assigning class rank if they must factor in the grades of varying populations, such as special education and vocational students. The latters' straight A averages don't reflect the same level of skill or achievement as students following a general or college prep schedule. School officials, in declining to assign rank, said ranking students under these circumstances amounts to mixing apples and oranges.

In the wake of roll-backs of affirmative action policies, many admissions criteria and formulas are being reconfigured to give consideration to educational and economic disadvantage. However, their is a simple rule of thumb for what colleges are looking for. Students who have some combination of the following characteristics:

do well academically

take challenging academic courses or take advantage of whatever rigorous courses are available at their school

perform well on admissions tests

demonstrate personal strength and character

In considering the following chapter abut challenging courses, and the continuing call for good grades and strong results on college admissions tests, keep in mind that there are still plenty of higher education options if your child is not breezing toward straight A's or outscoring all his classmates on standardized tests. The law of averages demands that most children will be somewhere around the academic middle. And the truth is, many colleges and universities do accept students who take few college preparatory courses, have average to poor grades, and report SAT/ACT test scores that other colleges scoff at. Schools with "Open Admissions" are open to most of those who apply.

This is true among some—but certainly not all—Historically Black Colleges and Universities. Their original missions were to uplift those denied the kind of quality public school education that results in top grades and scores.

A popular HBCU in Tennessee, for example, had these admission requirements for in-state students: 2.25/"C" grade point average, or 19 on the ACT, or 720 on the SAT.

Meanwhile, a Black college in Florida admits applicants with "B" averages in academic subjects, regardless of standardized test scores. This university also admits students who do not meet the academic requirements, "but who bring to the University other important attributes or special talents."

Edwin T. Johnson, admissions counselor at Morgan State University, explains that some colleges are open to underachieving students by mission and design. "We'll take you where you are and get you where you need to be." That's what this HBCU did with Horace Moo-Young. Apologetically, the admissions officers at a major university told him he was not university material and referred him to a community college. Morgan State, however, gave him a chance. Small classes and personal involvement with faculty helped Moo-Young excel. As Johnson tells it, during Moo-Young's four years at Morgan, he earned one "B." The rest were "A"'s.

Morgan likes to boast of this unlikely scholar who was named professor of Civilian Engineering at Lehigh University after earning a Ph.D. at the prestigious Rensselaer Polytechnic Institute.

Says Johnson, "Here was a student who, if it wasn't for an HBCU, wouldn't have been college-educated. There are a lot of phenomenal stories about students who are deemed not-college material."

One of the jobs parents take on is helping children to be the best they can be. This is not just an ethic for the academic elite. It has far-reaching practical implications. The better our children do, the more choices they'll have among colleges, the more chances they'll have for scholarship money. And excellence, besides being its own reward, can lead to benefits and opportunities unimagined.

To help your child do his best and widen his opportunities, you need to know how high the academic bar is set. You need to know what to aim for. Keep reading.

THE RIGHT STUFF
(HIGH SCHOOL COURSE LIST)

"They have to show us, in terms of their transcript,
that they can handle the college curriculum."
Temple University admissions official

Graduation requirements are the set number of credits in specific courses that your child needs to earn a high school diploma. Four years of English, plus some math, science, social studies, and physical education are standard graduation requirements. Depending on the college or university your student wants to attend, he may need additional math, laboratory sciences, and several years of the same foreign languages. Seems basic, but If your child is not in a college preparatory program he can easily graduate without the courses that colleges require.

High school freshmen should get a list of graduation requirements and refer to them whenever they sign up for new courses. But heed these words from an admissions counselor at the University of Alabama in Huntsville. "We're looking for the well-rounded student who has taken some of everything academically."

The following schedule is generally recommended for college-bound high school students. This kind of course schedule follows closely the requirements at selective colleges and universities. By following it, your student will likely have the courses needed to apply to any of the nation's 4,100 plus colleges and universities.

High School Course List for the College-Bound

English-all four years, including Composition, American Literature, British Literature, World Literature

Mathematics-three to four years of advanced courses, including Algebra I and Algebra II, Geometry, Trigonometry, Pre-Calculus/Calculus

Social Sciences-two to three years, including U.S. History, U.S. Government, World History, World Cultures, Civics

Laboratory Science-two to three years, including Biology, Chemistry, Physics

Foreign Language-two to three years of the same language

Visual and Performing Arts-one year of offerings such as Art, Dance, Drama, Music

Challenging Electives-one to three years, such as Economics, Psychology, Statistics, Communications, African American Literature, Ancient and Medieval History, Sociology, Television Production

If you read the chapter on Algebra, you know the importance of advanced math for all students—and society—not just science and math majors. In a longitudinal study, a whopping majority of students in grades nine through twelve—80 percent—said they decided on their own what math courses to take. On their own, many dropped math altogether once they met basic requirements. Dona Baker, who attended a rural Alabama public school, knows the consequence of this choice. "My first opportunity to take non-college prep courses, I chose Business Math. It was a big mistake. Business math is checkbook balancing. You need more than that in business. I ended up taking remedial math in college and having to pay for it."

Parents must be involved in selecting courses, just as the parents of a student from Cincinnati were: "Every semester, every quarter, my parents went over my course schedule to see if I had what I needed. The school follows what the parents want."

Advice From College Admissions Officers:

Stick with one foreign language. Your child needs to develop an ease and fluency in at least one language, rather than sampling many languages throughout high school. Colleges like to see the perseverance it takes to try to master a foreign language. In math, taking algebra and geometry as early as possible means your youngster will have a solid background for the college admissions tests. The math part of the SAT I, for example, tests algebraic and geometric concepts. The SAT I introduced in 2005 tests more advanced math, such as Algebra II. If your student doesn't take those courses until senior year, he'll be taking a major test before he learns all the skills that are being tested.

If your child makes it to high school without a course in computers or new technology, make sure they sign up for one. Your high schooler should at least know basic keyboarding and word processing, which will make writing reports and compositions easier. By now, all high school students should be internet savvy, too.

Encourage your students to take classes that interest them. Woodworking or Introduction to Business is okay. A class in speed reading and study skills may be an opportunity to acquire important skills. But don't overload on courses that don't prepare them for the rigorous academic work that lies ahead.

The Hardest Classes They Can Handle

Advanced courses in high school provide the preparation and background to do college-level work. Great numbers of African American students don't take them. For the Class of 2003, for example, 13 percent of Black students took calculus, compared to 43 percent of Asians and 26 percent of Whites. The results for that class on the SAT math section, then, were no surprise. Black students averaged 426, compared to 575 for Asians and 543 for Whites.

The U.S. Department of Education ranks "Who's Prepared for College" based on how many rigorous classes students take. It found that more than half of Black high school students are "marginally prepared" or "unqualified," based on the courses they take, and, consequently, their SAT scores.

Taking advanced high school courses, in some cases, is more important than whether a student attends a great school or a school that provides little more than the basics. One set of research found that public school students who took advanced courses did just as well on admissions tests as those who took the same advanced courses at private schools with strong academic records.

In almost any major school district, you will find this happening: In some of the roughest schools in the roughest neighborhoods, children of all colors are earning top grades and high SAT or ACT scores that send them on to some of the most prestigious colleges and universities in the nation. These are the islands of success where the students who challenge themselves and take the hardest courses available are prepared to compete with the best and brightest.

Why are so few minority students enrolled in advanced classes?

lack of preparation in middle school for advanced courses

lack of course planning during freshman and sophomore years

lack of availability of advanced courses at the schools children of color attend

academic tracking that guides students who aren't viewed as "college material" towards general courses

parents who don't insist that their capable children enroll in advanced courses

At predominantly Black schools, some students and parents are turned off by the so-called elitism they associate with honors and higher-level classes. One mother, a middle school counselor, declined to enroll her own son in an advanced program. "My son tested for [Talented and Gifted] but I wouldn't put him in… There's a lot of snootiness from TAG students and their parents. Too many of these parents push their children into TAG just so they can brag."

Okay, but what's that got to do with her son getting the education he needs?

At predominantly White schools, some Black students complain about being "the only one" in honors and advanced courses. An African American mother from Arkansas expressed her reluctance in a national news magazine interview. "Basically, your honors classes are Caucasian and you have teachers who are unfair. This is an opportunity for them to continue their racism," she said. "I never even considered enrolling [my daughter] in honors."

Okay, but what is she doing to get her daughter the tough courses that will prepare her to perform at top levels in high school and college?

Michon Lartigue, a graduate of the University of Oklahoma, knows what can be lost by the attitudes of those two mothers. She took advanced English in high school and, she says, it was her most valuable educational experience. "That class prepared me for a lot. A lot of writing—essays, opinion, analysis, literary criticism. I learned to meet deadlines. Every week, timed tests. I learned to write quickly. It was college level. A lot of reading, Shakespeare to *The Color Purple.*" She adds, "I only took the course because a teacher saw something in me and decided to care. I got into advanced English because of a teacher."

Concerns about the social dynamics and racial isolation in such situations are valid. But who loses when a student doesn't take advantage of demanding school work and demanding teachers? It's this simple: The highest scoring African American students on the SAT were five times more likely than lower-scoring Black students to have taken calculus and about three times more likely to have taken honors English.

Those who are tempted to load up on easy courses should know that colleges don't look at grades and GPAs out of context. College admissions people increasingly consider the grades in college preparatory courses, not in home economics. "We're looking to see if the student challenged himself, if he made the most of what was available or if he just took it easy," says a representative of Harvard.

Again, remember that advanced math courses aren't just for the technologically inclined or science-minded. "Advanced math and science provide the analytical skills that are going to help them with critical thinking. It's important for grasping concepts in social sciences, etcetera," says Monique Irvin, a recruiter for Loyola University in New Orleans. "It's all interrelated."

Finally, don't miss the point about taking the hardest classes *the student can handle*. What's most important is that a student learn and master each subject. If the Honors Spanish teacher never speaks English in class and your student is missing a lot, and the class is moving at a pace your student can't keep up with, it's fine to take regular Spanish. She'll spend less time struggling, and more time learning. That's the real goal.

Advanced Placement

Advanced Placement is a program of college-level courses and exams available in high school. AP courses involve work and demands well beyond that of even high school honor courses. AP students study a subject in the depth and scope of a college-level course with a heavy focus on writing, research, and analysis. Colleges use their own discretion in granting credit for Advanced Placement work. In one year, more than 30,000 high school students were eligible for sophomore standing in college based on their AP exams (a standardized test separate from the course grade given by a teacher; the AP exam requires a registration fee). AP courses once were available only in a few elite public and private schools. The programs are expanding, though, with efforts to put AP courses in more rural and urban schools so that more minority and highly able youngsters will have a chance to take them. If your child has a strong academic record, AP courses can raise her profile even higher. They are that prestigious. A high school transcript with AP courses is an immediate signal that your student is highly motivated and capable.

A transcript full of strong classes also can help overcome weak areas. A Temple University admissions counselor says, "If a student doesn't have the SAT scores, we'll accept lower. But they have to show us in terms of their transcript that they can handle the college curriculum. We'll look for Advanced Placement, honors courses. With that, they can pretty much get in."

Find out how many AP courses are available at the school your child attends. At last count, the courses were offered in thirty-one subjects in social sciences, languages, math, science, English, music, and art. Most schools offer only a handful, such as AP History, AP English, AP Chemistry, AP Government, AP Calculus. Some of the most competitive high schools offer as many as twenty-two AP courses. Most students decide to take AP courses in the subjects they are strongest in, although some of the most capable take them across the board.

Tracking

School counselors can hold enormous power over your students' future, and some of that power is in the form of tracking.

Kathleen, a mother of two girls, saw this firsthand when her tenth grader's schedule did not include the chemistry class she signed up for. Telling her guidance counselor about the oversight, her daughter learned it was intentional. She didn't need Chemistry, she was told, because she already had fulfilled her basic graduation requirements. "You don't need any more science," the counselor told her, adding doubtfully, "unless you were going to college."

Kathleen started some stuff up at the school after hearing that. "Why wouldn't she think my child is going to college? Just because she's brown-skinned?"

The Achievement Council, a Los Angeles organization that promotes equal education for poor urban students, documented the insidiousness of tracking when it searched for the reasons why few minority students were enrolled in advanced courses. Focusing on how algebra was assigned, they found that in one California school district Black and Latino students who scored high on math placement tests nonetheless were not recommended for algebra. More than half of the high-performing African American students were "tracked" away from Algebra I. Meanwhile, 87 percent of eligible Whites and all of the eligible Asian students got into the "Gateway to College" course.

The findings raise "questions about belief systems and expectations we have for different groups of students," the Council noted.

It would be interesting to know if the parents of those students who were tracked away from algebra ever knew what had happened. But this is a good lesson in understanding what your student needs for college and being involved in the process of getting it. Unless your child is severely disabled, don't easily accept someone else's opinion that he or she is not college material. (As noted many times in this book, many colleges exist for students whose grade point average is under 3.0—or even 2.5. That doesn't make them unfit for college or advanced study. A number of students-of all creeds and colors—just are not academically prepared or strong enough in high school for advanced work.) If this is suggested to you, ask for specific examples on paper that demonstrate your child's proper placement. If he's getting "D's" in lower level math, ask what you and your student can do to improve these grades; then ask what the school will do to help your child move up.

As in the earlier years, tutors and extra help before or after school and during lunchtime may make a difference. If your school doesn't do it already, ask if advanced courses can be designed for students who needs more time to grasp the concepts. School districts committed to seeing more students take advanced math now divide traditional one-year courses into three semesters or two years. Although it may take longer, they can finish algebra.

All of your student's classes should challenge her to do her best and prepare for the next level. In some school districts, a student may simply outgrow her high school. If your child's school doesn't offer the advanced courses she's ready for, consider enrolling her concurrently for one class or more at a nearby community college. Talk to parents of other students who are doing advanced work. Together you may be able to get the school to offer the courses your children need.

THE BIG TESTS

"We can look beyond [poor] grades but the SAT says a lot. You can't fake the SAT."

Hampton University Official

If children of color had the inferior mental capacities assigned them in books such as *The Bell Curve,* they would score poorly from the very beginning. But the national data show Black children doing well and excited about school in the preschool years. It's what happens between then and high school that is the problem for so many African American students.

That said, here's the breakdown on the SAT I for the Class of 2003 (maximum score: 800 for each section).

	VERBAL	MATH
White	529	534
Asian American	508	575
Hispanic/Latino	457	464
Black	431	426

As of 2005, the SAT will have three parts: Math (including Algebra, Geometry and Algebra II), critical reading (the verbal analogies are being dropped) and writing (a 20-25 minute essay). Each of the three sections of the new SAT I will be graded on the familiar 200 to 800 point scale, bumping up the "perfect" score to 2400.

The College Board changed the tests in part due to criticisms that they didn't reflect what was being taught in today's high schools. The addition of the writing exam is good news for girls, who typically do better in that area than they do in math. However, writing skills present the second largest gap in SAT scores among Black and White students who take the SAT II (formerly known as achievement tests) Writing test.

Many people understand that the scores on the SAT and other standardized tests are determined by the quality of the students' school and family life, the kinds of courses they take, parents' education and income, and enrichment opportunities. The tests also are widely believed to be "coachable" (hence, all of those prep courses).

Dr. James Comer, the Yale child psychiatrist and renowned educator, sums it up this way: "The tests by and large measure privilege. What you're looking at is the disproportionate amount of African American young people who grow up under difficult conditions, either poverty or alienation, marginality and the kind of antagonisms that African Americans experience in everyday life, and the low expectations and conditions in schools. Those are all conditions of under-privilege. When [standardized tests] compare African Americans with people who have not had those experiences ... that is not a just comparison."

Even so, Comer has worked wonders in school districts across the country where his School Development Program has dramatically lifted standardized scores among disadvantaged children. One New York school moved from thirty-fourth to first place in standardized test score ranking.

The tests persist. That's why this section focuses on standardized testing. Those looking to discredit and abolish them might find it counter to minority progress to focus on tests here. For parents and their college-bound students, however, standardized tests are a reality to be faced and understood.

Monique Irvin of Loyola University in New Orleans says, "Either we've got to do better on the exams or we can stand on the sidelines and not be a part of the opportunities. If we want our children to sit at the same tables of competition we've got to get past [complaints about bias and fairness]. Go as far as you can, take the higher ground."

Freeman Hrabowski, III, the first African American president of the predominantly white University of Maryland at Baltimore County, is unapologetic about the high SAT scores required for scholarships to his prestigious minority science program. "When people say we shouldn't be weighing [the SAT] as heavily as we do…I always ask, 'Who wants a physician who can't pass the test?'"

Even as we prepare our children for the Big Tests, the Black community must challenge the way in which tests that essentially measure opportunity, advantage, and preparation are used to determine who will receive additional opportunities, advantages, and preparation.

Why Admissions Tests?

All but about 400 colleges around the country require the SAT or ACT college admissions test. The reason is that high schools around the country differ vastly in the kind of education they offer and students they produce. High schools have different expectations, standards for effort, work, and proficiency. An average student at a school with high standards and a rigorous work schedule might be the valedictorian at a school that doesn't expect much.

Colleges and universities consider admissions tests a standard by which all applicants can be measured. Institutions of higher learning say they use them primarily to determine whether a student has the skills to handle the work at their campuses. High SAT scores are considered a good predictor of success in the first year of college, although say the best predictor in the quality of work done in high school (grades).

Among schools that require the tests, the weight given to them in determining admission differs, too. One selective women's college, for example, cautions that high scores are not enough to overcome a weak transcript. It is looking for students who work hard and do well in class, not just when it's time to take a standardized test.

Another school—particularly for math and science majors—strictly follows its minimum score requirements. It may be unrealistic to apply to such a school if your score is well below the minimum SAT they require.

All but about three hundred American colleges and universities around the country will require your teenager to take an admissions test, either the SAT I or the ACT. Other tests are not as widely required but they can be useful to schools and students.

The following lists the major tests college-bound students may be required to take. All require the students to register and involve a fee, which may be waived for those with financial difficulty.

PSAT/NMSQT. The Preliminary Scholastic Aptitude Test/

National Merit Scholarship Qualifying Test is administered in October to interested sophomores and juniors. It assesses critical reading, verbal reasoning, math problem solving, and writing skills. Some sophomores take the test for practice and again in the eleventh grade, when the scores are considered for the prestigious National Merit Scholarships and National Achievement Scholarships for Outstanding Negro Students. Taking the PSAT and filling out the accompanying questionnaire gets your child's name on mailing lists used by colleges and scholarship programs.

SAT I. The Scholastic Assessment Test (Scholastic Aptitude Test is the old name) introduced in 2005 has three parts, measuring critical reading, writing skills (students must write an essay) and mathematical reasoning. Students register to take the test through their school, although the test is not necessarily administered there. It is given about seven times a year. High school students in the East and West typically take SATs.

ACT. The American College Test is a given about five times during the school year. It measures English, social studies, math, and natural sciences. Scores are reported in each area as well as one composite score. High school students in the South and Midwest typically take the ACT.

TOEFL. The Test of English as a Foreign Language is designed to measure the level of English proficiency of non-native English speakers. Colleges and universities require most foreign students to submit TOEFL scores with their application.

SAT II. Once known as SAT Achievement Tests, SAT II exams test specific subject areas. Many colleges do not require any SAT II's. Requirements vary at other institutions, depending on a student's intended major. Some scholarship programs require applicants to take specific tests.

CLEP. The College Level Examination Program is for those who are ready for college but have come by their skills and knowledge outside of traditional schooling. For more information, contact a specific college about CLEP placement.

Advanced Placement (AP). Advanced Placement tests are taken by students who successfully complete courses designated as AP in high school and want to get college credit for these advanced courses, or exemptions from some introductory college courses. Students can learn more about the AP test when they enroll in an AP course in their school.

BEING COMPETITIVE

At a free introductory session for an SAT prep course, a high school counselor—a Black man who happened to be in the audience—stood and offered this advice to a group of African American parents and students. "Don't waste your time or money on SAT prep classes. We all know that Black students don't do well on the SAT. And anyway, most of our children go to schools that aren't looking for high SAT scores. You don't need high scores to get into college. Some people nodded their agreement. Others beamed with the look of sudden enlightenment, as if all that concern about good grades and test scores was unwarranted. Some just looked confused. The prep course speaker, a Caucasian sister whose job was to sign up students for the $600 course, was speechless.

It's true. Your student can enroll and do well in a community college or nonselective school even if he doesn't do well on admissions tests. An African American school superintendent, defending his district's low performance, spoke on the relevance of standardized tests with this sarcastic question to an audience of Black professionals. "How many of you got 1600 (a perfect score on the old SAT) on the SAT?"

This is not about spending money on a prep class (increasingly, school districts and private groups offer them at no cost, or subsidize the cost of private courses). As in all things, you want your children to do well on the tests, their very best. Don't be lulled into accepting mediocrity. Don't expect little from your children, as the opinionated counselor apparently does.

For one thing, stellar performance on college admissions tests can translate into big money. Simply put, "The higher the test scores, the better the grades, the more the scholarship money," says Audrey Hill, of the National Association for College Admissions Counseling. Hill offers these ideas about being your best.

"All kids on paper look almost the same. They all need the same number of things. You need to be in something that's going to make you stand out. If you are a good tester and your test scores are high, it makes you stand out. It shows you're a competitive student, and you do qualify for different scholarships or grants that are out there.

"The students who have the highest grades and the highest test scores, who go to HBCUs, are the ones who get all the scholarships. So, be competitive. I don't care if you're going to an HBCU or if you're going to an Ivy League school, be competitive if you want part of the money. But if you don't want it, then sure, be mediocre.

"I tell kids that all the time, 'Sure, anybody can go to college. College is available for everybody. For those of you who either have low grades or don't want to do testing, the community colleges have open admissions. But can you [do the work to] stay in the community college?'

"If you are an outstanding student and have to go to a community college, because of finances or you just want to stay near home, or whatever, a community college is an excellent education. Community colleges give scholarships. Who do they go to? The kids who have the highest test scores.

"It's all tied to being competitive. To be competitive, there are a

number of AP college courses students can take in their senior year. AP History, AP European History, AP Psychology. In order to be competitive with other kids who are applying to college, they should try to take a social studies course in senior year. But there are also outstanding electives, courses like Ancient and Medieval History, African American History, Economics and Law, Psychology, Sociology.

"If they can get into Algebra I by ninth grade, they can do Geometry in the tenth, Algebra II in the eleventh, and Pre-Calculus as a senior. If they started their algebra in eighth grade, they could start high school in Geometry and get to Calculus by the time they are seniors.

"Foreign language is that course on a student's transcript that really shows strong in-depth study. It shows the student has been consistent. I always tell kids as they come into high school, they should try to go as far into a foreign language as they can. If you take Spanish in ninth grade, you should definitely take Spanish II and Spanish III. Colleges like to see the more advanced languages.

"The higher you go in math and science, the better. Regardless of whether you're majoring in science or not, you should at least get beyond Chemistry. There are a number of sciences you could take: Physics, AP Biology, Anatomy, and Physiology."

If your family won't qualify for grants and financial aid for the neediest students, a strong academic record will help your child pay for college. In recent years, for example, Howard University has placed the following value on a strong high school record, including high SAT scores:

Presidential Scholarship. For students with at least a 1500 SAT (verbal and math) or 34 ACT and 3.75 GPA; or National Merit Finalist. *Tuition, fees, room and board, books, laptop computer, one round-trip ticket to and from the student's home.*

Founders Scholarship. For students with at least a 1400 SAT (verbal and math) or 32 ACT and 3.50 GPA; or National Achievement Finalist or National Merit Semifinalist. *Tuition, fees, room and board.*

Capstone Scholarship. For students with 1300 SAT or 29 ACT and 3.25 GPA. *Tuition, fees, and housing.*

Legacy Scholarship. For students with at least a 1200 SAT (verbal and math) or 27 ACT and 3.0 GPA. *Tuition and Fees.*

Hilltop Scholarship. For students with at least a 1100 SAT (verbal and math) or 24 ACT and 3.0; or first or second in Class Rank. *Tuition.*

After the results came in from their daughter's ACT, taken during her junior year, one family met with a financial aid officer at a school in the Midwest. "He opened his books for us and showed her in dollars how that score affected her aid," the father explains. "We'll see how she can do [on the tests] this fall."

Test-Taking Strategies

Take the PSAT in sophomore year as a practice test. If the scores are high, consider taking a PSAT/SAT prep course, or work with a tutor before taking the test again in the eleventh grade. Few people prep for the PSAT, but it's worth it for students whose scores, with a little practice and tutoring, can be boosted to the level that triggers scholarships and national awards.

Eleventh grade PSAT scores are considered for National Merit Scholarships and National Achievement Scholarships for Outstanding Negro Students.

Instead of enrolling your student in an expensive prep course, consider a few sessions with a private tutor. A tutor (a graduate student, a college professor or high school teacher) will focus on your student's individual strengths and weaknesses. Tutors are relatively expensive—as much as $75 an hour. But the cost of 10 sessions of individual tutoring can equal the cost of a prep class that has 50 students. You won't get individual attention in a prep class.

Many public schools and mentoring programs have prep classes, noting their importance in building confidence and test-taking skills. Other organizations offer scholarships for commercial prep courses, such as those given by the Princeton Review and Kaplan. Test prep courses are valuable in demystifying the tests. They give your student practice in budgeting time and understanding how the test is organized. Prep courses, as well as handbooks, give tips on whether it is better to guess or skip questions you can't answer.

If neither is an option, obtain a study book for whatever exam is being taken (available in bookstores or from the public library). Then get your student to use it. Here's how one young man managed a near-perfect score on the SAT (While in college, be came an SAT tutor.): He bought a study book, and a book with actual SAT exams from the past. Once a week, he took one of the practice tests. He graded the tests himself, identifying his mistakes and picking up answers to questions that might come up again along the way. By the end of the summer, he had taken 10 practice SATs: "People buy the books and don't use them, but I did. By the time the summer was over, I knew how to score high on the SAT."

Cramming for standardized tests is not a replacement for years of dedicated study and reading. If there are still a few years before the tests, students can prepare by reading a lot. Reading the newspaper editorial page every day builds vocabulary necessary to do well on the critical reading sections of college admissions tests. Some schools instruct their students to do this.

Make sure your student reads all the prep material that comes with the registration packet *before* the morning of the test.

Take the SAT I or the ACT for the first time at least by the spring of eleventh grade. Especially if you're considering a military academy, ROTC program, or early admission to college. Those schools/programs need to score reports in the fall. But the real purpose is to take a practice test. Get an idea of where your student's scores will fall. Taking the SAT or ACT again in the fall of the senior year—your child will be more comfortable, and more confident. This may lead to better scores, and by then your student should have an idea of the schools he's interested in. He will have to name the schools he wants to receive his test results.

Some schools actually encourage their least able students to take the SAT or ACT as late as possible. This may give a student another three to six months of study and time to prepare. Because the SAT reportedly measures skills developed over a long period, however, it may or may not help. And your student may not have time to take the test again and possible earn a higher score.

Ask the guidance counselor about fee waivers if you can't

afford testing fees, or if paying for more than one test is a financial strain.

Take the SAT I achievement tests as soon as possible after completing that subject's course in school. If your student finishes Chemistry at the end of tenth grade, he can wait around until senior year to take the Chemistry achievement test. Or he could take it after finishing the course when the material is still fresh in his head. This is a good strategy for students who have a strong sense of the colleges they want to attend, their major, and what achievement tests are required.

Fair Test, a national organization that works to ensure fairness in standardized testing, compiles a list of colleges that do not require the SAT for admission. Contact Fair Test at 342 Broadway, Cambridge, MA 02139, call 617 868 4810 or visit **www.FairTest.org.**

BUILDING THE HIGH SCHOOL RESUME

There's a saying among college recruiters, "Thick folder, thick kid." It refers to those eager students who send in reams of material listing all the clubs and organizations they've joined. They include recommendations from teachers, neighbors, church people, their parents' coworkers, and the lady who baby-sat for them in first grade. The folder that college admissions committees are left to review is "thick" with certificates of recognition and participation, sometimes dating back to elementary school. Who can hold anything against such wonderful young people who are doing what we ask: getting involved, taking the initiative, doing more than is required?

Unfortunately, not everyone sees it this way. The impression left with those who review these "thick" folders is not necessarily the one the "thick" student intends. It leaves some admissions review committees wondering how one person can contribute *in a meaningful way* to the chess club, Spanish club, future business leaders club, student government, and band boosters while putting in a regular and significant volunteer effort at a preschool, senior citizen center, and community tutoring program—and still have time for a rites of passage program, Saturday community clean-ups, weekend enrichment classes, and a part-time job.

The answer is, they probably don't. The "thick" folder is a

giveaway about someone who has sampled much but dedicated little to any one cause or activity. Students who "sign up for everything," as one young woman explained her resume, have a hard time keeping their commitments. Too often they become card-carrying, but inactive, members. Don't let your young people spend too much time loading up on activities that are not challenging or truly meaningful. The benefits, in the end, are negligible.

One businesswoman recalls getting the resume of a high school senior seeking an internship. The resume was a typed list of activities, hobbies, and awards and distinctions that filled three pages, single-spaced. It was longer than the professional resumes the organization had on file. "This girl was busy running around from one thing to the next and entering this contest and that. I'm glad to see she liked being involved. But looking through it all, there was no indication that she had ever focused on anything, accomplished anything significant."

This student didn't get a call-back. The internship went to a young woman who had organized a major fund-raiser at her school, and in her senior year won election as a class officer. She also played clarinet in her school's orchestra, a commitment of practice and time. She probably spent as much time on these three activities as the other student did on her three pages of activities.

Still, it's hard not to give credit to a young person with such energy and initiative. Consider the alternative, which is the more common African American experience: Black high school students appear to be less involved in school than others, and they become less engaged as they move through high school.

A national study, which tracked students beginning in middle school, showed that up to half of Black eighth-graders were involved in some kind of school activity. By senior year their involvement plummeted.

For a variety of reasons that include peer pressure, racial isolation, or feelings of uneasiness, Black students aren't participating in all that their schools have to offer. (See "Attitudes About 'Acting White.'") Some students have competing interests outside of school (negative and positive), jobs, younger siblings, or their own babies. Sometimes, they just don't have the adult support and resources they need, such as transportation and the costs associated with participating in some activities. Some of them are just used to sitting on the sidelines after so many years of television, video games, or just hanging out.

Not all the blame can be put on competing responsibilities, uninvolved parents or the kids themselves. Some of our nation's poorest schools don't have a school newspaper. Their varsity teams don't have the right equipment or a safe place to practice. At one school, the swim team did not have a pool to use regularly. Yet we want young people to be involved and enthusiastic!

Consider all these when your child enters high school. Do what you can by talking to your young person about checking out the clubs and activities the school has to offer. Getting involved early will help them sort through their interests.

Hopefully, by sophomore year they commit to one or two activities. By junior and senior year they'll be positioned for distinguishing leadership roles-club president, team co-captain, class treasurer.

"We just want students to be involved in something. It can

be one thing or a lot of things," explains a recruiter from Pitzer College, echoing the call of his peers. "We're not looking for someone who just comes to school and then goes home."

Most schools today arrange opportunities for community service; some give students academic credit for it or require it for graduation. If your child's school seems to have few opportunities for your youngster to explore interests, encourage your young person to look for positive things to do outside of school. Be creative. She can create her own club, organize friends in a community project, work from home on hobbies.

Support them the best you can, by giving rides and spending what you can afford on the related expenses. And consider the example you set. What are you involved in? Do you take time for the activities you enjoy and causes you consider important? Remember, you are a role model in all things.

Consider the following:

    academic achievement

    spiritual development

    family involvement

    healthy relationships with peers and friends

    community service

    participation in athletics/special interests

Work and School

Some students can't enjoy after-school sports, join the science club or jazz band, because of the pressing demands of family. Some of those demands include making money, not just for cell phones, but basic clothing and spending money.

If, after school and work or family responsibilities, your student has no time left for extracurricular activities, let somebody know. Inform counselors and teachers about outside demands on your child, whether it's a new baby, an ailing grandmother, or little brothers and sisters who need watching. When they review your child's file, or if they're asked to write a recommendation, they won't assume she's uninvolved by choice.

Fulfilling family and financial responsibilities while keeping up in school does count for something. It is another form of accomplishment that such students can be proud of. Later, on college applications and interviews, the student can explain these special circumstances more fully. "We just want to know a student doesn't leave school every day and go to the mall," explains one college president.

Saving to provide basic needs always is a good reason for working during the school year. But your student should be learning to save at least a small amount of earnings for life after high school—$150 in a money market account can go a lot farther than $150 worth of braids and extensions.

If the job supports an expensive wardrobe, extensive CD collection, monthly cell phone bill or keeps gas in a sports utility vehicle, teachers and college admissions people may be less sympathetic to the student's "need" to forsake everything in order to work.

Enriching Summers

Maybe it's time for parents who can afford it to stop insisting that their teenagers spend every week of summer working.

In the increasingly competitive world, more and more students are taking summer classes, going to summer school, or participating in some kind of academic or career enrichment program. Summer school, once the bane of those who didn't keep up during the school year, has become a must-do for those who want to get ahead.

During the summers between college, you'll find that some of the most prestigious internships—those door-opening, resume enhancers that impress colleges, graduate schools, and potential employers—pay little or nothing. Congressional and White House internships are a good example of trading pay for prestige. The real payment is in the experience, skills, and connections to professional mentors. One professor advised his students to take out a loan for school if they have to, but get an internship.

The benefits of spending high school summers in enrichment programs are similar.

This is wholly unfair to all those children who can't afford *not to earn money* during the summer. But consider if, during any of the high school summers, some of your child's time could be better spent in academic enrichment, leadership training, or perfecting a special talent. It may only require three weeks, and your young person can work the rest of the time.

Almost every college campus has some kind of summer program for high school students, whether it's a philanthropic, subsidized effort or profit-driven. If your student qualifies for some of the government or privately funded programs for students who are minorities, low income, or whose parents do not have a college degree, your child may be able to attend free. Ask a counselor about Upward Bound or Talent Search, the federally funded academic enrichment and college counseling programs that bring such students onto campuses around the country. Some programs pay a stipend.

Contact the universities and colleges in your area about on-campus programs during the summer. The school guidance office should have much of this information as well. For students with particular interests, many national organizations and foundations sponsor summer enrichment activities, such as NASA space camps and the National Science Foundation.

One of the most extensive sources of information on summer opportunities is in Peterson's *Summer Opportunities for Kids and Teenagers*. Most of the programs are pricey private affairs—but they offer financial aid. Also between the 1,300 some pages are programs that offer up to six weeks on a college campus for free. Ask for this book in your public library's reference section.

Whatever your family can afford, the high school years will likely be the last years your child will be able to avoid the world of work in order to explore his interests and better himself.

The following is the resume of an African American student whose parents got him involved in community and school activities beginning in preschool. The resume shows his accomplishments at the beginning of his senior year of high school. Notice the range of activities this young man explored, from basketball and track to poetry, law and singing in a youth choir. Combined with his academic record and strong SAT scores, the resume helped the student win six scholarships from colleges that didn't mind that he did not yet know what he wanted to major in.

High School Resume

EDUCATION

High School Courses: AP English, AP American History, AP Micro Economics, AP Macro Economics, Spanish III, Computer Science Tools, Physics, Pre-Calculus, Political Philosophy

AWARDS & HONORS

AP(Advanced Placement) Scholar, The College Board

"Outstanding Participant," National Achievement Scholarship Program

National Honor Society

Who's Who Among American High School Students (sophomore and junior years)

Johns Hopkins Center for Talented Youth, participant

SUMMER ACADEMIC ENRICHMENT

Summer Journalism Program- college sports writing class for high school students

Teen Law College - Six-week introduction to law program. Lead counsel of winning mock trial team

Community College - Web design class

Summer Center for Gifted Students - Creative Writing/Poetry camp

EXTRACURRICULAR ACTIVITIES

Freshman and Junior Varsity Basketball

Junior Varsity and Varsity Track (WCAC Champions)

COMMUNITY SERVICE AND INVOLVEMENT

McKenna Center – I help at a soup kitchen near my school during lunch hour once a week

Food and Friends – I help deliver food after school once a week to the homes of people with AIDS

Project GIVE – I spent a week living on a farm and helping senior citizens in a rural community

Project VIP – I spent a week in a Latino community helping to renovate a houses for poor families

United Methodist Church – Junior Usher, Youth Choir member, Rock for Jesus 2000 youth conference leader

WORK EXPERIENCE

Air and Space Museum - Exhibit guide and flight demonstrations presenter in the "How Things Fly Gallery," (summers and holidays)

Purple Eagle Basketball Camp - Counselor/Coaching assistant (summer)

REMAINING INVOLVED

At Home

Well before senior year, discuss with your student the different college options and ways to pay for higher education.

Plan a college prep schedule of classes for the next four years. Your child can change his mind about some things, but start a road map to high school graduation and college. To be most competitive, your student should take as many challenging academic courses as time allows, and Algebra I and Geometry by ninth and tenth grade, if not earlier.

Your role in homework diminishes as your children get older, but even senior high school students should be monitored. Most have earned more flexibility and independence to set their own schedules. Still, periodically check to see if their work is being done and given the proper amount of time and effort. Make sure your student is working on something each school night without disturbances and distractions such as the television, phone calls or instant messages on the computer (instant messaging is difficult to monitor; implement an honor system and get your teenager to agree not to do it while studying). Notice whether your student brings home books and notebooks regularly—and takes them back to school.

Set a going-out policy. A student involved in schoolwork, reading, and extracurricular activities shouldn't have much time left for going out socially on school nights.

Help your child manage time and meet deadlines. If necessary, put interim and final due dates for major assignments and long term projects on a calendar the student can check regularly.

At the middle of every term, ask your student how he's doing in each course. Ask to see exams, reports, and other graded assignments. Call a teacher and ask for a midterm progress report if you're unsure, or your child is, about his academic standing.

Don't assume no news is good news, even though most high schools alert students and parents of academic trouble. These warning or deficiency notices may be mailed or given to your student. Hopefully, you'll see them in time to do something about low grades.

Encourage and support your teenagers' outside interests and extracurricular activities. Hobbies are important, help her stay out of trouble, and can pay off with awards and scholarships and the self-confidence that comes from personal accomplishment. Don't let your young person spread herself too thin, however, or let extracurricular activity interfere with study.

Explore summer job or academic enrichment opportunities—anything to keep your teenagers productive during the summer. If your student can afford it, let him pass over the high-hourly rate job stocking grocery store shelves. Instead, he can accept that internship at modest pay or an academic enrichment program with a small stipend. Either will pay off later with new skills, impressive credentials, and professional connections.

Encourage your underachiever or late bloomer to pull up weak grades. Colleges are impressed by improvement, and as the grades go up, so will the number of opportunities. That's a powerful message for some youngsters.

Remember that adolescents are not "grown," though some look and act that way. You still need to be available, to set rules and offer guidance at a time when they are making decisions that will determine their futures.

At School

Continue to meet teachers, and make the counselor's acquaintance. Identify one of your teenager's favorite teachers as a point person, if no regular adviser is assigned. Keep an open line of communication by attending all parent-teacher conferences. Have prepared questions written down. Phone or email specific teachers if you can't attend the conference.

At the start of high school, tell your child's teachers and counselors to consider her college material. Then talk with the counselor or adviser about graduation requirements and courses recommended for college-bound students. Keep this material in a place for easy reference over the next few years.

Keep abreast of what's going on in school. Through daily conversation, find out about situations that hinder learning. Does your student have all the books he should? Is his geometry teacher certified and permanent, or is there an endless series of substitutes?

Answer the call for volunteers—pledge to help out with at least one school project each year. Attend sports events, talent shows, awards assemblies. Find reasons to come inside the school building.

Take ownership of the school career/college/or counseling center. That is, come in on your own time to see what's available. Your child may not like seeing you in there, but guidance counselors insist this is a good way for parents to be part of the process.

Something to think about: Sometimes, especially when a student is the last of several in a family, parents stop being as involved and excited as they were with their first child. They've been through it all before, spent a lot of work, time, and money. They're tired. The youngest siblings are left to do much on their own. That's not fair. All children deserve a parent's best effort. And if you file away all the interesting pieces of information you've been collecting, much of your work is already done.

PART FOUR

Start Your Search Engines

*"Success is not coming to you, you must
come to it. "*

Marva Collins, Educator

THE $400,000 SCHOLAR

HIGH SCHOOL: Northeast Comprehensive High School, Macon, Georgia

ACADEMIC RECORD: GPA: 4.67 on a 5.0 scale; 1190 SAT

HIGH SCHOOL COURSES: AP Calculus, AP English, AP Biology, AP American History (college credit for English and History)

ACTIVITIES: Academic Bowl Team Captain, newspaper teen board, literary magazine assistant editor, Red Cross volunteer, drama club, student council president

HONORS: 21 awards and scholarship offers totaling $400,000

Marianne Ragins likes to say she's living proof that in order to win scholarships you don't need to have the highest grades or SAT scores.

This is true, but Ragins is not a poster girl for the average or laid back. She was an outstanding high school scholar and community leader, with a record of involvement that dates back to elementary school. "I've been involved in a lot of things throughout my entire school career. I've always been into something," she says.

Ragins's extraordinary scholarship bounty is a tribute to her academic excellence and her involvement. But more than that, it was the result of a determined, organized search for college money planned and executed with single-minded purpose.

"There was a very big motivation. That was, to get in and out of college owing the least amount of money possible and not burdening my mother, who was a single mother (My father died a while ago). That was my driving force."

When Ragins's search was over, she had amassed awards and scholarship offers totaling $400,000. Two universities were in a bidding war over this young African American woman from Macon, Georgia. She eventually "signed" with Florida A&M after it sweetened its four-year free ride by making sure Ragins had $2,000 spending money every year.

A FAMILY AFFAIR

In Denver, the family of Christophe and Pensal McCray launched college and scholarship searches for their five children with equal boldness and resolve. In mother Pensal McCray's own words, here's what this family did:

"With five children in six years, I knew they were going to need some scholarships. I sent Telia to her public high school counselor at the beginning of her junior year to ask about scholarships. She had a 4.2 grade-point average. The counselor told her she didn't know of any scholarships.

"We knew something was wrong. So we went to the library. They had a section with nothing but scholarship books. After that I talked to people in bookstores, supermarkets. There's a Tylenol scholarship. Coca-Cola has a scholarship. Kmart. Target. They have scholarships. JC Penney. We'd talk to one company and they'd tell us of others.

"By the start of her senior year we had all of her four years of college taken care of. We even went to admissions, financial aid, the president's office. A college president has scholarship money that's not available through the financial aid office. The academic departments of a college have scholarships.

"She got a presidential scholarship to Bennett College. A Colorado Student Scholarship (for minorities in Colorado). Since she was interested in engineering, we checked out the National Society for math; women's engineering associations.

"We worked as a family. We gave everybody a job. The kids who typed best, typed. We sat around the kitchen table, in an assembly line, with the applications. Older kids came up with ideas for the scholarships' essay questions. We kept copies for future use and reference for our other kids.

"We always had official transcripts on hand—not copies—to send in with the applications. We went to the school and purchased about twenty at a time. Each one of our children had a file with their transcripts. We'd send them off.

"Each child applied for at least twenty scholarships. My son sent out forty applications. He got all four years of college paid at North Carolina A&T."

For undergraduate and graduate studies at Bennett College, North Carolina A&T, Hampton, University of Pennsylvania, University of Michigan, University of Colorado, "We never paid a dime," says proud father Christophe. "I just paid for telephone and travel back and forth," and as more awards and scholarships came in, "it got so I didn't have to pay for that."

Elder son Christophe was the most prolific at getting money, spending his Friday afternoons in college looking for new grants and financial awards. He kept winning them—"If you have an A average in physics, who can compete?" his father asks—to the extent that "he lived like King George while in college."

With all she learned through the experiences with their children, Pensal McCray founded the Ethnic College Counseling Center in Denver. Ragins put her experience in the book *Winning Scholarships* for *College,* written when she was in undergraduate school. Later, she wrote *Making the Most of Your College Education,* published as she began a career in marketing.

One more story, a short one. When nine-year-old Chris, who loved science, started talking about being a biologist, his mother began looking at scholarship books. Before he turned ten, she had identified half a dozen scholarships specifically for minorities in science. She took note of the qualifications and quietly set her son along a path to winning them. She enrolled him in math enrichment classes, Junior Ranger detail at a state park, science camps in the summer. At 15, he had narrowed his interests to wildlife management and environmental biolology. So he volunteered at a local nature center, which game him experience in small mammal care. He used that experience to become a certified Junior Naturalist. With that kind of resume, he was a sure bet for a summer position at the Smithsonian's National Zoo.

None of these activities kept Chris from the other things he loved, basketball and baseball.

Who knows if these scholarships will still be available when Chris is ready for college, or even if he'll still be interested in science? In any case, he was excited about the prospect of being, for example, a Meyerhoff scholar at the University of Maryland Baltimore County, a program for African American science majors) or going to Xavier University in Louisiana, an HBCU with a renowned science program.

At nine, Chris knew he had a lot of opportunities to look forward to, while his mother continued acquiring information useful to him—or some other young person. He could have changed his mind about biology (he hasn't), but the attitudes and habits he developed will be important no matter what area of study he eventually takes up in college.

Marianne Ragins, the McCrays of Denver, Chris's mom: in their own time, each started a deliberate search for colleges and ways to pay for them. That's what this section is about.

GATHERING THE INFOR-MATION

The start of high school—not senior year, as you know by now—is the time to seriously start accumulating information about colleges, admissions requirements, and financial aid, although many, like Chris's mom in the previous chapter, start a lot earlier. It's not uncommon to see parents of middle school children at college fairs and financial aid workshops. But if you come to all this relatively late in the game, it's okay. Back in Denver, Colorado, the McCray families' research for their eldest daughter began when she entered eleventh grade. And Marianne Ragins, the $400,000 scholar, didn't begin until her senior year had already started. The key to success in all cases is to be organized, be thorough, and, most important, to follow through.

As early as you can in high school, you and your student should start taking deliberate steps to explore colleges and admissions requirements and procedures. At the same time, begin collecting information about scholarships and awards, as well as learning about the financial aid process. Remember all the notices and brochures you were advised in previous chapters to bring home and file away over the years? You'll be calling those numbers and asking for applications sooner than you think. Begin early so you'll have time to methodically gather information and get applications ready.

The summer before twelfth grade, many students across the country already know where they want to go to college, have the application forms for their top choices, and have started filling them out. By then they've already taken many of the required tests. The summer before senior year, the most organized and aggressive are already requesting and receiving applications for all the scholarships and awards they have a good chance at winning. They know about essays they'll have to write, and start working on them without the additional load of schoolwork bearing down on them.

Imagine the difference between them and the family without a clue: Senior year has started and the student doesn't know anything about colleges or which ones he wants to attend. He doesn't know what's needed to apply, has no idea what it will cost or how to pay for it. During the next six months, both student and parents scramble to obtain all the necessary paperwork and fill out all the detailed forms. They must try, under looming deadlines, to make major decisions about the future.

Unfortunately, the latter scenario is more common than not. "Going to college is like a marriage. You don't just rush into it. "But most people do," says a financial aid officer at the University of the District of Columbia, exasperated by all the mistakes in applications to this Historically Black College. Consider what's at stake. Do you want to determine your child's future under deadline pressure or with the confidence that comes from prior knowledge? If you have the time, isn't your child's future worth advance planning and legwork?

Without it, he may have to settle for less than he should—a school he doesn't like or that doesn't suit him. There may be countless missed opportunities. Meanwhile, the both of you could end up paying more than you have to. Why do it this way if you know better?

You and your students can begin your research by setting up five sets of files, boxes, or portfolios, one each for the following:

Research on Colleges

Money for College

Enrichment Opportunities, such as internships and summer
   programs

Contests and Competitions

Personal Documents

If you've already begun collecting information, sort through it and file it in the appropriate place. Get updated information for things that your student is still interested in. You're doing this because it's not just for the benefit of one child. It's for any other students you know. If you have younger children, nieces, nephews, or kids living next door, consider their special needs and interests, too. Keep information that may be helpful to them later on.

For the Personal Documents file, your student should have a resume that highlights strengths, abilities, accomplishments, talents, and goals. Also keep copies of mementos, certificates of merit, and awards. Have a nice photo of the student (not a glam shot) available.

Many applications will ask for letters of recommendation. Your student should ask someone who knows the student well and has many favorable things to say. If the references are willing, ask them to write a generic "To Whom It May Concern" letter that you can keep on file to be copied and used with more than one application. Always provide an addressed, stamped envelope if your references need to mail their letters directly. Afterwards, send them a thank you note.

Make copies of everything that is sent out.

Remember the busy guidance counselors? Don't assume they have or will give your students everything they need. A young woman who went to a predominantly White high school in North Carolina never even knew about Historically Black Colleges and Universities: "The only schools I knew of were Winston-Salem, Johnson C. Smith, North Carolina State, and North Carolina Central. I just had the bare essentials. I didn't get the counseling from a majority White high school."

Even the most dedicated and helpful counselors cannot do everything for every student. So don't damn them with, "Nobody told my child about that scholarship!" You probably can find out the same information through your own research. There are a number of resources to explore.

College Fairs

College and Scholarship Guidebooks (in your school guidance center or public library)

The Internet

College websites

Your state department of higher education

U.S. Department of Education

As the research begins, your student should think about interests, needs, and preferences, such as:

Will I be more productive and happy at a large university or small college?

What do I want to major in?

Do I want to venture far from home, a few hours drive, or stay close by?

Will I be more comfortable on a campus in a big city or in a more

self-contained setting?

Am I interested in going to a Historically Black University or does it matter?

What special services do I need for any physical or learning disabilities, or family support?

What activities do I want to participate in at college?

HOW TO WORK A COLLEGE FAIR
(FOR STUDENTS AND PARENTS)

Knowing that she couldn't afford the sticker price at the schools her son wanted to attend, one mother approached the college fair with the seriousness of a job-hiring convention. Here's what she did in the spring of her son's junior year.

"I took a morning off and got there as soon as it opened—before the schools started dropping off kids. I pretty had it all to myself, so I scoped things out. Got brochures from the popular schools before they ran out. Then I did a walk through: I asked questions from schools I didn't know much about. If they fit my son's needs and interests, I gave them a copy of his resume and started talking him up. The recruiters weren't rushed that early in the day and they even gave me inside tips about applying to their school. The most important thing I did was identify those schools that had scholarship criteria that matched my son's qualifications.

"When I got back home, we went over the information as a family. My son and I emailed notes to the recruiters at the schools he was interested in. One of the recruiters stayed in contact with us throughout the whole process."

I'll tell you how it all turned out for this student at the end of the chapter, but for now you need to become acquainted with The National Association of College Admission Counseling organizes the National College Fair program. Each year, it assembles college recruiters and financial aid experts at sites around the country, such as convention centers and shopping malls. NACAC also sponsors Performing & Visual Arts College Fairs at major cities around the country from September to November.

Your teenager's high school should announce the dates of this major college fair when it comes to a locale near you. Individual high schools, private and parochial school consortiums, civic, and educational groups also organize college fairs at schools, malls, churches, and some college campuses. If the big NACAC College Fair doesn't come directly to your area, it still may be worth a one or two hour drive to check it out.

The college fair season runs from September to May. Few are held in March, when colleges are processing applicants for the next school year.

Fairs in public places are free and open to the public. Expect to see rows and rows of tables and booths where recruiters are on hand to answer questions. Your student can pick up brochures and applications and get on a mailing list.

This is the time to explore the types of schools best suited to a young person and to find out what kind of financial aid is available. Being selective is fine, you don't have to take every brochure or visit every table. But be open-minded.

At a college fair in one major city, recruiters from White schools watched as the predominantly Black gathering swamped the tables of HBCUs and in-state schools. "They may not want to come here, but they don't really know that if they don't talk to us," explained one recruiter from a small, private liberal arts college in the Northeast. He added, "We're a small school with a huge endowment that could pay all the costs of some of these students."

Come with prepared questions, such as:

How can I arrange a visit or speak further with a representative? What are the deadlines for admission and financial aid?

Based on my record or special circumstances, what scholarships or financial aid can I qualify for?

What percentage of students live on campus? Is there adequate housing for all who need it?

What additional academic services do you offer to students (tutors, study skills workshops, career or graduate school counseling)? Is there a summer bridge program for entering freshmen?

What enrichment programs are there for high school students? What is the graduation rate among African American students? Do most return after their freshman year?

Can federal student aid money be applied toward costs at this school?

If you start going to college fairs before senior year, your student can return at least once more and to expand his college search. The scheduling of the National College Fair is interesting. In some areas, it arrives in the spring, giving high school juniors a jump start on the process that begins seriously in the fall. If it doesn't arrive in your area until late fall, the twelfth grader who is just beginning the search will be at the end of the pack.

"The [students] most serious about college we find at the spring college fairs," says a recruiter from a private university in the South. "You'll see freshmen and sophomores. Their school system has already prepared them to go."

The most assertive and organized parents play a role, too. A college recruiter from a prestigious school in the South explains how communities of parents band together to position their students at prestigious, hard-to-get-into schools. "At one high school in Greenwich, Connecticut, the PTA assigns parents to take admissions officers home after the fair. [These parents] are doing research, asking their own questions, finding out all they can about the process, the competition, what's available. They have the Duke [University] representative eating dinner at their home, and they're asking, 'What about early admission?'"

Why would a PTA do all this? "The community has said getting their students into the best colleges is a priority," says the southern college recruiter.

College fairs are usually noisy and chaotic, as bus loads of teenagers usually arrive at the same time. There are crowds around the tables of "popular" schools, and few students get a chance to ask more than the generic questions (listed above). If you can arrange for your student to go on a weekend or evening, apart from the times when schools bus their students in, she'll be able to focus on the schools she's interested, get answers to questions specific to her, make personal contact with (and, hopefully make a good impression on) the recruiters.

Or, as a parent, you can stay involved in your child's affairs, like the mother at the beginning of this chapter. Her story shows how important it is for parents to stay involved and to be a part of the college admissions process. Many people, however, believe that by this time the entire responsibility for applying for college and scholarships should be left to the high school student. Young people need to grow up and take responsibility for themselves, right?

Each family can decide how much of the load the family will share (Review the story of the McCray family in Chapter 43, "The $400,000 Scholar.") For this mother, though, leaving her child's future entirely up to a sixteen year-old boy was not an option. He did his share by filling out applications, getting transcripts and recommendations. Writing essays, taking tests and going on interviews. He kept track of deadlines and got his applications in the mail.

And the mother's college fair visit led to $25,000 a year for four years in scholarship money from Xavier University in Ohio. The student received five other scholarship offers (from schools not contacted at the college fair) and accepted a scholarship to Wake Forest University. As a freshman, he worked in a volunteer project helping local high school students apply for college.

For information on college fairs in your area, contact National Association for College Admission Counseling at 1631 Prince Street, Alexandria, VA 22314-2818. Phone: 703-836-2222. Or visit **www.NACAC.com**.

All colleges do not come to every college fair. Some colleges only recruit in specific parts of the country. They don't venture to places around the country if a number of students from that area don't typically apply. So don't assume you've seen everything there is to see by going to college fairs. You may just see the same colleges over and over.

Your search should also include handbooks, guides, and the internet. If you're not on the web yet, libraries and bookstores carry most of the major commercial college guides, published by

Princeton Review, Kaplan, Peterson's, and *U.S. News & World Report,* to name a few. Some recent books specifically address the concerns of minority students:

> *The Black Student's Guide to Colleges:* 700+ Private Money
> Sources for Black and Minority Students (Madison
> Books), edited by Barry Beckham
>
> *Black Excel African American Student's College Guide,* by
> Isaac Black (John Wiley & Sons)

Each gives details on specific schools and information of particular importance to minority students on academic support and the campus environment. "You want to find out if it's a hostile environment," says Silas Purnell, who counsels minority college-bound students in Chicago. "You can't just look at a *Barron's* guide and pick a school like White parents."

The internet has become a one-stop guide for information about individual schools and directories for financial aide and scholarships. They are just a Google or Yahoo search away. Colleges have their own websites that tell you most of what you'd ask at the college fair. Many of these sites are interactive: You can download forms onto your computer, fill out an application, and submit it by U.S. Postal or via the Web.

THE MONEY TRAIL

People are either saying there's less financial aid available than there use to be, or, there's plenty of money "out there" to pay for college. The truth is, there's more money out there than there ever—a record $90 billion. Much of the aid, however, is though low-interest loans.

There are still grants and scholarships from state, local, and private sources, including corporations and the colleges themselves. In the early years of high school, your student can start searching for money for college from private sources while doing the initial research on colleges and universities she might want to attend.

Money from private sources is typically based on accomplishments, specific qualifications, demonstrated character or leadership, competitions-science fair, essay contest, performance-talents, and interests. Most major corporations and many small companies award scholarships. Ask around. Check the yellow pages. Contact organizations that are related to your student's special talents or college major by calling their community relations or human resources offices. Stop in at the customer's service desk of major retailers in your area to ask about scholarships for students in your community or local high schools.

Now also is the time to let friends, acquaintances, and family members know of your student's goals. Tell them. They may have information and personal contacts that can pay off.

Here's what Marianne Ragins, the winner of $400,000 in scholarships, says on the subject:

"Yes, there are merit scholarships that are based on grades only, and also standardized test scores. But there are also a multitude of scholarships that aren't... They're looking at the more well-rounded students who have participated in a lot of activities—whether in school, after school, in the church, in the community—who they feel can make a contribution to the university that they eventually attend. There are a lot of scholarships out there for well-rounded students that are for specific hobbies, interests, groups, and things like that.

"That's why I say you can still be successful as far as your transition from high school to college, especially if you're looking for funding, if you don't have the highest grades."

Focus your search for scholarships based on requirements and eligibility criteria your student meets:

    ethnicity/race gender

    high school grade-point average SAT or ACT scores

    college major/career interest special talents

    extracurricular activities and community service geographic
       location

    religious affiliation

    military background (paents' and student's)

    employers (parents' and student's)

    affiliations (parents' clubs, fraternities, sororities)

    special needs, disabilities

    personal circumstances (foster children, children of disabled
       veterans, for example)

parents' level of education (scholarships exist for "first generation" students whose parents aren't college educated)

In your money search, you and your student can review some of the same college guides, handbooks, and internet sites you use to explore colleges. In the same library stacks where you find college information, you'll find scholarship guides, too. Purchasing a major college or scholarship guide from a bookstore use to be a good investment but you can find much of the same information on the internet.

Where Else to Look
Bulletin Boards
Community newspaper announcements
Human Resources or Community Resources office of parents' employers
Labor Unions
Churches
Clubs and Organizations
The Community Relations office of the local shopping mall and other companies and corporations
Major employers in your community
Sororities and Fraternities
Professional Associations
Chamber of Commerce

Where Not to Look
Your high school student will begin to get mail from college scholarship services. They'll appeal to you emotionally with con-

gratulations on your student's outstanding achievements (how do they know your student's record?). They claim that getting all the money your "outstanding student" needs for college is the easiest thing in the world. They claim that "Millions Go Unclaimed Every Year." Toss any that also suggest the following:

A scholarship is guaranteed

This is the only source for the information

You must submit your credit card or bank account numbers to guarantee a scholarship

You must pay a fee

You're a finalist for a contest or award program you've never applied for.

Once you begin the search for college money, you'll realize that your student doesn't have to be valedictorian, senior class president, or captain of the basketball team to get decent money for college.

Congressman Albert Wynn (D-Maryland) told a group of parents and students that "scholarships exist in strange and unexpected places." A law school acquaintance asked him about his religion, he recalled, telling Wynn there was scholarship money for minority law students who were Methodists. Unfortunately, Wynn was a Baptist. But you get the point.

Your student, with your help, will have to do the work. How successful you both are depends on how aggressive your search. Initially, that means studying information that is already on the internet, or calling, writing or emailing to request additional information and applications. A short note with your name, address, and phone number may be all you'll need for the initial contact. In all cases, note whether the award or scholarship is a one-time award, whether it will be spread over four years of college, and if your student can reapply annually if it's not a four-year award.

Gather personal papers—activities list or resume, awards and certificates of merit, letters of recommendation, Social Security card, transcripts—and keep them in a file along with your other college-bound material. You'll need to refer to them and make additional copies of some of them when it's time to send out applications.

Unfortunately, a lot of scholarship money goes unclaimed. The reason is procrastination. A single mother whose research paid off in free tuition for two sons to Frostburg State College says, "It's true. We don't go after the money." Challenging listeners at a workshop on scholarships, she said, "See how many of you leave here—and follow up."

HELP FROM YOUR COUNTRY

The U.S. government provides nearly 75 percent of all college financial aid to American college students. With billions of federal dollars up for grabs, you need to understand what's available, the formula for determining your eligibility, and the procedures for applying for it.

In most cases, your student won't be able to apply for federal money until the twelfth grade. But it's worth knowing what's ahead. Prior knowledge about the financial aid process can help in your personal financial plan for college, as discussed in Part One. It'll make the process less daunting, and alert you to what you need to do to get done years earlier (saving, cleaning up your credit rating to qualify for a parent loan).

Financial aid from the U.S. government for undergraduates comes in the form of:

Grants: They don't have to be paid back.

Low interest loans: They do have to be paid back.

Work-study jobs: The government subsidizes a student's wages.

Who's Eligible?

In general, to be eligible for federal aid you must be a U.S. citizen or eligible noncitizen, have a Social Security number and in most cases have financial need. Students must register with the

Selective Service, if applicable, and maintain satisfactory grades in college. A student with a felony drug conviction might not be able to get federal aid. The following comprise the government's major Student Financial Assistance programs:

Gift Awards

Federal Pell Grants are awarded to needy undergraduate students. They don't have to be paid back. The amounts awarded typically depend on how much funding the program gets. The maximum grant in 2003-2004 was just over $4,000. This is the only federal financial aid program in which all eligible needy students are guaranteed a grant.

Federal Supplemental Educational Opportunity Grants (FSEOG) are awarded to undergraduates with dire financial need. Pell Grant recipients with the greatest need for funds are the first to be considered for an additional FSEOG grant. In recent years, these grants have ranged from $100 to $4,000 a year. FSEOGs are campus-based aid, which means they're administered by the financial aid office at schools that participate in this program. Schools get only a specific amount of money for these grants each year. If you apply too late, the money may be gone.

Self-Help Awards

Federal Work-Study provides part-time jobs to help needy undergraduate and graduate students. Work-study job holders are paid an hourly wage that is at least the current federal minimum wage. The money goes directly to students like a paycheck, to spend as they choose. There are limits on how much you can earn, depending on when you apply, your financial need, and the funds available through the college. In the last few years, community service projects, including tutoring youngsters in reading, have qualified as work-study jobs. Most jobs are on campus or with a private nonprofit organization or public agency.

Federal Perkins Loans are low interest loans for undergraduate and graduate students with exceptional financial need. Loan amounts depend on when you apply, the money available, and how much a student needs. In recent years, the annual limit was $4,000, maxed out at $20,000 for undergraduate study. Students don't have to pay this loan back until they stop attending school at least half time. There's a nine-month grace period before the first payment is due, typically with a ten-year payment schedule. A student who goes on to graduate school, or has an economic hardship, may be able to get their payments deferred.

Federal and Direct Stafford Loan rates are adjusted annually, but are capped at 8.25 percent. Funds for Direct Loans come from the government to participating schools. If the college your student will attend is not part of the Direct Loan program, the loan money can come from a bank, credit union, or other lender that participates in the Federal Family Education Loan Program (FFEL). If a student is considered *still in need* even after receiving other federal aid and scholarships, the government pays the interest on these loans while a student is in school and for a short grace period after that, or if the student gets a deferment. Under these terms, it is a *subsidized* Stafford Loan.

If a student is *not considered still in need* after receiving other forms of financial aid, a student can borrow a limited amount. The student is responsible for paying all of the interest. Under these terms, it is an *unsubsidized* Stafford Loan.

Plus Loans for Parents have variable rates that are adjusted annually, capped at 9 percent. These loans are available to those who do not have a bad credit history. Note the wording there. If you have no credit history, that's okay. But Plus Loans are difficult to get if you have bad credit. If that's the case, getting a cosigner who can pass a credit check will help. The money can be borrowed for educational expenses for a dependent student enrolled at least half time. There's no grace period for repayment of these loans. First payments are due as early as sixty days after receipt. The money typically goes directly to the college. Check with Your school or lending institution for specific terms.

How Much Can Your Get and How to Get at It?

The chapter on "Paying for College," introduced the basic points of financial aid to show you why you should start saving for college early. Here's a review and more details:

The Free Application for Federal Student Aid (FAFSA) determines how much federal aid a student is eligible for to pay the costs of one year of college.

Using information supplied by parent and student, the FAFSA employs a formula to determine how much a family should be able to pay for college. This amount is called the Expected Family Contribution (EFC). It will be reported on the Student Aid Report generated by the government and sent to the student and the colleges the student selects when filling out the FAFSA.

College financial aid offices determine the amount of financial aid a student needs to attend their school by subtracting the EFC from the cost of attendance. A simple example:

Cost of Attendance $9,500

-Expected Family Contribution $3,000

Financial Need $6,500

Unless your student receives a full scholarship for academics, athletics, music, dance, or achievement in other areas, the financial aid office will try to meet the student's need for $6,500 in other ways. The amount could be met with PELL and FSEOG grants for the neediest students, loans and work-study wages for others. The financial aid office tallies all of these, including any money the college awards, to come up with a student's financial aid package.

Hopefully, your student's scholarship search will turn up awards from private corporations, nonprofit organizations, groups, clubs, and churches. Since most students won't get a free ride for four years, however, the Expected Family Contribution is serious business. What if it seems downright crazy and unrealistic? What if, when all the grants, loans, and awards are tallied, you still can't meet your EFC?

Inform the financial aid office of colleges your student has applied to immediately about your "special circumstances." Maybe there's a relative you're helping to support. Although you can't claim them as dependents if you don't pay more than 50 percent of their support, the financial aid office should know the family sends $100 a month back home to Grandma or has to pay Granddad's medical bills. You don't have to wait until your student receives the Student Aid Report back from the FAFSA. Write a letter to the college explaining that you're paying tuition for the younger children's parochial school. The FAFSA won't take these real-life expenses into account, but college financial aid administrators can use some discretion. Let them know that the $3,000 they assume you have is already earmarked for St. Anne's Middle School.

Inform the college financial aid office immediately of any changes in your family's financial picture since filling out the FAFSA, such as a job layoff, death or injury of a major breadwinner, or a new baby.

In short, it can't hurt to talk to the people in the financial aid office, before and after you've applied for financial aid. If yours is a student they really want—assuming all the hard work, dedication, study, participation has paid off—financial aid administrators will work with you.

Truth in Applying—You Can Be Audited, You Know

Actually, it's not an audit. It's called verification, the process the U.S. Department of Education and colleges use to make sure the information on the FAFSA is accurate. Not all applications are verified. Some are singled out because of inconsistent information. Other applications are selected at random. In any case, you must supply copies of all sorts of documents. Try to avoid this by filling out your FAFSA completely, accurately and with information that supports your overall financial statement. You could lose federal aid and money from other sources if your application can't be verified.

For More Information:

U.S Department of Education
http://www.ed.gov/parents/college/pay/edpicks.jhtml?src=ln
The Student Guide   http://www.studentaid.ed.gov/

HELP FROM YOUR STATE

Some of the same types of financial aid available from the U.S. government may be available from your state and local government. Contact the offices of the governor, mayor, and elected city or town officials. Contact your state's department of higher education (see listing at end) and inquire about educational grants, awards, scholarships, and loans. Within the state higher education department, most states have a scholarship administration or agency. When contacting local and state agencies ask specifically about:

Educational Opportunity Grants for needy students

Awards/scholarships from elected officials. From the town council to your state's Senate and House of Representatives, elected officials typically have money set aside to acknowledge deserving youngsters in their districts. The awards may be based on need, academics, community service, or some combination of the three. The recipients may be selected by an independent panel appointed by the elected official whose office presents the award.

Awards to children of public safety officers or other state employees disabled or killed in the line of duty

Grants to students who plan to major in areas in which there are professional shortages. In recent years, aspiring nurses and teachers have benefited from these kinds of grants.

They usually require an agreement to work in the stat or locality for a specific period after graduation.

Each year, my home state awards more than $45 million in financial aid to more than 33,000 residents. Compare your state to what one relatively small state offers:

Child Care Provider Scholarship

Delegate Scholarship

Distinguished Scholar Award

Distinguished Scholar Teacher Education Scholarship (for students who plan to teach)

Educational Assistance Grant

Firefighter, Ambulance and Rescue Squad Member Tuition Reimbursement Program

Family Practice Medical Scholarship Guaranteed Access Grant

Health Manpower Shortage Program Tuition Reduction for Nonresident Nursing Students

Memorial Grant

Loan Assistance Repayment Program

Loan Assistance Repayment Program in Primary Care Services

Part-Time Grant

Physical and Occupational Therapists and Assistants Grant

Professional School Scholarship

Senatorial Scholarship

Sharon Christa McAuliffe Memorial Teacher Education Award

State Nursing Scholarship and Living Expenses Grant

Most states use the Student Aid Report from the FAFSA to make additional awards to needy students. Also, students should indicate their majors on the FAFSA even if they're not sure. Indicating a major can automatically make a student eligible for state scholarships for students interested in specific areas of study.

Many states require that state financial aid be used at public colleges or colleges within the state, unless no state school offers your student's major.

Always follow the news for what your state General Assembly and the U.S. Congress are doing for higher education. Funding changes from one year to the next. New programs and tax credits may be adopted without your knowing it.

WAYS TO CUT COSTS

Take Advanced Placement (AP) courses offered in high school. College credit may be given to those who score high on AP subject tests. That can lead to fewer courses in college and early graduation—and savings on tuition and time spent in school.

Stay in-state. Tuition is the least expensive for those who go to a public college in their own state. Also, many local, state, and community scholarships are available to state residents only if they attend a college within their state.

Start out at a two-year community college where tuition generally is lower than a four-year institution. A student can take some of the same kinds of classes at community college, and then transfer to a four-year school and receive credit for some, if not all, of the work done at a lower cost in community college.

Select a major in areas of study/careers where there are shortages. In recent years, nurse and teacher shortages have led to scholarships from private and government groups interested in increasing the ranks in those professions.

Serve your country. They're not for everyone, but the Army, Navy, Air Force, Merchant Marine and Coast Guard each has its own four-year program where tuition is free to good students. ROTC (Reserve Officer Training Corps) participants earn scholarships that cover some to all of their expenses. In recent years, other programs have been established to help pay for college by helping others.

Get a job at a college or university. Higher education institutions general grant tuition breaks to their employees, even part-timers. Employees can use the tuition discount for themselves or their children.

KEY FINANCIAL POINTS

Free money (grants and scholarships) is preferable to loans, but it takes more work. Students will have to write more essays, enter contests, go through interviews, prove their worth. In short, they'll have to compete. Get your child used to competing. Enter contests, big and small: local essay contests, science fairs, poster and slogan contests. There's a lot of local money available, and all your student has to do is write about "What I Want to Be When I Grow Up."

Scholarship search services exist for those with the money to spend on such things, but what they guarantee to find sometimes is no more than what you can find for yourself.

Parents can suggest that the groups, clubs, and organizations they belong to start a scholarship fund. Do this a few years before your student will need one, to avoid the appearance that your idea is solely self-serving. Many kids can benefit from $100 if that's all your group can give.

Colleges talk more seriously about financial aid and awards to those who are already admitted or indicate their school as the student's first choice.

Don't presume your income is too high for financial aid. You'll at least probably qualify for a low-interest loan.

Don't be ashamed that your income is low. Your federal and state governments have money set aside just for students who qualify for free or reduced price school lunches in high school, for example, or whose parents are not college graduates. It's a costly mistake to hide this kind of information, or not apply for benefits that are there for people in your situation.

Student loans are an honorable debt. They help young people reach their dreams. Much is being written about the fact that student debt has reached record highs. But some feel it is worth it if it gets you the kind of education that will place you among the top candidates for the best jobs. Parents who are footing the entire bill can be proud that their children will graduate without any debt. In many cases, though, some kids are going to low cost schools that are open to almost anybody. Such a choice may not make the student as competitive in the real world as they might be with a degree from another school. For some, it may be worth taking out a loan to attend a more expensive school or to have the once-in-a-lifetime experience of living on campus.

Borrow the least amount necessary, only what's needed for college. Too much debt can threaten your own finances as you get older or overburden your young person before he gets his first real job.

Have contingency plans. Job layoffs, a new baby, family illness, and divorce are some of the things that can affect the family's ability to pay what it could have paid just a month before. Or maybe your student doesn't get the financial aid package you expect. Consider what you'll do if Plan A falls through. Maybe the student will have to take a less expensive school or go part-time. Have a Plan B.

On-campus work-study jobs offer great flexibility. One student worked in the admissions office of Syracuse University, and later in the school library. Much of what she did on the library job was study, in between checking out books to others, of course. Although these jobs pay only minimum wage, where else can you routinely tell your boss you can't make it because of a test or paper, and the boss says, "That's fine"?

No law says you have to bankrupt the family to send a child to college. Students should consider the impact of their college wishes on the rest of the family. Parents have to have something left to live on when the kids are gone.

COLLEGE-BOUND CALENDAR AND CHECKLIST

When Your Child Is in:

Sixth to ninth grade

Let guidance counselors and teachers know your child is college bound, if it's not apparent. Ask your child's counselors or adviser to recommend courses that will help prepare your student for advanced studies in high school. Get a list of high school courses required for admission to your state-supported colleges and universities.

If your child has not already taken or is not currently enrolled in Algebra I, ask the counselor to set a timetable for when she should be assigned. The timetable should allow enough time during the next four years for Geometry and Algebra II, as well. Ask the counselor to plot out a schedule of math, science, and foreign language courses for the next few years.

Attend a college fair and financial aid workshop.

Encourage your child to sample extracurricular activities, join clubs at school.

Begin a file with information about summer enrichment programs, contests, competitions, scholarships, and awards your child may be eligible for during the next four years. Collect information from the school guidance office, libraries, churches, and community centers. Get in the habit of scouring bulletin boards, community newspapers, and junk mail for information that could benefit your child.

Get your young person involved in competitions: local essay contests, science fairs, sports, art and competitions.

Where there are choices, help your students select the courses to take. Continue to make sure they are being assigned to math, science, and foreign language courses that will keep them on a college track.

On family trips, such as vacations and reunions, stop at a college along the way.

In January of every year, start looking for fun and enriching summer activities. Deadlines for the most sought-after summer programs can be as early as January, but usually are in early or late spring.

Tenth grade

Have your child register at school to take the PSAT in October, as practice for taking it in the eleventh grade, when scores are considered for scholarships.

Attend college fairs and career workshops with your student. Ask about scholarship qualifications and other forms of assistance. Collect brochures from schools your student may be interested in. Mail back the postcards to get on their mailing lists.

Attend open houses and financial aid workshops at colleges in your area.

If you haven't already, begin three files: one for college

brochures, one for financial aid information and scholarships, another for special programs.

Encourage your child to commit to one or two extracurricular activities, and support these activities.

Follow up on the information you've been collecting, encourage your child to apply for summer or weekend enrichment programs, enter competitions that showcase young talent and ability.

Eleventh grade

In the summer before junior year—but no later than the summer of the junior year—have your student put together a list of colleges and arrange to talk to college representatives who are in your area. If you can't arrange a visit during the next twelve months, call the schools outside of your area and ask for names of local alumni and recruiters.

Check the admissions requirements of the schools on your child's list and compare them to your child's transcript and upcoming course assignments. Determine what admissions tests are necessary, particularly any subject (achievement) tests.

Ask your child's adviser for a reality check. Does he have a realistic chance of getting into the schools of his choice? Identify "safe bet" schools that your student has the best chances of getting into.

Have your child register to take the PSAT again in the fall. Strong scores may lead to scholarships from the National Merit Scholarship program or National Achievement

Scholarships for Outstanding Negro Students.

In the spring, have your child register to take the SAT I. Also at this time, your student should register to take any SAT II tests in subjects in courses just completed. Refer to the test requirements at the narrowed-down list of colleges your child is considering.

Students interested in military academies, which have earlier deadlines, should contact their U. S. senator or congressman in the spring for a nomination form.

Encourage your child to take a leadership position in school and community. Encourage your student to fulfill community service requirements this year.

Get your child to identify teachers and other adults to ask for recommendations.

Continue researching scholarship sources. Get applications and note the deadlines.

Encourage your child to take a leadership position in school and community. Encourage your student to fulfill community service requirements this year.

Get your child to identify teachers and other adults to ask for recommendations.

Continue researching scholarship sources. Get applications and note the deadlines.

Students should tell their school counselor what majors they are interested in, and give updates when things change. Hopefully, the counselor will have your young person in mind when that program for aspiring artists crosses her desk.

Twelfth grade

In summer and early fall, finalize the list of schools to which your student will apply. (The average among African American students is four colleges). The student should call or write for the application and financial aid information. Make copies of the original application form and fill out the copies as practice. Make a folder for each school.

Your student should prepare or update a resume of accomplishments, activities, work experience, and awards to refer to when filling out applications. Give copies to those asked to write recommendations.

Encourage your student to look at the essay and interview questions on admissions and scholarship applications, and think about how to respond to them well before she needs to start working on the forms. This will help her to develop ideas and themes fully, rather than completing them with whatever comes to mind as the due date nears.

Keep a calendar in a prominent place in your home that lists important dates and deadlines-test dates, applications for admission, scholarships.

Narrow top college choices, then begin a dialogue with the financial aid officers at those schools. If a major has been decided on, contact the heads of those departments at schools you're interested in. If they're interested/ eager to have your student, they may put in a word to the financial aid office. The jazz ensemble director, desperate for a good string bassist like your child, could point this out to the admissions and financial aid officers.

Remind your student to ask teachers for recommendations early in the school year, before everyone else does. Teachers may be swamped with requests to write dozens of these. The most thought and effort are likely to go into the first ones a teacher has to write. Your student should include appropriate forms, stamped envelopes, and a resume/list of activites with the request. Afterward, the student should send a thank-you note.

Have your child register for the SAT in the fall, especially first-time takers or those who need higher scores to get into the colleges of their choice.

Send in completed applications in the fall, usually in November, if you're seeking an early admission decision. CHECK FOR EXACT DEADLINES. Other applications can be completed and mailed by the end of the year, although final deadlines are usually around February or March.

Look over a copy of the Free Application for Federal Student Aid (FAFSA) in the fall and attend a college financial aid workshop. Start collecting financial aid forms and the information you will need to fill them out. Mail the FAFSA in early January.

Senior Slump

When your student is popping off about being all done with applications, essays, and transcripts, remind him of the Fat Lady. Even by spring, when the acceptance notices arrive, the future is not set until a college receives the final senior year grades. The final semester is no time to slack off. For one thing, it can bring down class rank and overall grade-point average. Colleges frown when they see that a student they considered hardworking and ambitious has zonked out at the final stretch. Most acceptances are pending the final transcript.

Another form of senioritis is when your student learns she has all the credits and courses required for graduation and to get her where she's going. When this is the case, many public school districts, but *few* private schools, allow students to leave school early each day. Some reasons for early dismissal involve jobs, internships or apprenticeships, family responsibilities, courses at another school or at a college, or other outside endeavors. These are legitimate uses of a young person's time. But don't agree to an early dismissal if your child has no place to go and nothing to do. Remember the adage, "Get all the education you can get...." For most of us, high school is the last time education is totally free—and you can get as much as you want.

PART FIVE

Detours Along the Way

"You must do the thing you think you cannot do. "

Eleanor Roosevelt

OVERCOMING BAD GRADES

Silas Purnell got involved in college placement unwittingly while he chatted up youngsters behind the counter at a Walgreen's. "I couldn't understand why the kids had senior class rings on and were working at Walgreen's. There were so many opportunities out there." He asked why, the story goes, and they said they never thought about going to college—they didn't have the money. Asked if they would go if they had a chance, they answered, "Yes."

For more than thirty years, Purnell assisted about forty thousand young people in enrolling in more than two hundred colleges and universities. Purnell was a businessman until he found his calling helping the least likely candidates for college.

Purnell's work is an inspiration to young people (and hope for their parents) who may never have planned for college or, for whatever reason, don't have got the credentials to enroll. Besides a high school diploma or its equivalent, Purnell's single criterion for college placement candidates is "desire to go."

"Bad grades, bad test scores, and bad attitudes. If a kid wants to go to school, I'm going to place him. Those other things will change in college."

Purnell's story is about moving beyond the negative, finding hidden potential, overcoming odds, making a late start, getting a second chance (in many cases, a first chance).

Purnell worked his magic from an office in the basement of a Chicago public housing complex, with funding from a federal education project that identified students not likely to go to college without outside counseling and direction. "Some of my best students are armed robbers," Purnell says. The law prohibits him from asking about criminal activity or taking it into account in deciding whom he'll help. One of the solutions to lack of academic preparation in the students he sees is, "family, family, family."

This section talks about how parents can help young people when things don't go as hoped. Many students are not prepared for all that they want to do; some need more creative alternatives than the standard high-school-to-college approach, others have major obstacles to overcome.

This section includes information on admissions policies and programs for students who wouldn't be admitted to specific colleges otherwise. Later in this section you'll find information on how community colleges can be a helpful and affordable first step in obtaining a four-year degree. There's also a discussion about students who have done well, by most standards, but want an extra boost that will make them even more competitive when it comes to scholarships and selective schools.

Open Admissions, Alternative Admissions

Schools with Open Admissions accept almost all who apply, regardless of academic credentials. Most do require a high school diploma or General Equivalency Diploma, and in some cases only that a student is at least eighteen years old. For the most part, average to low grades and SAT/ACT test scores aren't a barrier to enrolling.

Many colleges and universities adopted open admissions policies in one form or another in the 1970s, on the heels of 1960s' civil rights movements that focused attention on the vast numbers of women, minorities and people with low and modest incomes who had been locked out of higher education by generations of inadequate public education. Colleges like the City University of New York (CUNY) developed remedial programs to help admitted students who had not been academically prepared for college.

In the 1990s, CUNY reversed the policy. The system of public colleges reported that half of its students had failed at least one basic skills proficiency exam. CUNY was spending 13% of teaching time on work that should have been mastered in high school. It closed the door to its four-year campuses and started sending students without strong academic backgrounds to two-year community colleges. One higher education official declared at a press conference, "We are cleaning out the four-year colleges..."

Open admissions policies have been abandoned in public colleges in Kansas and elsewhere, but for the trend has not caught on. Most state and private institutions have some form of open admissions. As few as 150 colleges have highly selective admissions standards. In short, almost any student who is willing to do the work necessary to succeed in college can be admitted somewhere. A guidance counselor can direct your family to those kinds of schools, whether it's a community colleges or state university.

When colleges with defined admissions standards bend their

rules, it's called Alternative Admissions. If your student wants to set high goals but hasn't got the academic record to reach them, a school with Alternative Admissions may be the answer. Requirements and offerings to students admitted through Alternative Admissions vary. In recent years, the University of Massachusetts Dartmouth College has offered College Now and START (Steps Toward Abstract Reasoning and Thinking). Students in both programs get additional counseling and academic help. START programs focuses on students interested in science and technology majors (engineering, computer science) but didn't get or do well in advanced courses in high school necessary to begin those programs in college.

Students who are considered for Alternative Admissions may fall into one or more of the following categories:

low to average grades and scores on college admissions tests

low to average grades, with acceptable test scores

acceptable grades with low to average test scores

low grades in the early high school years, but improvement in later years

previous good work interrupted by personal problems or special situations

federal low-income eligibility status

limited English proficiency

first generation family member to attend college

disabled

Consider alternative admissions if it means:

getting in, or not getting into a college

getting into a selective college that would not accept the student otherwise going to the school the student is set on, even if the student doesn't qualify on paper

Some schools have specific policies or programs, Conditional Admissions, Provisional Admissions, Freshman Incentive, Academic Development, Guided Study programs. Standards vary depending on the college, just as standard admission requirements vary from school to school. What may be low to one school is an acceptable test score or grade-point average to another. You'll know how your student's record fits the standards of different schools by looking at the admissions requirements listed in college brochures and guides.

Students who enter college under these conditions may be required to take remedial classes in math and/or reading. Their choice and number of courses may be limited, and they may be limited to taking classes with other Alternative Admission students.

Some colleges conduct structured Alternative Admissions programs that begin with summer "bridge" sessions before freshman year. During this time, students are coached in study skills, take placement tests and remedial classes, and are counseled about campus life. If there's an offer for a summer program, ask if the college will provide financial aid for it. Some funding has been eliminated for bridge programs that target minority students (the affirmative action backlash).

Many of Silas Purnell's students are accepted into colleges through Alternative Admissions programs or policies. We can't all get Purnell to help our child, so if your student's academic record isn't outstanding, ask the admissions staff at schools that interest him about Alternative Admissions. Find out if there is a separate application process.

High school counselors and college admissions offices may be able to refer you to programs in your area, such as federal Talent Search programs for low-income students and those whose parents didn't go to college.

If your student is motivated and has potential but has not done well because of difficult circumstances (including going to a school not focused on preparing students for college), this is a strong selling point to schools that might consider him. A guidance counselor or other interested adult can help you and the student explain the situation. Call and arrange an interview—or do it by email or over the phone if you can't travel. This is the chance for your student to show off the personal qualities that don't come through on an official record. Let him explain, honestly, the story behind his poor or average performance and how determined he is to do better in college and in life. A personal display of maturity and dedication can go a long way. Generally, colleges accept only a limited number of students this way. So don't plan on Alternative Admissions. It's only something to fall back on.

THE TWO-YEAR STOP ON THE WAY TO A FOUR-YEAR DEGREE

President Bill Clinton put community colleges on the map when he called for making two years of schooling after senior high a universal educational benchmark. This vision of K-14 education as a standard put a spotlight on community colleges, which for generations have served many functions.

Community colleges, supported with local and state taxes, are a good idea for those who don't want to invest in four years of higher education and have career plans that don't require it. (See "Different Kinds of Colleges.")

For those who do aspire to a four-year bachelor's degree and beyond, community college is a good way to begin. The American Association of Community College reports that 46 percent of African American undergraduate students attend one of the nation's 1,173 community colleges. (About half of all community college students are not pursuing classes for degree credit.)

Community colleges students take advantage of their relatively low-cost courses for different reasons. For some, community college is an important link in preparing those students who haven't acquired many basic academic skills, even though they hold a high school diploma. Though they don't like to put it this way, many are remedial education centers where students can gain basic reading and math skills. African American students, many of them stuck in schools that haven't served them well, have needed remedial education to a greater extent than some others: Nearly 30 percent of our students in four-year programs and 25 percent of those in community colleges have to take remedial courses in college.

Success at community college is a way to overcome a less than stellar high school transcript and prove to a four-year institution that your student can succeed in higher education.

Community colleges are also a great bargain. Your student may enroll in a community college where tuition and fees are a fraction of the costs of a public university or private college. For hundreds or thousands less, your student spend two years at a community college and transfer to a four-year school.

Do the math: average annual tuition at community colleges in 2004 was $1,518. Tuition and fees at a public four year college was running at $4,694. The figures for a private four-year college was about $19,710. A community college student's first two years cost about $3,000. Meanwhile, others are spending much more in meeting the $9,000 price tag for two years at the state university. Yet both eventually can earn the same degree and the State U.

The counselor at a well-to-do suburban high school where community colleges are looked down on lamented, "There's a stigma, but a lot of kids don't realize the English 101 at the community college is the same as English 101 at a four-year school." Well, not always. There are benefits to being on the campus of a four-year college. But starting out at a community college is a good alternative.

Your student will have to pay close attention to make sure that the courses she takes will be accepted at any school she transfers to. Credit for remedial courses aren't accepted by most four-year colleges.

THE THIRTEENTH GRADE

The thirteenth grade can be a good thing, although few of us have ever heard of it and few students are able to take advantage of it. I'm including a brief discussion of it here, however, because it demonstrates the value in exploring and researching all the options available to students. Hopefully, by understanding that there are so many options and opportunities for today's young people, you will be encouraged to do the work to find out about the ones that suit your students' needs.

So here goes:

The thirteenth grade of school is not freshman year of college. It is an additional year of high school—after a student has already received a diploma. This additional year of high school is a tradition that is at least a hundred years old. Also known as Postgraduate Study or the Postgraduate year, the thirteenth year is offered at about 180 private schools around the country. In school catalogues you'll see it listed simply as "PG." Northfield Mount Hermon School in Northfield, Massachusetts, enrolls between sixty five and eighty PG students every year.

Students attend a thirteenth year of high school for the following reasons:

They have made progress in high school and want to show another year of improvement before applying to college.

They are dissatisfied with the college choices available based on their high school record. Another year gives them a chance to take more college prep courses and boost their scores on college admissions tests.

They are young for their class and want a chance to catch up academically, socially, or for purposes of athletic competition.

They like the idea of living away from home for the first time in an environment that offers more academic support and structure than most colleges provide.

Northfield Mount Hermon has launched its PG graduates into some of the nation's most prestigious colleges—Brown, Cornell, Johns Hopkins, MIT, Oberlin, Rensselaer, and the Naval Academy, to name a few.

Unfortunately, the schools that offer a thirteenth year are some of the most expensive private schools in the country, with tuition for a single year equaling a pricey college—more than $25,000 a year. Yet even in these cases, there are scholarships and financial aid for those who have the foresight to see how another year in high school can boost their college and career options.

A man, now a doctor, reveals that he was already a good student when he graduated from high school, but spent a 13th year at a private school getting his grades and SAT scores up so that he could be accepted at an Ivy League university.

Here's another example: A high school football coach suggested a thirteenth year at a college prep boarding school for a youngster named Malik. Malik was a "young" high school senior—he turned seventeen a few months before graduation from a public high school—and his coach thought another year in high school could help him mature physically, and boost his grades and SAT scores so that he could be a strong candidate for a football scholarship at a major university the next year.

The boarding school was eager to have him and offered Malik a $13,000 scholarship for a thirteenth year. He declined it. Most of his friends and family had never heard of such a thing as returning to high school after graduating. The idea was just too tough to sell.

Malik ended up at a small state school, which his parents paid for. He did well there, but didn't play college football. He graduated, nonetheless. Today, he's a successful business man.

TEEN PARENTS

Political Science major Michelle Garrett, Math major Tara Robinson, and Monique Perry, her major still undecided, made the dean's list their freshman year at North Carolina Central University, all posting 3.0 grade-point averages. Amanda Johnson, a Criminal Justice major, earned an A average in her first year at the school.

Each was an excellent student. Each was a teen mother.

North Carolina Central State University helped these young mothers adjust and move beyond the consequences of teen pregnancy through its "Strivin' and Survivin'" Single Parent Support project. A teen parent scholarship and support program, it awarded scholarships based on a personal potential and financial need to full-time students who are single parents.

Mostly mothers, the students in recent years earned about $4,800 in scholarship money to help pay for books, tuition, or child care. Most students lived on campus—one came all the way from Connecticut. All were their children's primary caretakers, but they left their youngsters in the care of family members while they were away at college.

During group meetings and activities, social worker Pam Tingley counseled them in such areas as child development, birth control, and campus life. The program was started by law school professor Cheryl Amana. She was expelled from her high school for getting pregnant. Even without much outside support, she was determined to attend college. Amana persevered, earning a Bachelor's degree and becoming a lawyer.

Years later, speaking at a program for teen moms in high school, Amana pledged to help any who wanted to attend college. Through her efforts, eleven teen mothers enrolled at NC Central through a grant from the Z. Smith Reynolds Foundation.

North Carolina Central's program is not unique, as a number of other colleges recognize that teenage pregnancy, while a very bad idea, should not end the dreams or potential of young women. In recent years, the state of North Carolina sponsored scholarships for single parents who attend two-year state colleges.

Oxnard Housing Authority in California also recruited parents from public housing to attend nearby Oxnard College. Supported with a federal grant aimed at ridding public housing of drugs, participants in the Teen Parent Program got help with child care, career, and their studies.

Bennett College, the Historically Black women's school in Greensboro, N.C., called its student-mothers "unique Belles" and offered counseling and support through its Women's Leadership Institute.

At some colleges, support for teen parents is limited to the housing set aside for students with families, or on-campus child care. At a small college outside of Los Angeles, students and staff simply supported single parents in college by collecting Christmas toys for their children.

Tingley, the social worker at NC Central, says families can help their daughters move forward after pregnancy and birth by getting over the hurt and disappointment. "You have to clear up the judgmental thing for a young woman to go forward. You've got to support her. You've got to say, `It's not easy, it can't be done alone, but this is not a tragedy. College is doable, it can be done.'"

As with all young people, however, plans to go to college should be set in place in their early years. "If you've never talked to anyone about going to college before, why should you talk to them about it [once they're pregnant]?" says Tingley.

Contact the colleges your pregnant or parenting teen is interested in and inquire about support for undergraduates who are young or single parents. Many programs for young parents (guys included) are spin-offs of programs for displaced homemakers and older women returning to school.

Contact your state's social services agency, especially if your teen is eligible for Temporary Assistance to Needy Families (TANF). Welfare reform mandates increasingly offer help with education and advanced training.

GLOSSARY

ACT Standardized college admission test published by American College Testing. Many colleges in the South and Midwest require applicants to submit their scores from the ACT. Students typically take the ACT or the SAT I in their junior and senior years of high school.

Alternative Admissions Separate requirements or programs for students who don't meet a college's regular admissions requirements

Advanced Placement High school courses taught at a college level through a national program supervised by The College Board; students who have a high score on AP exams can get college credit for the course.

Americans With Disabilities ACT (ADA) The federal law that prohibits discrimination based on disabilities. It requires postsecondary institutions to provide certain academic adjustments, including auxiliary aids and services, to ensure that the school does not discriminate on the basis of disability. Provisions of the Individuals with Disabilities Education Act that guide elementary and secondary education (IDEA) are different than those of the ADA and do not apply to colleges and universities.

The College Board Association of educators and administrators focused on the transition from high school to college. It oversees the SAT college admissions test and provides information for the college-bound.

The College Fund/UNCF The higher education assistance organization that provides scholarships, programs, and funds for thirty nine Black colleges and universities.

Expected Family Contribution (EFC) The amount a family is expected to pay toward a child's postsecondary education, determined by a government formula that takes into account family income, assets, and benefits, compared to necessary family expenses, such as medical bills and the college tuition of other students in the family. The EFC is used specifically in determining eligibility for financial aid from the federal government.

FAFSA Free Application for Federal Student Aid. The standard form used to determine aid, scholarships, and grants. Used for all federal and most state government financial aid, as well as most college need-based awards. College students must fill this out each year they seek financial aid.

First Generation College-bound students whose parents never got a college degree are dubbed "first-generation." Many public and privately sponsored enrichment programs that offer tutoring and college guidance are designed for first-generation students. Admissions and scholarship committees also may give special consideration to first generation students and will ask your student to indicate this on an application.

Ford Federal Direct Loan Newer federal program through which students may obtain federal loans directly from their colleges with federal funds instead of through a private lender.

Grant Money given to a student to help pay college costs. Grants do not have to be repaid.

HBCUs Historically Black Colleges and Universities.

Kindergarten redshirting A practice in which children old

enough for kindergarten are kept out of formal education for an
additional year so they'll be more advanced than their classmates.

Merit-based aid Financial awards for reasons other than financial need. Most merit-based aid is based on academic performance or special talents and interests, community service, and
given in the form of scholarships or grants.

Need-based aid Financial awards based on need, determined by
student/family's ability to cover all the costs of college.

Open admissions The practice among those colleges that admit
most or all students who apply. At some schools anyone who has
a high school diploma or GED may enroll. Other schools may
accept anyone over eighteen.

Pell Grants Federal grants to the neediest students.

Perkins Loans Low interest federal loan program for exception-
ally needy students.

Plus Loans Federal loan program in which parents may borrow
money for their childrens' college education.

Postgraduate Study (PG) Additional year of study after high
school graduation but before college, meant to boost standardized test scores and grades for college admission or to improve
students' weak areas. Many private high schools offer postgraduate study. **PSAT/NMSQT** Preliminary Scholastic Assessment
Test/National Merit Scholarship Qualifying Test is a practice
test for the SAT I. The PSAT is usually administered to tenth
and eleventh graders. Those who do very well in eleventh grade
may qualify for the National Merit Scholarships or National
Achievement Scholarships for Outstanding Negro Students.

ROTC Reserve Officers Training Corps program. The U.S. military covers the cost of tuition and fees in exchange for a commitment to serve in the military after college.

SAT I Scholastic Assessment Test, said to measure math, critical reading and writing skills, is used by many colleges in the East and western U.S. as part of the college admissions process. Many students take the SAT I more than once to improve their scores. Required by most colleges as part of the admissions process.

SAT II Special subjects tests that are designed to measure skills in specific subjects, such as foreign languages, biology, chemistry, and high level math such as calculus.

Selective colleges Those institutions that have significantly more applicants than they can admit. The more selective the school, the higher the grades and test scores of students accepted. Ivy League colleges are among the most highly selective.

Tracking Grouping students according to their abilities or achievement. This can begin as early as kindergarten, with some children going into the "top" reading group or gifted classes, while others are labeled average or below average. Tracking continues through high school, where some students are assigned to an academic or college prep track and others get a general or vocational diploma.

Transcript The list of all courses a student has taken with the grades earned in each course. Colleges require a high school transcript as part of the admissions application.

Title IX The federal law that requires that student-athletes be provided equitable athletic opportunities, regardless of gender, and that female and males receive athletics scholarship money proportional to their participation.

Work-Study programs Federal college work program that provides salaried, part-time jobs, typically on campus, as part of a student's financial aid package.

WHAT TEACHERS WANT US TO KNOW

Saying things like, "Oh God, I'm scared to death of the water," when a child is learning to swim; turning your nose up at things you don't like, like different kinds of foods or mathematics, keeps children from wanting to explore new things.

Don't disagree with educators in front of the child. It undermines teachers' authority. Don't accept your child's word as gospel. Get all sides of the story.

Black parents give too much criticism and don't praise enough.

We've seen science projects you know a nine-year-old didn't do. Be there as a resource and support but don't do the work.

Some parents spend too much time on activities that isolate them from the family, whether it is watching TV alone or talking on the phone or doing community and church work that doesn't involve their children.

Some parents have unrealistic expectations. The mother of a two-year-old was upset that he wasn't bringing home seat work or learning to write the alphabet. The hands of a two-year-old aren't developmentally ready to hold a pencil!

Do "active" things such as cooking together, playing sports, working in a garden, picking apples at an orchard. Instead, time that is spent together is often in doing passive things that don't require a lot of interaction between parents and child, such as going to the movies or a concert. Parents can help prepare a child for an exam by giving drills, calling out spelling words, giving practice questions or math problems.

Make it clear how happy you are that "Our family does well in school." I would reward not so much with outside rewards, but more inside, feelings of pride in the family.

Put projects on the coffee table, frame the artworks.

The best reward is to show genuine interest in your child's work. Concrete rewards for achievement mistakenly place emphasis on the reward rather than on the learning.

Read books to the slow starter about children who catch on later. For older children and youth, read inspirational books about people who overcame bad starts and went on to success. Make it fun and happy for the child to achieve. Never threaten or punish a child for poor performance.

Convince the slow learner he can do more, then give opportunities for success. Start with little assignments or tasks that you know he knows and can do well. That will encourage him to move on to the next harder thing.

Everybody's success is not going to be academic. Whatever they're good at, let them show that off.

I think helping a child develop a deep interest is very important. The subject is not very important, it could be anything. In my first grade class students do an in-depth study and develop an expertise about the beaver or the buffalo, and different Indian tribes. This kind of in-depth study provides a hook on which many lifelong learning strategies can be hung. The key: Competence and confidence go together.

Sometimes when a child says he's bored, he's really frustrated or doesn't understand the work. Check the situation out. It might be something else.

Don't over schedule your child. Allow time for school projects and homework. Kids also need time for relaxing. It shows up in school when children don't have time for fun at home.

Discuss the news, the world, life with your children. Then encourage them to discuss things and ideas, and give reasons for their opinions.

The parents of successful students are generally interested in learning themselves. They show their children the importance of learning by reading, studying, visiting museums themselves. In this way, children see that improving your mind and learning about new things are part of life.

What College Students Can Tell Us

I'll be honest with you: fast cars, nice houses, and financial peace of mind keep me pounding the papers.

-George Washington University

I knew I wanted to be a success. I could do things to get me in trouble or go to school and have options. I just thought if you have options, you can live the way you want.

-Morehouse College

A graduate and undergraduate chapter of Alpha Kappa Alpha sorority was having a high school debutante cotillion. I saw all these college age women and I wanted to know what it was all about. I first realized I could go to college after seeing these college women.

-Columbia University

I began thinking about going to college in middle school when I was chosen to take a special test. I felt special and intelligent. I felt I must be college material.

-Florida A&M

I could not get a decent job. The only skill I had was typing. So

I went back to school.

-University of the District of Columbia

I was subject to indirect motivation to go to college when I saw many examples of how I did *not* want to be. I knew that going to college was something I had to do in order to be more successful than my older siblings who were in jail or having babies.

-Florida A&M

I attended a program at Purdue University called Minority Introduction to Engineering (MITE). The program lasted two weeks and taught me about college life and about the different fields of engineering.

-Morehouse College

When I was going into the eighth grade I spent two weeks on the Chesapeake Bay. I was in a six-week program at the Oregon Museum of Science and Industry. These programs allowed me to mature in ways I wouldn't have otherwise. In different environments I learned how to respond to different situations. They're not as expensive as regular summer camps. I got scholarships.

-Georgia Tech

I read a lot but I wish I had read more than just what I liked. I should have read more of *Time* and *Newsweek* instead of just *Ebony* and *Glamour*.

-Northwestern

The ability to organize and prioritize is one of the most important skills in college.

-Northern Virginia Community College

Be able to compromise. A lot of projects involve a collective effort.

-Hampton

Those people who fail don't know how to manage their time. Listening. Reading. Time management.

-Morehouse College

Juggling different things: classes, personal matters. Balancing studying and social life is important.

-Georgia Tech

Stay away from credit cards. Many kids are in serious financial trouble from one year in college.

-University of Oklahoma

Sometimes you don't want to study an extra night, an extra hour when it could have a big effect on your future.

-University of West Virginia

Lack of self-confidence. Doubt holds you back by not taking risks, not believing in yourself.

-Clark Atlanta

Get kids involved in positive, productive activities that make them feel they have accomplished something. Once an achiever, always an achiever.

-Catholic University

Make sure kids read and write a lot. No matter what you major in, you're going to have to write essays and papers.

-Howard University

Don't always take the easy route. Be challenged. If you do the hard work in high school, you'll be used to it in college.

-Morgan State University

Remember what you like doing and do well. That's the best step in determining what you want and can be successful at.

-University of Michigan

WHAT COLLEGES WANT US TO KNOW

When they set foot in high school, get your child thinking, "Everything I do from now on determines if I'm going to get into college, if I'm going to get an academic scholarship."

-Morgan State University

When students come in for an interview, we ask the parents to sit out in the lobby. We want to hear if the student can articulate well, explain his situation, ask thoughtful questions.

-Temple University

At the college fairs, students don't know why they're here. They don't know what to ask.

-DePaul University

Students need to come out of high school loaded with academics. There's no other time you can get that for free after high school.

-University of Alabama, Huntsville

The college admissions officer's job is not to be pushy or a salesman. It's my job to give information and tell you why it's a good school. The students should do the homework, should find out that we have a good psychology program if that's what they're interested in.

-Pitzer College

State schools are less subjective. We look at grades and test scores. A private school can take a C student just because they need a dancer {that student].

-University of Vermont

Students can't wait until their senior year to say they want to do well to go to college. We look at grades in ninth grade on through. If they've been able to improve their grades, that's positive, but we're looking at all of them.

-Syracuse University

Visiting a college is one of the more important things you can do with your child. It comes down to finding out, "Is this a place where I can fit in or grow into by age twenty-two?"

-University of Massachusetts, at Amherst

Everybody wants to hurry up and get into the job market. But you need the "jeopardy preparation." The people on that [TV] show have a broad range of knowledge. You need the depth and broad range of knowledge to be competitive.

-Bennett College

We have family housing, and day care for students and staff.

-University of Michigan

There's a financial aid estimator parents of high school seniors can fill out even before they apply.

-Oglethorpe University

Too many kids [when considering college majors] think about paychecks instead of their skills and interests.

-Wentworth Institute of Technology

Parents and students don't do research. What would be good for this kid? Instead, it's I want him to go there because it is a good school.

-Bryant College

Business students, even liberal arts students, need the math skills to handle research.

-Loyola University

Learning has to do with how your future turns out.

-Chicago State University

HISTORICALLY BLACK COLLEGES AND UNIVERSITIES

"When we sang the Alma Mater [at Howard University] my soul stood on tiptoe and stretched up to take in all that it meant.... I felt the ladder under my feet."
Zora Neale Hurston,
Harlem Renaissance Writer

ALABAMA
Alabama A&M University
Alabama State University
Bishop State Community
College Concordia College
Gadsden State Comm. College
J.F. Drake Technical College
Lawson State Community College
Miles College
Oakwood College
Selma University
Shelton State Community College, C. A. Freed Campus
Stillman College
Talladega College
Trenholm State Technical College
Tuskegee University

ARKANSAS
Arkansas Baptist College
Philander Smith College
Shorter College
University of Arkansas, Pine Bluff

DELAWARE
Delaware State University

DISTRICT OF COLUMBIA
Howard University
University of the District of Columbia

FLORIDA
Bethune-Cookman College
Edward Waters College
Florida A&M University
Florida Memorial College

GEORGIA
Albany State College
Clark Atlanta University
Fort Valley State College
Interdenominational Theological Center
Morehouse College
Morehouse School of Medicine Morris Brown College
Paine College
Savannah State College
Spelman College

KENTUCKY
Simmons University Bible College
Kentucky State University

LOUISIANA
Dillard University
Grambling State University
Southern University and A&M College, Baton Rouge
Southern University, New Orleans
Southern University, Shreveport-Bossier City Campus
Xavier University of Louisiana

MARYLAND
Bowie State University
Coppin State College
Morgan State University
University of Maryland, Eastern Shore

MICHIGAN
Lewis College of Business

MISSISSIPPI
Alcorn State University
Coahoma Community College
Hinds Community College, Utica Campus
Jackson State University
Mary Holmes College
Mississippi Valley State University

Natchez Junior College
MISSISSIPPI (continued)
Rust College
Tougaloo College

MISSOURI
Harris-Stowe State College
Lincoln University

NORTH CAROLINA
Barber-Scotia College
Bennett College
Elizabeth City State University
Fayetteville State University
Johnson C. Smith University
Livingstone College
North Carolina A&T State University
North Carolina Central University
St. Augustine's College
Shaw University
Winston-Salem State University

OHIO
Central State University
Wilberforce University

OKLAHOMA
Langston University

PENNSYLVANIA
Cheyney University of Pennsylvania
Lincoln University

SOUTH CAROLINA
Allen University
Benedict College
Claflin College
Clinton Junior College
Denmark Technical College
Morris College
South Carolina State University
Voorhees College

TENNESSEE
Fisk University
Knoxville College
Lane College
LeMoyne-Owen College
Meharry Medical College
Morristown College
Tennessee State University

TEXAS
Huston-Tillotson College
Jarvis Christian College
Paul Quinn College
Prairie View A&M University
St. Phillip's College

TEXAS (continued)
Southwestern Christian College
Texas College
Texas Southern University
Wiley College

VIRGINIA
Hampton University
Norfolk State University
St. Paul's College
Virginia Seminary and College
Virginia State University
Virginia Union University

VIRGIN ISLANDS
University of the Virgin Islands, St. Thomas Campus

WEST VIRGINIA
Bluefield State College
West Virginia State College

RESOURCES

A Better Chance - A national program that helps place academically talented minority middle school children into some of the nation's most prestigious and rigorous college prep high schools, both private and public. The schools provide financial aid and scholarships. Best chance for consideration for the next school year is by completing application and registration materials by October. www.abetterchance.org

ACT-SO - Afro-Academic, Cultural, Technological and Scientific Olympics (ACTSO) is the NAACP's year-long enrichment program for African American high school students. The program centers around mentors and coaching to promote academic and artistic excellence. Students in grades 9 through 12 participate through their local NAACP chapter. The program culminates with local and national competitions in the sciences, humanities, and performing and visual arts, and scholarships of up to $1,000. Contact your local NAACP branch or the national office at 4805 Mt. Hope Drive, Baltimore, Maryland 21215.
http://www.naacp.org/work/actso/Factsheet.shtml

The Algebra Project - A math literacy effort aimed at helping low income students and students of color master higher-level math skills. www.algebra.org/index.html

AmeriCorps - Domestic community service programs in which you can earn money for college. Call 1-800-94-ACORPS. http://www.americorps.org/

Black Excel - This "college help network" provides help with college selection, admission, scholarships, and financial aid: http://www.blackexcel.org/

The College Board - The premier national organization serving the needs of colleges and college-bound students through services and programs for college admissions and testing. It administers the SAT, the PSAT/NMSQT, and the Advanced Placement programs. www.collegeboard.org

Concerned Black Men - A civic organization in more than a dozen cities that emphasizes mentoring to boys. To locate a local chapter, call 215-276-2260.or contact CBM at 7200 North 21st Street Philadelphia, PA 19138-2102

The Family Education Network - This is a commercial site includes a section called "What Kids Need to Know." This has a simple list of things children of different ages should know in different subjects. If you want to go further, you can look at different activities, exercises and games to help children of various ages in different subjects. Find advice on different aspects of education and learning from preschool to 12th grade. A parent's section offers ideas on handling school and social issues. http://www.fen.com/

FastWeb - This interactive scholarship sites provides customized searches and sends regular alerts about new scholarships to registered users. http://fastweb.monster.com/index.ptml

Federal Student Aid Information Center - Find general information about federal student aid programs and assistance in completing the Free Application for Federal Student Aid (FAFSA). P.O. Box 84, Washington, D.C. 20044; a toll-free number, 1-800-4-FED-AID. Help in completing the FAFSA is available online at http://www.ed.gov/prog_info/SFA/StudentGuide/ and http://studentaid.ed.gov

Financial Aid Information Page - A free, comprehensive, independent guide to other financial aid resources, including special interest groups for women, international students, and minorities: httpa/www.finaid.org/

First Book - A nationwide nonprofit group that provides new books to low-income children through community-based family literacy programs, tutoring and mentor programs. http://www.firstbook.org/

GEAR UP - The federal Gaining Early Awareness and Readiness for Undergraduate Programs identifies low-income middle school students and their families in specific for mentoring, tutoring and special programs through high school graduation. Contact your Board of Education or state department of higher education.

GreatSchools.Net - A nonprofit online guide to K-12 schools that provides detailed information about specific public, private and charter schools in all 50 states. Using data schools are required to submit to the U.S. Department of Education, the site lets you see the profiles of individual schools. You can enter than name of a school and location and get data on tests scores and comparisons to other schools in the same district. www.greatschools.net.

Home2School.com - This site provides specific information on what children of different ages should be learning. In order to help your children with homework, the site gives you "Two Minute Tutorials" on any subject by grade level, up to grade 8. You can also set up a specific education plan for your child, based on grade and your state's educational requirements. http://home2school.com/

Inroads - Works with corporations to sponsor internships for minority high school and college students. Contact Inroads at 10 South Broadway, Suite 700,St. Louis, Missouri 63102 (314)241-7488 Email: info@inroads.org. Also at http://www.inroads.org/

LEAD - Leadership Education and Development Program in Business, Inc. selects minority high school juniors for a Summer Business Institute at one of several prestigious graduate business schools around the country. The program then follows LEAD scholars through college, helping them to win internships and launch professional careers in corporate America. Visit http://www.leadnational.org/summer.cfm

National African American Parent Involvement Day - Gives information about this annual event, the second Monday of every February. The site includes a parents' guide for visiting schools on NAAPI Day and setting up events in your communities. http://naapid.org/. Or call 800. 351.4097, or write NAAPID, P. O. Box 2043—Ann Arbor, MI 48106-2043.

National Association of Student Financial Aid Administrators - www.nasfaa.org/parents

National Parent Teacher Association - The website for the national center for parent-teacher school organization. It has information about how to get involved in your school's PTA, as well as general advice and support for parents. Phone: 312-670-6782 or 800-307-4PTA (4782); Fax: 312-670-6783; http://www.pta.org/

NCAA Guide for the College Bound Student-Athlete - Available in school guidance offices and online, it outlines eligibility requirements, how to deal with recruiters and coaches. Or contact NCAA at 317-917-6222.

NCAA Initial Eligibility Clearinghouse - Has information on high school requirements for high school athletes preparing for NCAA-level sports. http://www.ncaaclearinghouse.net;

The Parent Institute - This site is focused on helping adults to help with schoolwork, deal with teachers, and a number of different school situations. Its sells products, such as student study

guides and parent information booklets, including "Why Study
& How Much Should Parents Help?"
http://parentinstitute.com/

SchoolSuccessInfo.org - This website is designed to help parents
get involved in their children's education. There are sections that
give general parenting tips, such as how to help a child with reading
or homework, or how to prepare for a parent-teacher conference.
The site is the result of a project between People For the American
Way Foundation and NAACP. http://schoolsuccessinfo.org/

Federal Student Aid on the Web - This website takes students and
parents through the entire college admissions process involving
financial aid, from choosing schools, applying, finding funding,
attending and repaying loans.
http://www.studentaid.ed.gov/

**Students with Disabilities Preparing for Postsecondary
Education: Know Your Rights and Responsibilities** - To order
call 1-800-872-5327 (1-800-USA-LEARN), fax to 301-470-1244
or e-mail a request to edpubs@inet.ed.gov.

Upward Bound - The federal government's program for promoting
college among low-income high school students and first-generation
students (those who don't have a parent with a college degree).
Upward Bound projects must provide instruction in math, laboratory science, composition, literature, and foreign language, along with
tutoring and mentoring programs. Information available from
school guidance offices.

RECOMMENDED READING

Bad Teachers: How to Fight for Your Child's Education by Guy Strickland (Pocket Books).

Basic Black: Home Training for Modern Times by Karen Grigsby Bates and Karen Ellyse Hudson (Doubleday).

Beating the Odds: Raising Academically Successful African American Males by Freeman A. Frabowski III, Kenneth I. Maton, and Geoffrey L. Grief (Oxford University Press).

The Black Student's Guide to Colleges: 700+ Private Money Sources for Black and Minority Students (Madison Books), edited by Barry Beckham

Black Excel African American Student's College Guide, by Isaac Black (John Wiley & Sons)

The Color of Water: A Black Man's Tribute to His White Mother by James McBride (Riverhead Books). The author's mother sent all twelve children to college by working the school system to get them in the better schools and, frequently, just plain threatening her kids to do well.

Freedom Challenge: African American Homesehoolers edited by Grace Llewellyn (Lowry House).

40 Ways to Raise a Nonracist Child by Barbara Mathias and Mary Ann French (HarperPerennial).

In Their Footsteps: Travel to African American Heritage Sites by Henry Chase (Henry Holt).

Maggie's American Dream by James Comer. The Yale child psychiatrist's memoir about how his father, a steel-mill worker, and mother, a domestic, insisted on the high standards that led this family to thirteen college and graduate degrees.

Marva Collins' Way: Returning to Excellence in Education by Marva Collins and Civia Tamarkin (Tarcher/Pumam).

The Measure of Our Success: A Letter to My Children and Yours by Marian Wright Edelman (Beacon Press).

The Mis-Education of the Negro by Carter G. Woodson (Africa World Press, Inc.).

Money for College: A Guide to Financial Aid for African American Students by Erlene B. Wilson (Plume/Penguin).

Morning By Morning: How We Homeschooled Our African

American Sons to the Ivy League by Paula Penn-Nabrit

The Mother Daughter Book Club by Shereen Dodson. An African American mother tells how she set up literary discussions with young girls. Plenty of reading suggestions and discussion ideas.

The Multicultural Students' Guide: What Every African American, Asian American, Hispanic and Native American Applicant Needs to Know about America's Top Schools, by Robert Mitchell (Noonday Press).

Radical Equations: Civil Rights From Mississippi to the Algebra Project by Robert P. Moses with Charles E. Cobb, Jr. (Beacon Press)

Silver Rights: A True Story from the Front Lines of the Civil Rights Struggle by Constance Curry (Algonquin Books of Chapel Hill). This story is about a Mississippi sharecropping couple's struggle to educate their thirteen children in the 1960s.

The Sport o f Learning: A Comprehensive Guide for African-American Student-Athletes by Vince Fudzie, Andrew Haves, and the Boyz (Doubleplay Publishing Group).

Swimming Upstream: A Complete Guide to the College Application Process for the Learning Disabled Student by Diane Wilder Howard (Hunt House Publishing).

Winning Scholarships for College: An Insider's Guide by
Marianne Ragins (Henry Holt). A Black high school
student from Macon, Georgia, tells how she earned
$400,000 in scholarships.

WHO WENT WHERE

Yolanda Adams - gospel singer (Tennessee State University)

Debbie Allen - choreographer, director (Howard University)

Ed Bradley - broadcast journalist (Cheyney University)

Erykah Badu - singer (Grambling University)

Rep. Frank Balance Jr. - Congressman (D-NC) (North Carolina Central University)

Rep. Sanford Bishop - Congressman (D-GA) (Morehouse College)

Dr. Benjamin Carson - pioneering neurosurgeon (Yale University)

Johnnie Cochran, Jr. - lawyer (UCLA)

Bill Cosby - entertainer, educator (Temple University)

Sean "P. Diddy" Combs - rapper, entertainment mogul (Howard University)

Common - actor, hip hop artist (Florida A&M University)

Bryant Gumbel - television journalist (Bates College)

Kwame Kilpatrick - youngest mayor of Detroit (Florida A&M University)

Toni Morrison - Nobel Prize winning author (Howard University)

Thurgood Marshall - Supreme Court Justice (Lincoln University)

Colin Powell - retired general, former U.S. Secretary of State (City College of New York)

Condoleezza Rice - U.S. Secretary of State, former National Security Advisor (University of Denver)

Rep. Jesse Jackson, Jr. (D-IL) - (North Carolina A&T University)

Rep. William Jefferson (D-LA) - (Southern University)

Rep. John Lewis (D-GA)- (Fisk University)

Rep. Kendrick Meek (D-FL) - (Florida A&M University

Rep. Gregory Meeks (D-NY) - (Howard University

Rep. Major Owens (D-NY) - (Morehouse College)

Dr. Mae Jemison - astronaut, medical doctor (Stanford University)

Robert L. Johnson - Black Entertainment Television founder (Princeton University)

Oprah Winfrey - talk show host, philanthropist (Tennessee State University)

Keenan Ivory Wayans - actor, producer (Tuskegee University)

Tiger Woods - golf pro (Stanford University)

Montel Williams - talk show host (U. S. Naval Academy)

2005 Publication Schedule

January

A Heart's Awakening
Veronica Parker
$9.95
1-58571-143-9

Falling
Natalie Dunbar
$9.95
1-58571-121-7

February

Echoes of Yesterday
Beverly Clark
$9.95
1-58571-131-4

A Love of Her Own
Cheris F. Hodges
$9.95
1-58571-136-5

Higher Ground
Leah Latimer
$19.95
1-58571-157-8

March

Misconceptions
Pamela Leigh Starr
$9.95
1-58571-117-9

I'll Paint a Sun
Al Garotto
$9.95
1-58571-165-9

Peace Be Still
Colette Haywood
$12.95
1-58571-129-2

April

Intentional Mistakes
Michele Sudler
$9.95
1-58571-152-7

Conquering Dr. Wexler's Heart
Kimberley White
$9.95
1-58571-126-8

Song in the Park
Martin Brant
$15.95
1-58571-125-X

May

The Color Line
Lizette Carter
$9.95
1-58571-163-2

Unconditional
A.C. Arthur
$9.95
1-58571-142-X

Last Train to Memphis
Elsa Cook
$12.95
1-58571-146-2

June

Angel's Paradise
Janice Angelique
$9.95
1-58571-107-1

Suddenly You
Crystal Hubbard
$9.95
1-58571-158-6

Matters of Life and
Death
Lesego Malepe, Ph.D.
$15.95
1-58571-124-1

2005 Publication Schedule (continued)

July

Pleasures All Mine
Belinda O. Steward
$9.95
1-58571-112-8

Wild Ravens
Altonya Washington
$9.95
1-58571-164-0

Class Reunion
Irma Jenkins/John
Brown
$12.95
1-58571-123-3

August

Path of Thorns
Annetta P. Lee
$9.95
1-58571-145-4

Timeless Devotion
Bella McFarland
$9.95
1-58571-148-9

Life Is Never As It Seems
June Michael
$12.95
1-58571-153-5

September

Beyond the Rapture
Beverly Clark
$9.95
1-58571-131-4

Blood Lust
J. M. Jeffries
$9.95
1-58571-138-1

Rough on Rats and
Tough on Cats
Chris Parker
$12.95
1-58571-154-3

October

A Will to Love
Angie Daniels
$9.95
1-58571-141-1

Taken by You
Dorothy Elizabeth Love
$9.95
1-58571-162-4

Soul Eyes
Wayne L. Wilson
$12.95
1-58571-147-0

November

A Drummer's Beat to
Mend
Kay Swanson
$9.95

Sweet Reprecussions
Kimberley White
$9.95
1-58571-159-4

Red Polka Dot in a
Worldof Plaid
Varian Johnson
$12.95
1-58571-140-3

December

Hand in Glove
Andrea Jackson
$9.95
1-58571-166-7

Blaze
Barbara Keaton
$9.95

Across
Carol Payne
$12.95
1-58571-149-7

Other Genesis Press, Inc. Titles

Acquisitions	Kimberley White	$8.95
A Dangerous Deception	J.M. Jeffries	$8.95
A Dangerous Love	J.M. Jeffries	$8.95
A Dangerous Obsession	J.M. Jeffries	$8.95
After the Vows	Leslie Esdaile	$10.95
(Summer Anthology)	T.T. Henderson	
	Jacqueline Thomas	
Again My Love	Kayla Perrin	$10.95
Against the Wind	Gwynne Forster	$8.95
A Lark on the Wing	Phyliss Hamilton	$8.95
A Lighter Shade of Brown	Vicki Andrews	$8.95
All I Ask	Barbara Keaton	$8.95
A Love to Cherish	Beverly Clark	$8.95
Ambrosia	T.T. Henderson	$8.95
And Then Came You	Dorothy Elizabeth Love	$8.95
Angel's Paradise	Janice Angelique	$8.95
A Risk of Rain	Dar Tomlinson	$8.95
At Last	Lisa G. Riley	$8.95
Best of Friends	Natalie Dunbar	$8.95
Bound by Love	Beverly Clark	$8.95
Breeze	Robin Hampton Allen	$10.95
Brown Sugar Diaries &	Delores Bundy &	$10.95
Other Sexy Tales	Cole Riley	
By Design	Barbara Keaton	$8.95
Cajun Heat	Charlene Berry	$8.95
Careless Whispers	Rochelle Alers	$8.95
Caught in a Trap	Andre Michelle	$8.95
Chances	Pamela Leigh Starr	$8.95
Dark Embrace	Crystal Wilson Harris	$8.95
Dark Storm Rising	Chinelu Moore	$10.95
Designer Passion	Dar Tomlinson	$8.95
Ebony Butterfly II	Delilah Dawson	$14.95

Erotic Anthology	Assorted	$8.95
Eve's Prescription	Edwina Martin Arnold	$8.95
Everlastin' Love	Gay G. Gunn	$8.95
Fate	Pamela Leigh Starr	$8.95
Forbidden Quest	Dar Tomlinson	$10.95
Fragment in the Sand	Annetta P. Lee	$8.95
From the Ashes	Kathleen Suzanne	$8.95
	Jeanne Sumerix	
Gentle Yearning	Rochelle Alers	$10.95
Glory of Love	Sinclair LeBeau	$10.95
Hart & Soul	Angie Daniels	$8.95
Heartbeat	Stephanie Bedwell-Grime	$8.95
I'll Be Your Shelter	Giselle Carmichael	$8.95
Illusions	Pamela Leigh Starr	$8.95
Indiscretions	Donna Hill	$8.95
Interlude	Donna Hill	$8.95
Intimate Intentions	Angie Daniels	$8.95
Just an Affair	Eugenia O'Neal	$8.95
Kiss or Keep	Debra Phillips	$8.95
Love Always	Mildred E. Riley	$10.95
Love Unveiled	Gloria Greene	$10.95
Love's Deception	Charlene Berry	$10.95
Mae's Promise	Melody Walcott	$8.95
Meant to Be	Jeanne Sumerix	$8.95
Midnight Clear	Leslie Esdaile	$10.95
(Anthology)	Gwynne Forster	
	Carmen Green	
	Monica Jackson	
Midnight Magic	Gwynne Forster	$8.95
Midnight Peril	Vicki Andrews	$10.95
My Buffalo Soldier	Barbara B. K. Reeves	$8.95
Naked Soul	Gwynne Forster	$8.95
No Regrets	Mildred E. Riley	$8.95
Nowhere to Run	Gay G. Gunn	$10.95

Object of His Desire	A. C. Arthur	$8.95
One Day at a Time	Bella McFarland	$8.95
Passion	T.T. Henderson	$10.95
Past Promises	Jahmel West	$8.95
Path of Fire	T.T. Henderson	$8.95
Picture Perfect	Reon Carter	$8.95
Pride & Joi	Gay G. Gunn	$8.95
Quiet Storm	Donna Hill	$8.95
Reckless Surrender	Rochelle Alers	$8.95
Rendezvous with Fate	Jeanne Sumerix	$8.95
Revelations	Cheris F. Hodges	$8.95
Rivers of the Soul	Leslie Esdaile	$8.95
Rooms of the Heart	Donna Hill	$8.95
Shades of Brown	Denise Becker	$8.95
Shades of Desire	Monica White	$8.95
Sin	Crystal Rhodes	$8.95
So Amazing	Sinclair LeBeau	$8.95
Somebody's Someone	Sinclair LeBeau	$8.95
Someone to Love	Alicia Wiggins	$8.95
Soul to Soul	Donna Hill	$8.95
Still Waters Run Deep	Leslie Esdaile	$8.95
Subtle Secrets	Wanda Y. Thomas	$8.95
Sweet Tomorrows	Kimberly White	$8.95
The Color of Trouble	Dyanne Davis	$8.95
The Price of Love	Sinclair LeBeau	$8.95
The Reluctant Captive	Joyce Jackson	$8.95
The Missing Link	Charlyne Dickerson	$8.95
Three Wishes	Seressia Glass	$8.95
Tomorrow's Promise	Leslie Esdaile	$8.95
Truly Inseperable	Wanda Y. Thomas	$8.95
Twist of Fate	Beverly Clark	$8.95
Unbreak My Heart	Dar Tomlinson	$8.95
Unconditional Love	Alicia Wiggins	$8.95
When Dreams A Float	Dorothy Elizabeth Love	$8.95

Whispers in the Night	Dorothy Elizabeth Love	$8.95
Whispers in the Sand	LaFlorya Gauthier	$10.95
Yesterday is Gone	Beverly Clark	$8.95
Yesterday's Dreams, Tomorrow's Promises	Reon Laudat	$8.95
Your Precious Love	Sinclair LeBeau	$8.95

ESCAPE WITH INDIGO !!!!

Join Indigo Book Club©
It's simple, easy and secure.

Sign up and receive the new releases
every month + Free shipping and
20% off the cover price.

Go online to www.genesis-press.com and
click on Bookclub or
call 1-888-INDIGO-1